TROUBLING WOMEN

feminist educational thinking

Series Editors:
Kathleen Weiler, Tufts University, USA
Gaby Weiner, Umea University, Sweden
Lyn Yates, La Trobe University, Australia

This authoritative series explores how theory/practice and the development of advanced ideas within feminism and education can be fused. The series aims to address the specific theoretical issues that confront feminist educators and to encourage both practitioner and academic debate.

Published titles:

Titles in preparation include:

TROUBLING WOMEN

Feminism, leadership and educational change

JILL BLACKMORE

OPEN UNIVERSITY PRESS
Buckingham · Philadelphia

Open University Press
Celtic Court
22 Ballmoor
Buckingham
MK18 1XW

email: enquiries@openup.co.uk
world wide web: http://www.openup.co.uk

and
325 Chestnut Street
Philadelphia, PA 19106, USA

First Published 1999

A catalogue record of this book is available from the British Library

ISBN   0 335 19479 6 (pb)   0 335 19480 X (hb)

Library of Congress Cataloging-in-Publication Data
Blackmore, Jill.
    Troubling women:feminism, leadership, and educational change /
Jill Blackmore.
        p.   cm. – (Feminist educational thinking series)
    Includes bibliographical references (p. ???) and index.
    ISBN 0-335-19480-X (hardcover). – ISBN 0-335-19479-6 (pbk.)
    1. Feminism and education–Australia   2. Women school administrators–
Australia.   3. School management and organization–Social aspects–
Australia.   4. Educational change–Australia.   5. Educational leadership–
Australia.   I. Title.   II. Series.
LC197.B53   1998
371.2'0082-dc21   98-25024
                                                                          CIP

Typeset by Type Study, Scarborough
Printed in Great Britain by Biddles Ltd, Guildford and King's Lynn

For my mother, Jean Crewther, and in memory of my father, Bill Mee (1916–1998), both committed educators

For strong women

A strong woman is a woman who is straining.
A strong woman is a woman standing
on tiptoe and lifting a barbell
while trying to sing Boris Godunuv.
A strong woman is a woman at work
cleaning out the cesspool of the ages,
and while she shovels, she talks about
how she doesn't mind crying, it opens
the ducts of the eyes, and throwing up
develops the stomach muscles, and
she goes on shovelling with tears
in her nose.

A strong woman is a woman in whose head
a voice is repeating, I told you so,
ugly, bad girl, bitch, nag, shrill, witch,
ballbuster, nobody will ever love you back,
why aren't you feminine, why aren't
you soft, why aren't you quiet, why
aren't you dead.

A strong woman is a woman determined
to do something others are determined
not to be done. She is pushing up on the bottom
of a lead coffin lid. She is trying to raise
a manhole cover with her head, she is trying
to butt her way through a steel wall.
Her head hurts. People waiting for the hole
to be made say, hurry, you're so strong.

Marge Piercy (1980)

Contents

Series editors' preface

At the end of the twentieth century it is not a new idea to have a series on feminist educational thinking – feminist perspectives on educational theory, research, policy and practice have made a notable impact on these fields in the final decades of the century. But theory and practice have evolved, and educational and political contexts have changed. In contemporary educational policy debates, economic efficiency rather than social inequality is a key concern; what happens to boys is drawing more interest than what happens to girls; issues about cultural difference interrupt questions about gender; and new forms of theory challenge older frameworks of analysis. This series represents feminist educational thinking as it takes up these developments now.

Feminist educational thinking views the intersection of education and gender through a variety of lenses: it examines schools and universities as sites for the enacting of gender; it explores the ways in which conceptions of gender shape the provision of state-supported education; it highlights the resistances subordinated groups have developed around ideas of knowledge, power and learning; and it seeks to understand the relationship of education to gendered conceptions of citizenship, the family and the economy. Thus feminist educational thinking is fundamentally political; it fuses theory and practice in seeking to understand contemporary education with the aim of building a more just world for women and men. In so doing, it acknowledges the reality of multiple 'feminisms' and the intertwining of ethnicity, race and gender.

Feminist educational thinking is influenced both by developments in feminist theory more broadly and by the changing global educational landscape. In terms of theory, both poststructuralist and postcolonial theories have profoundly influenced what is conceived of as 'feminist'. As is true elsewhere, current feminist educational thinking takes as central the intersecting forces that shape the educational experiences of women and men. This emphasis on the construction and performances of gender through both discourses and material practices leads to an attitude of openness and questioning of accepted assumptions – including the underlying assumptions of the various strands of feminism.

In terms of the sites in which we work, feminist educational thinking increasingly addresses the impact of 'globalization' – the impact of neo-laissez-faire theories on education. As each of us knows all too well, the schools and universities in which we work have been profoundly affected by the growing dominance of ideas of social efficiency, market choice, and competition. In a rapidly changing world in which an ideology of profit has come to define all relationships, the question of gender is often lost, but in fact it is central to the way power is enacted in education as in society as a whole.

The books in this series thus seek to explore the ways in which theory and practice are interrelated. They introduce a third wave of feminist thinking in education, one that takes account of both global changes to the economy and politics, and changes in theorizing about that world. It is important to emphasize that feminist educational thinking not only shapes how we think about education but what we do *in* education – as teachers, academics, and citizens. Thus books within the series not only address the impact of global, national and local changes of education but what specific space is available for feminists within education to mount a challenge to educational practices which encourage gendered and other forms of discriminatory practice.

Kathleen Weiler
Gaby Weiner
Lyn Yates

Preface

In this volume, Jill Blackmore takes up the issue of 'leadership', educational administration and feminism on a very broad front. Commonly the literature (and the practices) have kept separate what Jill sets out to put together: the concerns and strategies about getting more women into power, the life histories and experiences of women who work in education, the historically specific forms of education and the ways these shape and restrict possibilities for women, and the self-critical debates within feminism about its differences, its practices and its effects. Jill Blackmore's discussion confronts the assumptions that shape these different fields and builds for the reader a set of ongoing questions about the shape of education possibilities at present and about the shape of useful strategies for women.

Jill started her academic career as a historian, and one of the strengths of her work is not only the contextual historical discussion of the setting up of education systems, but an ongoing interest in historical specificity. In particular she sets out very clearly some changes in recent years from an era where distributive 'social justice' agendas were favoured, to a time when neoconservatism, corporatization and privatization dominate the restructuring of schooling. This historical sensitivity in Jill's work exposes the inadequacies of much of the 'women and leadership' literature, which assume this issue to be a topic requiring a set of techniques as the answer.

More recently, Jill has worked on a number of projects based in schools and in educational bureaucracies. She has observed, 'participated', interviewed, noted the stories of women, observed their problems and assessed the outcomes of reforms (both feminist and non-feminist). In this book, she tells some of these stories to show the tensions that the women experience and to reflect on assumptions of previous feminist reform. Showing what the issues for women in leadership positions look like produces a large canvas of discussion. It ranges from the most concrete and 'everyday' issues of dress and emotionality as these are experienced by the women, through deeper issues of how the body and the emotions are constructed as appropriate or inappropriate by the history and broader forms of the institution of schooling, and again through political changes, both micro and macro, that change the conditions and reception of feminist practices. As Jill Blackmore notes in her conclusion,

> Centralized-decentralization has therefore produced many leadership paradoxes [. . .] Discourses of good educational leadership stress ambiguity, shared visions, bottom up change and creativity; yet self-management has meant top-down, principal-led and managed change encouraging compliance. [. . .] The leadership literature stresses teaching, learning, and people management in learning organizations, yet self-managing schools prioritize entrepreneurship, financial management, and 'strong', if not authoritarian, leadership.

In the face of this and in the face of feminism's own current self-questioning, Jill Blackmore advocates an approach that recognizes ambiguities, that acknowledges difference and that keeps alive *both* 'strategic' and 'tactical' visions. This is a book whose discussion of feminist educational thinking very clearly locates that in a dialogue of theory with experiences, and in a dialogue of strategy with appreciation of the political forces and constraints of the contemporary education context.

Lyn Yates

Acknowledgements

Changing structures does not necessarily change values. This is borne out in my own workplace where the value of my colleagues' commitment and creativity to improving education for all, both theoretically and in practice, is inestimable. It is also, thankfully, persistent in the face of increasingly debilitating managerialist and conservative political cultures which work against critical social inquiry in education. As colleagues, they contribute much to my thinking and my desire to continue to reach and do research. So thanks to my Deakin colleagues Jenny Angwin, Lindsay Fitzclarence, Noel Gough, John Hodgens, Louise Laskey, Barbara Kamler, Jane Kenway, and Peter Watkins as well as ex-Deakin colleagues Chris Bigum, Marie Brennan, Bill Green and Robin McTaggart. Special thanks to Bernie Hernon, Anne Davies and Judy Bowly, each of whom have worked with me in the difficult role of research assistant, and to Judy in particular for her brilliant efficiency in the final 'housekeeping' stages of the book. The text benefited greatly from Lyn Yates's incisive and insightful editorial comments in its last stages while my research partner, Judyth Sachs, provided me with ideas, encouragement, emotional support and humour. I also wish to acknowledge copyright holders for permission to draw from work previously published but which has undergone considerable revision for this text. This includes the chapter 'Breaking out of a masculinist politics in education' in *Gender and Changing Educational Management*, ACEA Handbook of Educational Administration edited by B. Limerick and B. Lingard (1995, Edward Arnold, Sydney), 'Doing emotional labor in the educational market place: stories from the field of women in management' in a special issue of *Discourse*, 1996, 17(3), and 'Policy as dialogue: feminist administrators working for educational change' in *Gender and Education*, 1995, 7(3). But most of all, my thanks to the generous offer of time, energy, interest and commitment by the many teachers and administrators, many of whom were my students, and who informed my thinking, but who cannot be held responsible for the result.

Introduction: troubling women – new leaders for new hard times?

> Gender trouble is inevitable and the task is how best to make it and what best way to be in it.
>
> (Judith Butler 1990: vii)

Troubling women

Women have long been troubled by the notion of 'leader' and the images it conveys. In a casual discussion with two female principals the issue arose of how we, as women seen to be in leadership positions, 'represented' ourselves to others. Each of us recognized the importance of 'naming' ourselves, but no one descriptor could portray the multiplicities of self that we felt constituted who we were or could express all the contradictions we experienced on a daily basis of simultaneously being teachers, learners, mothers, daughters, partners, administrators, workers, leaders, and indeed feminists. I was particularly troubled by one principal's depiction of herself as first and foremost 'a leader' who would one day take her skills into private industry. At first I was concerned by the potential loss of a good female principal to public education due to burnout. At another level I was puzzled by her uncritical acceptance of contemporary management discourses that portray leadership as a value-free practice or set of generic competencies that were readily transferable into any domain of activity. In particular, I was surprised at her rejection of the label of feminism, for her leadership practices had suggested otherwise. I wanted to ask: 'What are the principles you wish to uphold? What ambitions and desires do you wish to fulfil other than the experience, the pleasure and pain of leadership itself? What are your criteria for judgement on how to act as a leader?'

My experience in schools during the 1970s and universities in the 1980s and 1990s has told me that change occurs in diverse and complex ways, and that leadership cannot be as readily identified and categorized as management theories suggest. As a young teacher, my personal and professional identity was closely bound up with radical pedagogies and teacher union activism, and not the least the women's movement. Leadership was to me about working creatively with colleagues, sometimes subversively, to produce educational change and reduce social inequality, more often despite, not because of, the principal. To be seen to be a 'leader' in the male dominated hierarchy of schools then, when my concern was about democratization of decisionmaking and teacher professionalism, was particularly worrisome, largely because the equation of formal authority to leadership had connotations in the 1970s of structured inequality and control and therefore being fundamentally anti-collegial. Leadership has continued to be problematic to me, because how it is usually conceptualized in theory, policy and the dominant images of top-down 'visionary' leadership or strategic management, does not match my experience of 'good leadership' initiated and worked on from the bottom up amongst teachers and academics.

So ironically, after many years rankling against those with formal status and seniority, I find myself researching leadership. I am highly aware that I am perceived within my institution, as a senior female academic, to be in a privileged position, with all the expectations that go with being one of a few. I am writing this book at the point in my life when some colleagues are challenging me to apply for 'formal' leadership positions but when all academic work, both teaching and research, is under threat, being made subject to market forces and reduced government funding. At the same time, my research data is full of the stories of women in formal positions of leadership who find the contradictions too great, the emotional labour and physical work too demanding. They express the need for some time and space for pleasure, leisure and self-indulgence. I also have stories of women who do not seek formal leadership positions because they see the price women pay for 'doing the emotional management work of a system in crisis' (Blackmore 1996), either for being feminist or not feminist, too caring or not caring enough, who have decided they 'do not want to be like that' or that their familial responsibilities reduce their 'choices'. Just as many women in schools express the desire to stay in teaching because it still gives them pleasure, I am likewise attracted to research and teaching at this moment in my life in preference to an administrative role, particularly when the latter may further detract from time spent with my 8-year-old son, Jesse.

The rapidly and radically changing political, social and economic context has produced new theoretical and political agendas for feminist educators in Australia, as elsewhere. The re-formation of the social relations of education, work and family in the past decade positions women in leadership, particularly those who are feminists, in highly contradictory ways. This text is about 'troubling women' in new hard times around three central issues. First, the underrepresentation of women in positions of power and authority is now seen to be a problem at a time when political authority itself is in trouble in the context of the unsettling economic, social and political relations of postmodern times. The lack of women in leadership is now troublesome in that it undermines male claims to leadership and authority in times of cultural pluralism and changing workplace and familial arrangements. Some new management discourses, such as those expressed in the Karpin Report on management education (1995) suggest that the failure to recognize that women are powerful political and economic constituencies as consumers *and* producers in an increasingly feminized workplace will cause trouble, trouble that is, largely in terms of productivity rather than human rights (Aburdene and Naisebett 1992; Pillinger 1993).[1] How does this impact upon feminist claims upon the state for equity?

Second, women who get into leadership are also trouble. 'To be a woman in a masculinist culture is to be a source of mystery and unmeasurability for men'(Butler 1990: vii). In particular, strong women are difficult and dangerous because they trouble dominant masculinities and modes of management by being different. Feminists are particularly disruptive because they seek social change to achieve gender justice. As both insiders (as managers) and outsiders (as women) in male dominated cultures, women in leadership are often positioned as change agents, and as such bear the brunt of organizational and personal anxieties. Those who also seek to promote gender equity further challenge the 'natural order of things', which has historically favoured men in schools and bureaucracies. As a professional development consultant to principals and teachers, I am often expected not to rock the boat by mentioning gender too often, given that this makes many men 'uncomfortable', although foregrounding gender is of great comfort to most women. In a market era, making your more powerful 'clients' nervous about their gender identity is downright dangerous. Equally often, however, women are cast as resisters to change when they defend the past gains of gender equity reform in decisionmaking forums. How do we deal with the ambiguities surrounding contemporary educational reform?

Third, we also need to trouble women themselves and feminists in particular. Feminism as a social movement and disciplinary knowledge has developed its own normative and regulatory tendencies, producing its own universalizing discourses, which make being a woman in leadership in new hard times a risky business. Populist versions promoted in the media of feminist discourses about women's styles of leadership being more caring and sharing have conflated 'being female' to 'being feminist' in highly essentialist ways. It is a conflation that ignores both the differences amongst women and the difficult political context in which leading women now work. The tendency to treat the issue of women in leadership in dominant management discourses as merely a matter of upgrading women's skills to meet the demands of current modes of leadership is also blind to the gender politics of educational change. Educational restructuring, with its emphasis on efficiency, accountability and outcomes, privileges 'hard' management and entrepreneurial discourses of leadership over less instrumental, more holistic and 'softer', 'feminized' leadership discourses. The former discourses decontextualize, distort, and depoliticize the issue of gender in their refusal to see to how educational restructuring and shifts in cultural values continue to reshape, and indeed constrain, the possibilities for feminist leadership practices.

Meanwhile, the focus upon women as 'the problem' has deflected attention away from the close connections between discourses of masculinity, rationality and leadership and left relatively intact, despite two decades of gender equity reform programs, the asymmetrical and unequal nature of the social relations of gender. While feminist discourses have gained some ground, in particular those of sexual harassment and equal opportunity, dominant discourses of masculinity have successfully been reconstituted over time within different management paradigms. White, middle-class, heterosexual males continue to wield cultural and financial power derived from contemporary educational discourses that circulate about 'good' leadership – discourses that associate masculinity with economic rationality, being strong, making 'hard' decisions, the 'hard' knowledge areas of science and technology, and entrepreneurship. Leadership, the central concept of educational administration, has once again become the solution to the problems of education for more pluralistic and team-oriented postmodern times. Paradoxically, postmodern management texts emphasize change, fluidity and flexibility as critical to effective change. Yet there is a sense of determinism about the rhetoric of change that has become 'the unexplored focus that is asserted rather than demonstrated and elaborated' (Mac an Ghaill 1996: 171). Indeed, close examination indicates that leadership practices as shaped by recent reforms towards devolution in the 1990s signal the reassertion, not dissipation, of organizational hierarchies; that we are experiencing a hardening, not softening, of the enduring gendered division of labour in educational management.

Indeed, in times of scarcity and the radical restructuring of the social, economic and political relations due to economic globalization and cultural uncertainty, new opportunities for resistance to gender equity and social transformation of gender relations arise. This is evident in Australia, as elsewhere, with more overt antagonism towards feminism and feminist agendas (equity, equal pay, child care, reproductive rights) and broader issues of social justice for indigenous people in the mid-1990s, reflecting both cultural and structural backlash (Blackmore 1997a).[2] Structural backlash is when the male biases embedded in educational organizations, processes, structures and values are able to be mobilized, consciously and unconsciously, in some, but not all, men's favour through the actual processes of restructuring e.g. job redefinition and reallocation. Cultural backlash takes the form of populist discourses circulating that are resistant to gender equity. Together, these backlash discourses uncomfortably co-exist beside more emancipatory discourses, which laud women as the new leaders and change agents for postmodern times.

Leadership: the solution or the problem?

Broadly, I argue that the capacity for feminism, and feminists in leadership, to work for social justice generally in public school education, and gender equity for women in particular, is currently at risk. First, because educational restructuring is merely one manifestation of a fundamental change in the nature of the state in many western liberal nation states (Blackmore 1998). In Australia, as elsewhere, the conjuncture of globalization with the rise of ideologies of neoconservative politics and market liberalism has produced a less interventionist state in the area of gender equity reform. Second, not only does the state tend merely to mediate market relations, modifying its more extreme aberrations only, but the corporatization and privatization of education have meant emerging education markets increasingly shape the daily practices of schooling in highly gendered ways (Blackmore 1996). The trend is towards education labour markets, globally and locally, to become more feminized, casualized and deprofessionalized (Ozga 1993a; Chen and Addi 1993; Milligan *et al.* 1994; Whitty 1994; Blackmore 1997a).

Despite these radical changes in the nature of educational work, official texts, when they attend to gender equity at all, equate equity to getting more women into leadership positions. Such texts of reform also call upon the more optimistic accounts of postmodern educational workplaces as being about change, diversity, flexibility, teamwork, collaboration and consensus building. This not only deflects attention way from wider issues of structured gender inequality, but also does not challenge dominant leadership discourses, practices and policies that tend to be more repressive than emancipatory for women. Instead, leadership is presented as the simplistic solution to complex educational problems rather than the means to a desired end. 'We become so fascinated with the means by which we pursue our goals that these means ultimately take place of the goals themselves' (Hargreaves 1994: 23). The emphasis on principals' leadership is justified by particular truth claims circulating about how good leadership directly improves student outcomes, a common misreading of the effective schools literature used to justify top-down principal-led reform linked to performance pay, whereas evidence suggests that it is teacher–student interaction (preferably with principal support and facilitation) in classrooms and playgrounds that impacts most on student learning. Furthermore, as leadership is treated in these policy texts increasingly in a more technicist fashion as a set of generic competencies rather than holistically, the social, ethical and political dimensions of leadership are leached out. One is rarely encouraged to ask: leading to what end and for whom – for the national interest, for individual students, for social justice in a democratic society?

For feminists, focusing upon women and leadership means it is difficult to cast aside the very category we seek to critique. It risks making women *the problem* in educational leadership rather than problematizing the concept of leadership itself relative to wider dominant power/gender relations. Not surprisingly, the benchmark of leadership remains white, middle-class, heterosexual and male. Christine Sleeter (1993: ix) comments

> What is ironic is that the principalship is the one role in the school that is most likely to be occupied by a member of multiple status positions (white, male and well educated) that benefit from existing social arrangements. While all these facts do not condemn administrators in general, and principals in particular, they do position administrators in a particular way: to take for granted much of the institutional structure of schools and their context, and the justifications for why things are as they are.

In this text, I use leadership, the linchpin of administrative theory and practice, as a conceptual lens through which to critique the gender politics of educational reform. I conceptualize leadership in its most inclusive sense based on the view that leadership is practised by many teachers, principals and parents in a range of educational sites and in a number of informal as well as formal administrative positions (principals, executive officers, policy developers). Leadership is practised in a variety of ways by classroom teachers and professional development managers. Educational leadership is something that good teachers, good bureaucrats and not just good principals or CEOs do. Failure to recognize the multiple dimensions of leadership within the various leadership paradigms that have proliferated in recent years means leadership is still viewed as something exceptional rather than everyday practice. This treatment of educational leadership as something different from what teachers do on a daily basis, I suggest, has deterred many women from assuming more formal leadership roles as they do not imagine their work as leadership. Their ongoing 'reluctance' to aspire to leadership has also been exacerbated by the reassertion of hierarchy in restructured educational organizations that has reallocated leadership to formal executive positions (e.g. principal, advanced skills teachers).

Casting the feminist gaze simultaneously upon leadership and educational restructuring indicates how leadership is constantly being reconstituted in the light of wider political, economic and social change. While what is seen to be effective leadership changes over time in particular contexts – whether it be the rise of new social movements in the 1970s, the new managerialism in the 1980s, or the market in the 1990s – what endures is the ongoing constitution of the unequal social relations of gender embedded in leadership practices. This is despite what now appears to be significant and fundamental shifts in relations between the state, education and the individual since the late 1980s, just as there were fundamental shifts in the late nineteenth century and in the liberal democratic educational settlement after World War II, which is producing a regendering of social relations. Widening the gaze to examine how restructuring and change informs the discursive practices of leadership high-lights the political and material effects for women both as a 'class' and as active subjects. I ask: What are the material and discursive conditions that privilege particular readings of feminism, leadership and educational change at certain moments? What are the strategies women leaders and gender reformers have used most effectively at such times?

The research projects

The research derives from a number of projects focusing upon women, leadership and educational restructuring in self-managing schools and the education bureaucracy in the Victorian state education system.[3] The studies were qualitative, based on in depth interviews, some participant observation and case studies (Minichiello *et al.* 1995). The major case study (Hillcrest Secondary College) was undertaken during the first two years of a con-servative coalition government (1992–93) which radically restructured the state education system towards self-managing schools. I selected a school that had previously experienced only male leadership at all levels, but whose local selection committee had appointed a female principal. The dual aim was to gain a sense of how perceptions of female leadership were altered in the initial years of her management and to explore the nature of the gender politics in two schools undergoing radical change. It was coincidental that Hillcrest was a rural coeducational college, a former boys' technical school, and that the female principal was appointed as a change agent expected to negotiate an amalgamation with a high school in a period of radical and rapid restructuring of the state education system. In the 30 interviews under-taken with the principals, male and female staff, parents and students, dis-cussions about leadership couldn't be disassociated from wider issues of restructuring and organizational change.

In 1990, another study focused upon a small group of women in the Vic-torian education bureaucracy under a Labor government, and how they, many of them feminists (commonly known as femocrats in Australia), worked through the state to achieve their educational and equity agendas. The data emerging from this study magnified the centrality of gender in the process of policy production, and the significance of the body and sexuality as a key to understanding how organizations work through, with, and upon gendered subjects. I revisited this site of policy formation within the central state education bureaucracy when I became a member of a Ministerial Review on Employment Equity for Women Teachers instituted by the Vic-torian state government and meeting regularly over a two year period during 1994–95. As a participant and observer in this active process of policy pro-duction, I confronted first-hand the contradictions, tensions and ambi-valence many of the femocrats in the earlier study had articulated about working within the bureaucracy, but this time in a more conservative political context. This later study indicated important continuities in gender power relations in bureaucratic life centred around discourses of bureaucratic rationality and the embodiment of authority in particularly masculinist forms. Together these studies highlighted significant discontinuities in the discursive construction of gender equity over time within different political contexts, and how policy could shift the vocabulary in ways that redefined what equity came to mean for those working for gender equality in education. While only 16 bureaucrats were interviewed overall in these two studies, the sample constituted about half the female executive managers in the state education bureaucracy at any one time.

Through networks of feminist teacher unionists and gender equity practitioners, leadership workshops, principal collegial groups and personal association, I was able to identify and interview a further 35 individuals and numerous focus groups in rural, provincial and urban schools, at primary (Prep–Year 6) and secondary (Year 7–12) level. These school-based studies and interviews with gender equity practitioners enabled me to trace the shift towards school self-management in different policy contexts at the school and system level over the period from 1990 to 1995. Together with the interviews, participant observation of policy production, and considerable professional development work in the area of leadership and educational change with schools, principals and teachers, these studies provided a range of insights into the production, circulation and reception of discourses about educational reform and gender equity for women in a range of sites – schools, regional and central.

Victoria, the location of the research presented here, has been typified as model for devolution and school self-management for both other Australian states and other school systems. The Victorian model, *Schools of the Future*, drew aspects from earlier reform models in England (e.g. education markets), Canada (e.g. Edmonton with regard to global budgets) and New Zealand (e.g. school charters). As such, Victoria is an example of how particular globalized policies promoted by key international bodies (OECD, UNESCO and World Bank) and right-wing think-tanks, are circulating and articulated locally in highly context- and gender-specific ways (Hyman 1994; Taylor *et al.* 1997). It is significant in that in Australia, as in Third World countries, 'reports of the "progress" of reform in one context have thus become resources in the struggle for reform in others' (Whitty 1997: 5). This study seeks to problematize what we mean by 'progress' by focusing upon the gender effects of such reforms in one particular site, Victoria. The study raises future equity concerns for other public education systems undergoing similar reforms (Weiner 1995a). Victoria, as a case study in gender equity and education reform generally, exemplifies a high level of feminist activism in education and a strong history of school-based decision-making which is atypical of most other Australian states and indeed other western education systems (Arnot and Weiler 1993; Limerick and Lingard 1995; Kenway *et al.* 1997). In that sense, this analysis can offer much to those concerned about gender equity in particular and reform strategies in general. As a case study of reform in action, it also points to the similarities in the changed nature of educational work and public administration generally across many western liberal democracies, and alerts us to how discourses of restructuring and economic reform circulating globally play out with significant differential material and social effects at the level of the local (Taylor *et al.* 1997; Wylie 1997).

Educational restructuring, leadership and gender: global/local resonances

This research was undertaken during a period of radical restructuring in Australian education under both Labor and Liberal/National coalition (conservative) governments at federal and state levels after 1987. The restructuring of Australian education is one manifestation of global trends arising out of common political responses to global markets, cultural diversity and the collapse of time-space with the emergence of new information technologies. Despite historical and cultural differences, globalization has produced a frenzy of policy-borrowing of educational solutions across western nation states (e.g. UK, New Zealand, Canada, USA, Sweden, Norway, and Australia) to what appear to be common social and economic problems. Policy has also become a solution to the legitimacy problems of governments, pressured on one side by the claims of interest groups such as women's, multicultural and indigenous movements lobbying the state for greater equity; and on the other hand, the often competing demands of international financial institutions and global markets for national economies to be more productive (or at least balance national budgets). Scarcity of jobs and resources in a time of economic, social and cultural uncertainty for both nations and individuals has also provoked a resurgence of neoconservative politics and a crisis of national and individual identity. These conservative ideologies have interesting mixes of new and old educational concepts of choice, diversity, core curriculum, strong leadership, markets, discipline, vocationalism, standards and equity that confuse the logic of older discourses of social justice (e.g. 1993 Education Act in England). They have also inspired public sector reform based upon idealized private sector models of management that seek to reduce public expenditure on education, health and welfare (Wylie 1995).

Restructuring is gendered in its re-formation of social, political and economic relationships in a number of ways. Public sector administrative reform in health, education and welfare emulating private sector models, in Australia as elsewhere, has radically altered the role of the state, the mode of educational governance and the nature of educational work. Education has been mainstreamed, and is now treated as an industry. Administrative responsibility has typically been devolved to small local units with a dominant trend towards self-managing schools in Australia, self-governing schools in New Zealand, local management of schools (LMS) and grant maintained schools in England, decentralization in Norway and Sweden, and site-based management in the USA. The managerialist practices accompanying devolution have sought to maintain the capacity of the centre to 'steer, not row' the margins (schools) through policy frameworks (national curriculum) and financial management mechanisms (global or block funding grants to schools) and to maintain control of implementation and effectiveness through monitoring. This control usually is in the form of transparent accountability measures (standardized test scores and performance management) that provide feedback to the centre. Devolution has produced a shift in focus in educational management in many western states away from inputs and processes to outcomes – generally in the form of measurable standards or benchmarks of performance (standardized test scores) which allow for comparisons of students, teachers, schools, systems and nation states.

Research on devolution in many public education systems in the USA, Norway, Sweden, Canada, New Zealand, England and, even more recently, in South Africa, indicates a common tension experienced by principals and teachers in self-managing schools arising from the stronger centralizing tendencies of line management and outcomes orientation and weaker decentralizing tendencies of devolution which espouse community participation and process (Codd and Gordon 1991; Moller 1993; Ball 1994; Watkins 1996). As Wylie (1995: 2) remarks: 'The price for individual institutional freedom is accountability'. For federal systems of government (USA, Australia, Canada), where states are largely responsible for education but federal governments seek to intervene, as in *America 2000* and *Goals 2000*, there is also an added tension in federal–state relations. With school self-management, centralized-decentralization means that principals operate in highly ambiguous relationships – responsible both to the centre through line management and to parents through school councils, boards or governing bodies – all within resource restrictions of global budgets or block grants.

Restructuring has also been characterized by the emergence of quasi-markets in education in most, but not all, instances (e.g. Germany and Japan), with varying combinations of parental choice, school autonomy, government regulation and public accountability in specific nation-states (Whitty 1997). Reduced per capita expenditure and formula-funding based on enrolments (Australia, Canada) or average teacher salaries (England and New Zealand), together with deregulation of catchment areas and open enrolment policies (UK), means schools now act in many instances more like small businesses seeking clients. Individual schools now compete with other government and non-government schools for clients in order to survive, blurring public/private boundaries as more popular government schools become more selective (Kenway *et al.* 1993; Gewirtz *et al.* 1995; Whitty 1997). Schools are thus highly susceptible to market forces that can lead to amalgamations or closure.

Survival in the market leads schools to shift focus onto image management, entrepreneurship and financial management and away from curriculum and pedagogy (Ball 1994; Blackmore *et al.* 1996). Schools with poor images cannot attract either students or sponsorships, and small schools cannot offer competitive comprehensive programmes. Productivity (measured by quantifiable outcomes against reduced inputs) and performativity (being seen to perform) are the names of the game. Research on the new performative school, the product of the outcomes focus of accountability mechanisms and market perceptions of 'good' schools, indicates a shift in emphasis of school leadership and resources (energy, funds and time) away from the core work of teaching, leading and learning, as well as equity issues (Blackmore *et al.* 1996; Blackmore 1997c). Paradoxically, as I have argued elsewhere, 'the market exacerbates differences between schools on the basis of class, race and ethnicity, but does not encourage diversity in image, clientele, organisation, curriculum or pedagogy' (Blackmore 1995: 53; Gewirtz *et al.* 1995). Social justice, as democracy, in this context, is becoming too difficult, too time consuming, too costly and outmoded, unless a school can tap into a niche market (e.g. all-girls' schools in middle-class areas). Given that women leaders are typified as being student centred and curriculum focused, this creates particular dilemmas about what constitutes successful leadership. Furthermore, any concern for democratic practice or social justice, often the reason for which they are appointed, can actually work against women leaders (Court 1995).

Public sector reform cross-nationally also indicates the trend towards the user pays attitude. Schools increasingly rely upon voluntary parental financial contributions and labour for essential equipment (e.g. computers) and services (parents undertaking administrative work on school boards and councils); (Dehli 1996). There is a shift in educational costs to parents (privatization) and for parents to become active consumers in school–industry based sponsorship deals (e.g. Apple/Coles program in Australia and the UK Tesco/Computers in Schools initiative). The trend to privatization is echoed in school systems in the USA, Canada, Australia, UK, Sweden and New Zealand,with privately managed profit seeking schools in the USA. The overall effect of privatization and marketization, research suggests, is a widening of the gap between rich and poor schools (Gordon 1994a). Given that in many school systems women principals tend to be concentrated in schools in poorer socioeconomic areas with greater cultural diversity, women are more susceptible to failure.

Finally, school self-management, within the constraints of global or bulk funding, relies upon greater staff flexibility. Restructuring has inevitably been accompanied by workplace and industrial relations reform of teachers' and principals' work. The Employment Contracts Act in New Zealand has replaced centralized awards with individual contracts (Hyman 1994). In Australia, the first move from a highly centralized award system to decentralization under enterprise bargaining, although introduced by the former federal Labor government, has been radically extended by the conservative Howard government under the Workplace Relations Act 1997. The Canadian provinces are also restructuring, with the demise of highly feminized educational jobs and supplanting of teachers with less qualified contract labour as 'assistants', similar to the new instructor class of teacher in Victoria (Coulter 1996). Government-established teacher registration boards and standards councils, often tendered out to private consultants, now determine what constitutes 'good teaching'. The effect, particularly in more conservative environments, has been to undercut union influence as state employers now seek to move to short-term employment contracts in order to gain local flexibility. In Victoria, the principal has become the employer of contract staff. Women teachers constitute, in most countries, an increasing majority of part-time and contract staff (Blackmore 1997a).

Simultaneously, teacher career structures have been reviewed, producing less democratic and collegial workplaces, with the codification of teaching practice (teacher competencies in Australia, Standard Attainment Tasks in England); and the development of skill hierarchies amongst teachers (Advanced Skills Teachers in Australia and proposed in England, Leading Teacher in Sweden) and between principal and teachers, with a general shift in power to principals or head teachers. Research in most western industrial nations indicates that teachers' work has intensified with increased hours, class sizes, administrative duties, reduced support systems and greater accountability, testing and recording. Many teachers express a sense of loss of professional autonomy and judgement, particularly with the recentralization of curriculum and assessment in Australia, England and Canada (Ozga 1993a; Coulter 1996). Governments have further effectively weakened teacher organizations' control over their profession by reshaping teacher education, professional development, certification and competency standards through the establishment of the Teacher Standards Council (Victoria), the Teacher Training Agency in the UK, and the College of Teachers (Ontario) which, while 'purportedly making teachers more 'professional' and autonomous [when], in reality, they are very significant new method of surveillance and control' (Coulter 1996: 93). The reassertion of principal power through performance management and control over staff allocation, promotion and employment is matched by the imposition of more prescriptive curriculum and assessment with national curriculum or curriculum frameworks being initiated in England and Australia (Ozga 1993a; Lingard and Porter 1997; Wylie 1997).

The principalship has also been transformed. New skills are demanded from principals beyond education qualifications and teaching experience; competency regimes require additional training, certification and expertise in non-educational areas of financial management linked to performance based pay awards (Ball 1994; Grace 1995). The emphasis is on measurement, hierarchy and regulation. Ball (1994) argues English head teachers now feel more controlled in that they merely manage the prescribed national curriculum, whereas in the past they negotiated with teachers and LEAs on curriculum matters. Similar sentiments have been expressed by Victorian principals (Blackmore *et al*. 1996; Townsend 1997). Regulated autonomy by the managerial state comes in the form of indirect guidance through curriculum and assessment practices (Curriculum Frameworks in Australia, National Curriculum in UK and New Zealand) and not direct administrative rule and regulation. It is also control by overload as head teachers rush to carry out the work of the state, with, for example, women principals in Victoria working, on average, longer hours than men (Caldwell 1994).

At the same time, devolution to schools in most systems has meant the 'hollowing out' of middle management, as regional curriculum and professional development support staff have been sent back to schools while finance and policy (on curriculum) have been retained at the centre. In New Zealand, with a population of 2 million, there are no intervening layers of support for accountability or control between schools and the centre (Wylie 1995). In Victoria, over three times the size of New Zealand, regional school support services have been cut, reducing resources and personnel support particularly in areas of disadvantage (equal opportunity, integration of students with disabilities, non-English speaking language services, counselling, health and welfare services) or outsourced to educational consultants, universities and teacher professional organizations (Blackmore 1994; Marginson 1994; Tickell 1994). In England, there has only been a partial bypassing of the local education authorities by the Education Act of 1988, as many schools have maintained their links voluntarily. In many states, however, the simultaneous processes of hollowing out and outsourcing have tended to neutralize the capacities of regional networks and local bodies, more often the site for policy initiatives and practitioner support for race and gender equity programs in schools. This has led to the dissipation and loss of significant professional and educationally informed experience and knowledge in equity reform, generally resulting in institutional amnesia (Weiner 1995a).

Finally, while the policy texts of self-managing, self-governing and grant maintained schools alike promise parents increased choice and participation in local schools, research in England on school governors now informs us that only some parents, the more active educational consumers tending to come from the professional and managerial classes, have more choices and greater opportunities for school involvement (Ball 1994; Deem *et al*. 1995). School councils in Australia, as boards of governors in England, tend to be unrepresentative of their school communities in terms of class, race and gender. School boards, previously an enclave of women community activity in Canada, are now under threat of amalgamation or being replaced by school councils that are voluntary and less powerful (Coulter 1996). Indeed, despite the rhetoric of parental participation and teacher professionalism, a common feature of newly devolved systems inspired by public choice theory, principal-agent theory and managerialism is that it has been top-down ideologically-driven reform focusing upon principal-led change, rather than bottom up community-initiated reform (Ball 1994; Townsend 1997). Wylie comments than in New Zealand, 'parental voice at the school level does not necessarily lead to more parental choice' (1995: 2). The formal organizations representing the constituencies of teachers (unions) and parents (parent associations) have largely been excluded from the processes of educational policymaking on the grounds that they have vested interests, although individual parents are still expected to implement policy as school governors or counsellors. Business, by contrast, has been actively included in key education policy reports shaping the nature of education (e.g. the Finn and Mayer Reports in Australia; Picot Report in New Zealand). So while the trend has been for principals to accumulate considerable power *relative* to teachers and parents in self-managing schools, they are more often constrained in what they can do in schools by central policies, accountability demands, the intensification of their workload and lack of resources (Ball 1994; Wylie 1995; Whitty 1997). These shifts in school/system power relations, replicated in all education sectors and the workplace more generally, have ramifications for women teachers' career choices, their perceptions of leadership and the type of leadership that is expected of them once they become principals.

The trend to localization (or bureaucratization), as a mode of educational governance, is not intrinsically bad, however. Highly centralized public education systems have been able to achieve equitable outcomes (Davies 1990). Progressivist educators have also focused upon school-based decisionmaking to promote equity – as in Australia in the 1980s, and the USA Coalition of Essential Schools in the 1990s. Devolved systems, as in New Zealand, have indicated a capacity to pay attention to some equity interests (Maoris), although not others (gender equity), which is similar to the USA where site-based management and racial desegregation are interconnected issues (Court 1995; Wylie 1997). School-based management, or visionary leadership for that matter, in themselves do not improve student outcomes (Hannaway and Carnoy 1993). What research does suggest is that it is particular combinations of reforms that have the potential to produce inequitable effects, although with considerable variation in different socioeconomic and political contexts. It would appear that devolution, in conjunction with the rise of quasi-markets in education and neoconservatism, has produced a significant value shift towards viewing parents as clients rather than citizens, and students as consumers of a product and more often produced inequities between schools and students. Devolution has also provided the means to fax any perceived crises of the state down the line to schools, for it is principals and teachers who deal on a daily basis with the ambiguities arising from competing discourses of equity and efficiency, quality and outcomes, devolution and democracy.

While all principals face the contradictions mapped out above, I argue that women principals and leaders in self-managing schools and 'lean and mean' bureaucracies, and feminists in particular, find it doubly difficult because the global/local discourses circulating about women and leadership position women differently. Women leaders have been typified in the media, professional development workshops, management discourses, and research on women and leadership, as being more democratic, collegial, caring, curriculum and student focused as well as being good change agents. Furthermore, policy texts produce new regimes of truth that allow the performative state to steer from a distance by establishing boundaries of practice, given that policy texts have the capacity to privilege particular discourses. Hence policy focuses upon performativity, strong leadership, entrepreneurship, discipline, hierarchy, accountability, efficiency, and line management places considerable constraints upon the capacity of women leaders to undertake their preferred leadership practices. This complexity requires a theoretical framework that could can explain these macro–micro linkages.

Useful theory

Theoretically the focus upon how gender reform policies for women teachers have been produced, read and acted upon required a theory that could link the macro to the micro in ways that explicated the complex nature of the micropolitics of schools and the broad sweep of structural and cultural change. A useful theory for feminism, as defined by Jean Anyon (1994: 129), which informed the theories and concepts I call upon in this text, is one that

1 'does not derive its value merely in reference to other theories but as a result of a dialogue between one's goal and current activities';
2 'would be neither total (and therefore seamless and deterministic) nor completely ad hoc and applicable only to one locale', but would recognize the complexity of social life and develop middle range theories that would 'connect local activity to widespread social constraints';
3 'makes theoretical recommendations which are capable of enactment'; and
4 would 'identify actions to be taken'.

The focus upon educational change throughout the text brings these elements together. I constantly ask: How can we better theorize change in ways that move the feminist politics of education forward, what have we learnt, what is different about our current conditions of practice?

Overall I work from a feminist poststructuralist position, but one with a strong materialist bent (Hennessey 1993; Kenway *et al.* 1994). Central to feminist poststructuralism and this text are the concepts of discourse, subjectivity and power. Discourse is a useful concept because it links the macro (global, national, state) to the micropolitics of schools through the ongoing formation of human subjectivity. Discourses, as systematic sets of meanings, circulate around practices of particular institutions (education), but also globally and locally, around certain cultural and social practices (e.g. feminism, economic rationalism, the New Right, management). Discourses 'regulate how we understand who we are, as well as how we understand our limits and possibilities in the social order' (Kelly 1993: 10). Discourses are the institutionalized use of language, which can occur at a disciplinary, political, cultural and small group level. Discourses shift to accommodate, modify, appropriate and resist more disruptive elements in order to maintain hegemony, and thus produce new, although often fragile, settlements between discursive fields. Thus new management theories gain ascendancy by incorporating, co-opting and transforming more emancipatory feminist leadership discourses. While discourses shape boundaries through the power of their internal logic, which privileges some readings over others (e.g. efficiency over equity), they are also unpredictable in their readings and effects in particular contexts. There is power through discourse however, in that the interests of some particular groups can be furthered because of their capacity to impart legitimate meanings while subjugating the meanings of other groups (Kelly 1993: 10). Discourses therefore have material effects (distribution of resources), in that they arise out of, as well as produce, particular historical (and therefore material) conditions.

Policy can be viewed as both text and discourse (Ball 1994). Policy as a text is written, read and reinterpreted as text, with a level of openendedness in its reception, although policymakers seek to create a 'correct reading'. Policy is a discourse in that ensembles of policies produce certain discursive truths. Thus the ensemble of policies on performance management, industrial relations, curriculum and assessment reform surrounding the Schools of the Future programme in Victoria mean self-managing schools are discursively portrayed as being more responsive and flexible to meet individual student needs better, community based, and conducive to professional autonomy, thus producing discursive truths about self-management, leadership and education (Kenway *et al.* 1994). In turn, policy texts and discourses are reshaped and rearticulated in often unexpected ways through practice, through their 'popu-larization', simultaneously tapping into, and creating, common-sense understandings about the nature of education. Thus discourses about women in leadership are informed by wider discourses about the politics of gender relations. Policy as a communicative practice is also about prioritizing and the allocation of values; and shifts in discourses and vocabularies of practice can lead to significant shifts in value (Gewirtz *et al.* 1995; Taylor *et al.* 1997). The notion of equity can, for example, through such discursive shifts, produce new meanings at different historical moments.

Feminist poststructuralists suggest that discursive practices both constrain and shape possibilities for action, and therefore have the capacity to be both emancipatory and repressive (Sawicki 1991). Individual subjects 'position themselves within discursive practices in multiple ways – in opposition to some discourses, in agreement with others' (Bartky 1990: 75). To be *constituted* by discourses is not to be *determined* by discourse, however. Subjectivity conceptualizes identity formation as an ongoing contradictory, precarious and complex process. It imparts a sense of agency, reflexivity and contradiction often lost in theories of the unitary self. It recognizes the contradictory nature of how power works, in that individuals can feel both powerful and powerless in different discursive spaces. Power here is 'exercised rather than possessed', by individuals on themselves as well as over others, and is 'not primarily repressive, but productive' (Sawicki 1991: 21, 25). The exercise of power does not necessarily require coercion; rather, power is exercised in many ways by individuals on themselves through self-discipline or self-regulation.

Power is contingent on particular social arrangements or networks of relations rather than on discrete elements and not located only in one source, but multiple sources (capitalism, patriarchy; Brown 1988: 207). The relations of gender are structured in three primary ways – through the division of labour, power and by emotional attachment which work in confluence and flux across the private and public domain (Connell 1987); and 'where there is power, there is resistance . . . We're never trapped by power; it's always possible to modify its hold, in determined conditions and following a precise strategy' (Foucault 1978: 95). Such a view of power recognizes that individuals may appear to 'choose' to act or be complicit in their own oppression. While recognizing the contingent nature of power and resistance, I suggest that this view of power can be extrapolated to consider links between systematic nodes of domination (patriarchy, capitalism) and sites of resistance, for example social movements (Sawicki 1991; McNay 1992). Such a perspective provides a framework for thinking about the irrationality and unpredictability of gender education reform, but also how global discourses about education reform, feminism and leadership play out in quite patterned forms in particular contexts in schools and bureaucracies.

Organizing the text

The text is organized to provide a broad historical sweep of the historical construction of gender/power/knowledge relations in educational administration in Part I, with a progressive focusing in Part II on how policy production actually works in an educational bureaucracy, and then in Part III, upon how policy is read and acted upon in specific sites. Part I focuses upon the ongoing renegotiation of the gendered division of labour in education in which men manage and women teach. The first chapter traces how educational administration has historically been constituted as a 'technology of the masculine' which associates leadership with rationality and autonomy, in opposition to teaching as a 'pedagogy of the feminine' associated with emotionality and care, thus constructing gender inflected images of 'good teachers' and 'good leaders' (de Lauretis 1987: 2–3; Theobald 1996). I explore how administration as a discursive field generates new regimes of truth associating particular hegemonic masculinities with a transcendental image of strong masculinist leadership that survives colonial, bureaucratic and marketized systems of educational governance.

The second chapter explores the forging of connections between masculinity, knowledge and power as educational administration came to be constituted as a disciplinary field by tapping into other powerful knowledges (science and economics) and fields of practice (business, psychology and management) to gain public legitimacy and epistemological authority. I argue that while feminism destabilized the claims of positivist theories of administration to objectivity and universality during the 1980s, administrative discourses have indicated the capacity to rework, co-opt, subvert and incorporate potentially oppositional feminist leadership discourses. Equally, feminist leadership discourses have indicated a capacity to be normative, reinforcing rather than challenging the gendered binaries between rationality and emotionality, for example, by promoting notions of women's styles of leadership which could be read in essentialist ways. At the same time, as the life histories of women teacher–leaders illustrate in Chapter 3, individual women read, interpret and act upon feminist as well as administrative and professional discourses in selective and subversive ways, although feminism, as a social and theoretical movement, remained for many women leaders critical to their gender identity formation and sense of being a leader.

In the second part, I argue that gender equity reformers, both in bureaucracies and schools in the 1990s, confront a radically different political and educational context. Because gender equity policies and practice have focused upon changing women, but less so upon changing organizations, changing men, or transforming the social relations of gender, they have not achieved their early promise. Gender equity reform imperatives have also been partly derailed due to the coincidence of gender equity initiatives (eg. affirmative action legislation) with restructuring and the closer alignment of education to the economy and state policy after the mid-1980s. This is marked by the shift from the welfare to the competitive or contractualist state (Yeatman 1993). Indeed, as mapped out in Chapter 4, changing state/education relations in the context of the new contractualism of market liberalism now jeopardize feminism's claims. I trace the shifts in the meaning of gender inequality in policy texts in Australia away from terms such as 'social justice' to those of 'managing diversity' in the context of more conservative organizational politics. The Victorian case studies, stories and critical incidents cited in Chapter 5 illustrate the contradictions and resistances experienced daily by those feminist bureaucrats (femocrats) who sought to produce gender equity reform by working through and within the state in the production of policy. Chapter 6 then examines the nature of the structural backlash and how male resistance to gender equity reform is discursively played out through the appropriation and misreading of gender equity discourses.

Part III focuses upon the micropolitics of gender in schools and points to significant silences in the women in leadership and change theory literature about masculinity, emotionality, authority, sexuality and the body. Chapter 7 highlights the gendered nature of the 'emotional management work' increasingly being done by principals, the middle managers of a system in crisis, and its effects on women principals in particular. Chapter 8 casts the feminist gaze upon how authority continues to be embodied in highly masculine ways in both bureaucracies and schools, positioning women as 'other' and incapable of authority, and the tactics women develop to assert their authority as leaders. Chapter 9 recognizes that while Australian white middle-class feminism provides powerful discourses of solidarity and collectivism, discourses from which individual non-feminist women have also benefited, such discourses have failed to problematize the category of woman. By marginalizing issues of race, class and ethnicity, as well as different political value positions, such discourses can become essentializing, silencing alternative ways of conceptualizing leadership. Together, these chapters question the hegemonic discourses that conflate 'being female' with 'being feminist', which, in homogenizing the category of women, perpetuates the bipolarity between rationality/emotionality, mind/body upon which women's subordination has long been premised.

In the conclusion, while I acknowledge the considerable successes of feminism so far, I point to how feminists may need to rethink both their short-term tactics and long-term strategies in an era of educational self-management and the market, and suggest some principles upon which a feminist postmasculinist politics may be based. In particular, I argue that a feminist postmasculinist politics should not flinch from the normative dimensions underpinning leadership and educational change, or about asking why we are changing, and who benefits?

Notes

1 There are two new management discourses – the softer version that derives from the human resource management and democratic workplace approach of the

1980s, and the hard version of the 1990s that assumes strong top-down leadership through the concept of re-engineering .

2 Lingard and Douglas make a similar point in their book on masculinity in this series.

3 My thanks to the Australian Research Council and Deakin University for funding the various projects informing this text, Women and Educational Leadership (1993, Small ARC) and Women in the Educational Bureaucracy in particular. The research was also informed by my involvement in professional development activities with teachers and principals within the Victorian state education system from 1990–96.

Part I

DISCIPLINARY TECHNOLOGIES

1 The gendering of educational work

To reinstate women's presence in the past provides spaces for women's voices and actions in the present. History also reminds us that social institutions and organizations are socially constructed, not given, and are in an ongoing process of transformation. History informs political actors of a sense of the possibilities of and impediments to, as well as the unpredictability, of change. In the next three chapters, I unravel the genealogies of the technologies of gender constituting educational work. Gender is 'the product and process of a number of social technologies' such as administration and schooling, of 'institutionalized discourses, epistemologies and critical practices, as well as practices of daily life' (de Lauretis 1987: 2–3). Theobald (1996) in *Knowing Women* argues that educational administration, as a technology of the masculine, produced its own truth claims, discourses and practices. Teaching was positioned as the 'other', a pedagogy of the feminine, in systematic, but not always predictable, ways. In this chapter I explore the connections between the particular regimes of truth associating rationality to masculinity in leadership, and thereby emotionality with teaching and femininity. I consider how these regimes of truth came to be and how they retain their hegemony. I document the counter-hegemonic discourses and various strategies called upon by feminists seeking to make administration more gender-inclusive. I shift the feminist gaze onto the 'politics of male privilege' to consider how the gendered division of labour has been sustained and reinvigorated.

Discourses of leadership and administration, in their ongoing reconstitution, draw upon various educational discourses circulating about the way schools are organized, about what students should be taught, how and by whom; professional discourses about child-centred pedagogies; as well as discourses about masculinity and femininity. They are products of particular historical moments and particular readings. Some discourses of leadership have been privileged in education. For example, there was the discourse of patriarchal masculinism institutionalized by, and into, the regulative practices of emergent state educational bureaucracies during the late nineteenth century. This was partially displaced by the discourse of paternalistic masculinism encapsulated in the ideal of the rational, neutral bureaucrat, which came to dominate the postwar social democratic educational settlement that shaped the modern welfare state. Now there is a discourse of strategic masculinism embodied in the image of the multiskilled, visionary, entrepreneurial post-modern manager in the era of self-governance and market liberalism of the last decades of the twentieth century. As the next three sections in this chapter indicate, these discourses, products of particular historical structural, cultural and social relations, some more enduring than others, coexist and compete for dominance, while their underlying thread is the ongoing association between masculinity and leadership.

Throughout the text I use Brittan's (1989) valuable distinction between masculinity, masculinism and patriarchy. Whereas masculinity refers to the features of male behaviour that can change over time, masculinism denotes the ideology that naturalizes and justifies men's domination over women. Patriarchy is the structure of unequal power relations sustained through this ideology (Brittan 1989: 3–5). Discourses about different masculinities and femininities, and what constitutes the norms of masculinity and femininity, are continually reconstituted. Hegemonic masculinities, while challenged and contested, continue to maintain their hegemony by discursively positioning as weaker and lesser 'other' masculinities (homosexuality) and all forms of femininity (Connell 1995). Masculinism remains relatively intact and is maintained through various homophobic and misogynist behaviours played out organizationally as sexual harassment and discrimination (Itzin and Newman 1995). The enduring paradox is that 'male heterosexual identity, which is a highly fragile socially constructed phenomenon' continues to be 'represented as an apparently stable and unitary category', a transcendental essence of rational man (Mac an Ghaill 1996: 7).

Local school management and patriarchal masculinism in an era of colonial governance

Benevolent paternalism was the mark of nineteenth-century Australian education. The Australian colonies did not develop educational 'systems' in the modern sense until the late nineteenth century when representative government and free immigration created the impetus for educational growth. In a localized market, denominational and state aided schools competed with private working-class dame schools to meet the needs of a emergent professional and commercial middle class. Teaching offered an independent and relatively autonomous occupational niche for many working-class women prior to the establishment of free compulsory and secular state systems in the 1870s in most western industrial nations (Acker 1996). Teachers, male and female, worked as independent contractors who decided upon the 'subjects they taught, set the level of fees, employed, paid and trained their own pupil teachers and assistants and sometimes built and owned their own school houses in a deregulated market' (Miller 1986: 25). These early schools existed in a highly competitive environment, reliant upon an inspector's paternalism and parental and community goodwill to maintain numbers and prevent closure. At that time, teaching was not secure employment. Teachers were subject to hiring and firing at the whim of school boards. For their survival, teachers, many of them women, often forged local community alliances with clergy and business. 'The free market of education before 1872 shaped an élite of teaching matriarchs, respected by parents and inspectors alike, who were accustomed to wielding power' (Theobald 1996: 146). But as women, they worked within the bounds of acceptable female behaviour prescribed at that time – as carers and nurturers of the young.

In the relatively autonomous but still embryonic bureaucracies of the more systematized national and denominational schools, a gendered division of labour quickly emerged. Male inspectors worked through patronage to produce a 'star system' of rewards. From the beginning, the culture, values and regulations institutionalized male advantage in this new profession. Women were paid 80 per cent of the male wage regardless of equal work, promotion was predicated on seniority, salary augmentations only went to head teachers (mostly men) and favoured larger urban schools (largely male teachers). Payment by results, which made teachers' salaries dependent upon pupil performance at external examinations, meant head teachers (mainly men) were more generously rewarded than assistants (largely women) (Theobald 1996: 184).

> The creation of the teaching profession cannot be seen in isolation from the mission of middle class men to create a bailiwick outside the uncertain pursuit of wealth in the marketplace. The invention of the professions, the expansion of the public service, the bestowal of power and civic subjectivities through democratic institutions . . . were the building blocks of middle-class masculinity in the nineteenth century. Territory had to be marked out, and in its defence, the administration of gender was central.
>
> (Theobald 1996: 174)

Compulsory free mass elementary state education was established in Victoria in 1872, as in other Australian states and most western liberal nations during the 1870s. Its establishment was initiated by an increasingly powerful middle-class male élite in response to the erratic provision offered by state endowed and religious schools of education in the local market. This new élite was also influenced by the desire to promote consensual social and moral order through a literate (male) citizenry. As in most western nation states during the 1870s, the bureaucratic formation of state education systems made women's presence in education both 'threatening and necessary' (Theobald 1996: 175). The state increasingly relied upon a pool of working-class female pupil teachers in a quasi-apprenticeship system to staff its expanding system of one-teacher rural schools (85 per cent of all pupil teachers in Victoria in 1888 were female). Patriarchal control was maintained through male school inspectors; surveillance being both of a sexual and professional nature, the male checking for female moral impropriety as well as poor work, as well as contracts establishing appropriate behaviour of female teachers in terms of dress, accommodation and decorum. The power of these 'administrative professionals', backed by the authority of the state, supplanted the earlier localized authority of professional males (local businessmen or clergymen), but consolidated the association between middle-class masculinity and public authority.

At that critical moment in the late nineteenth century, the 'naturalness' of the categories of 'man' and 'woman' and their conventional attributes as defined by popular constructs about gender roles in the family went unquestioned. Women's association with nature, as that of men's with culture embedded in Enlightenment thought, meant women were positioned as the biological inferior, requiring protection by the transcendent spirit of males who dominated the material world. Women as teachers were 'mothers-made-conscious' (Steedman 1985), with an incapacity to 'manage the material' matched only by their innate abilities for nurturant and emotive tasks (Reiger 1985: 21). The administration of public life required a natural paternal authority, the male's innate capacity to control the material world. In turn, the conflation of teaching and maternal care and the discursive construction of the 'pedagogy of the feminine', was particularly evident in the late nineteenth-century child-centred pedagogy. 'Love rather than coercion, became the centrepiece of the new pedagogy, and, with love replacing fear (or authority), was the woman teacher' (Walkerdine 1993: 62). While the pragmatics of women's employment in teaching was based on assumptions about their 'natural' skills of maternal care as well as their cheapness, the discourse legitimating their presence was that of moral danger (Theobald 1996). 'Women had to be the guardians of that moral order and the regulation of their sexuality and its channelling into nurturance was central to that regulation' (Walkerdine 1986: 63). Women teachers brought both moral and domestic virtues into the civil domain, and stood as complementary to men's propensity for moral weakness. Indeed, the association of the unmarried male teacher with moral danger and potential transgression, meant schools run by married couples were often favoured. Thus

> the mutual colonisation of the educational state and the teaching family constituted an early manipulation of the teaching labour market which allowed the authority of the husband over the wife to be translated into the authority of the male teacher over the female teacher . . . Yet from

the beginning women were seldom heads of any but the smallest coun-
try schools where no man could be found to take the position. This
unwritten law excluding women from the manifest rewards of the head
teachership was a crucial mechanism in their professional confinement.

(Theobald 1996: 191)

Because women's authority was premised upon the dangerous grounds of
sexual propriety and not technical expertise, femininity was thus cast in
antithesis to professional and public authority. There was a need, however,
to facilitate the entrance of the bourgeois daughter into the 'new' profession
of teaching, which combined respectability and short-term independence
before marriage. In order to remove the threat of being considered 'deviant'
or 'unsexed', discourses of masculinity and femininity were reconstructed
around the 'new woman' and 'the good teacher', which emphasized the
asexual and the maternal.

The legislative and organizational gate-keeping mechanisms excluding
women from leadership established during the late nineteenth century were
therefore predicated upon the naturalness of male authority and female
unsuitability for authority. While teachers were ranked and classified first on
the basis of gender, seniority and then merit (qualifications plus experience),
the feminization of teaching during the 1870s gave rise to what is now a
recurrent 'discourse of male anxiety' arising out of the threat to the formation of a masculine identity so closely bound to authority over women
and paid work. This anxiety underpinned legislation protecting male
teachers in the late 1880s, which barred women from being principals of
larger schools; which reclassified women so that promotion opportunities
disappeared; which continued to pay women four-fifths the male wage and
which disallowed employment of married women teachers (Biddington
1994: 287). After 1872, 'the educational project of the state did not set in
train the feminisation of teaching; it set in train the bureaucratisation of
women's teaching labour' (Theobald 1996: 175). The rise of mass state education was more 'the transition of patriarchal forms rather than the transition to capitalism', given that Australia did not experience full scale
industrialization until after 1945, as the characteristics of the father were
readily transported into the public roles of principal, administrator and professional (Miller and Davies quoted in Theobald 1996: 198).

The regulatory welfare state and paternalistic masculinity

With the federation of the Australian colonies in 1901, there was agreement
between conservative, liberal and labour ideologies about the power of science and technology. There was a convergence between new economic discourses of human capital that saw education as contributing to the economic

growth of the nation state and older discourses of social capital that envisaged education as promoting nationalism, social cohesion and racial purity. The now highly centralized state education bureaucracies took seriously the welfarist legacy of the state-run economies of Australia's colonial history, viewing centralization as offering both uniformity and equality in educational provision. This cultural reliance upon a strong state to deliver equality was maintained in the shift from the 'benevolent authoritarianism' of the colonies in the nineteenth century to one of 'benevolent paternalism' in the twentieth-century nation state. As education became increasingly critical to national advancement and efficiency in the discursive construction of the new nation, state intervention and regulation over education and teachers' work increased. The demise of most private academies after the 1906 Registration Act regulating all schools effectively constrained the career opportunities for educated middle-class women. The irony was that together the bureaucratization and professionalization of state education systems consolidated, if not exacerbated, the division of labour in which men managed and women taught (Hansot and Tyack 1983).

The construction of women teachers' work as marginal was part of a wider social redefinition through official policies of the new nation state that depicted women's work (paid and unpaid) as unproductive. Underpinning the emergent welfare state was the assumption that women were dependants of the paternalistic state rather than of individual men, as in the previous century. It was a maternalist and protective state that privileged the perspective that women's rights lay with their reproductive responsibility as 'racial mothers' (Biddington 1994: 32). Labour laws and administrative practices were modelled on a preferred image of the bourgeois family that became institutionalized during the 1900s into the industrial relations system under the policy of the minimum 'living family wage' in which the family unit was constructed as a male breadwinner, his dependent wife and two children. Underlying these administrative and juridicio-legal regimes were liberal theories of citizenship and the social contract that pseudo-included women under the universal rubric of 'man' and which implicitly contained a sexual contract naming the husband as the public representative of the family unit (Pateman 1988).

This new mode of governmentality in the decades after federation in 1901 coincided with a period in which the 'radical knowledges' of nationalism, Darwinism and socialism flourished, informed by Enlightenment ideas of the capacity of *man* to control *his* environment and nature through science, thus consolidating the public/private division. Women were excluded from this equation of control and science, thus translating into the cultures and knowledge hierarchies of mass education the 'mutually impoverishing split between masculine "rationality" and "feminine intuition"' at a time when the patriarchal ordering of society was renegotiated under 'organised capitalism' (Theobald 1987: 162). Somebody within this new and disturbing society must retain those qualities of nurturance and selflessness necessary in a just and liberal society. This ideological formation, informed by middle-class values of the nuclear family, equated masculinity with the public and technical rationality while femininity was equated with the private and the affective.

> This representation of bourgeois woman as moral and men as material-istic served to support the removal of moral, spiritual and interpersonal values from the public world of industry and commerce. Safely located with women in the domestic sphere, they were devalued and margin-alised but kept alive in a haven for the work-worn alienated male.
>
> (Reiger 1985: 21)

Some of the main features of the bourgeois model of the family became institutionalized in modern organizations at this time: discourses associating masculinity with administration stressed the rational, unemotional, logical and authoritative aspects of human behaviour as for example, those embod-ied in Weberian bureaucracy (Bologh 1990). Discourses of femininity saw woman as 'a container which soaks up and contains the irrationality which she best understands', doing the work of emotional labour in the private sphere of the family and as the handmaiden in the public quasi-professions of service: education, health and welfare (Walkerdine 1986: 59). Hegemonic middle-class masculinities that embodied rationality and neutrality and predicated upon expertise thus supplanted the tradition-centred notion of paternalistic masculinity in which authority was primarily derived from being the family patriarch.

> Over the period in which both the modern state and the industrial econ-omy was produced, the hegemony of this form of masculinity was chal-lenged and displaced by masculinities organised much more around technical rationality and calculation . . . This did not eliminate other masculinities. What it did was marginalise them: and this created con-ditions for new versions of masculinity that rested on impulses or prac-tices excluded from the increasingly rationalised and integrated world of business and bureaucracy.
>
> (Connell 1987: 130–1)

Meanwhile, the 'cult of true womanhood' only superficially disguised the contradictions inherent in the relationship between the bourgeois family model, education and the workplace. Educated middle-class women were among the emerging class of professional managers, experts in the field of education, health, welfare and psychology, who began a progressive program of social engineering in the early 1900s in the name of science (Reiger 1985). The professionalization of teaching, as other new professions, illustrated the capacity of the 'new middle class' to control technical and ideological resources in order to mark themselves off from the working class and achieve social mobility. Within organizations, new authority relations emerged premised upon the mental/manual division of labour with all its gender and class inflections. While professionalism offered some strategic possibilities for women, it also contained sources of entrapment. Women teachers gained some ground by tapping into the discourses of professionalism. For example, they gained new career paths for women into the principalship denied to them in coeducational schools, by advocating domestic science schools on the grounds of their feminine expertise in the new 'science of the domestic' (Biddington 1994). Feminist teacher unionists argued that teaching could not become a profession while women, who constituted the majority of the occupation, were treated as second class citizens. Yet the professionalization of teaching was seen by state employers and male teachers to be predicated upon an increased male presence rather than improving the status of women teachers beyond 'administering the feminine'.

The bureaucratization and professionalization of education, therefore, was largely at the expense of women's individuality and autonomy but to the benefit of burgeoning capitalism and middle-class masculinity. Claims for greater leadership for women were now contained within the parameters of the paternalistic state rather than those of the patriarchal father. While the claims of first wave 'modern' feminism focused upon human rights and equality as espoused in gender-neutral ideologies of professionalism, gender was central to the ways in which educational leadership was both constructed to, and measured against, the male norm, even though what was normative masculinity in education was not the same as in other workplaces. Being male administrators in a feminized profession meant the principal's work identity and authority was premised less on the traditional masculine boundaries in industry of mental (effeminate/soft) and manual (masculine/hard), but instead on new professional hierarchies distinguishing between hard (finance and administration) and soft (curriculum and pedagogy) knowledge (Roper 1994). Indeed hegemonic heterosexual masculinity in educational management early on assumed the cult of toughness, a desire to assert authority while haunted by the fear of effeminacy.

Hegemonic heterosexual masculinities also positioned those single women who 'made the wrong choice' between career and marriage as deviant. By the 1950s, the rigid code of compulsory heterosexuality and Freudian dictum that woman's anatomy was her destiny dominated, although the modern woman was still described in gender neutral languages (Weiler 1988; Bacchi 1990). The new sciences of sociology and psychology normalized a view of sexual identity that portrayed heterosexual sex within marriage as natural and healthy in a way which 'increasingly stigmatized celibate women, spinsters and lesbians' as 'deviant and threatening' (Weiler 1994: 16; Acker 1996). Thus single women teaching in the public domain were seen to become too 'masculine' while there were significant attempts to attract 'manly men' into teaching. There was a simultaneous desexualization of public life around notions of bureaucratic neutrality and rationality and a subtle resexualization on the basis of paternalistic heterosexual familial roles (Blount 1994). In this way, state paternalism

> facilitates a reduction of the tension surrounding management and individual masculinities by simulating typically patriarchal, family-like relations where power is exercised for the 'good' of the recipient . . . The reduction of tensions renders employees more compliant and predictable and, therefore, the lives of those exercising power more comfortable . . . adopting a paternal role helps legitimise the managerial prerogative both in the eyes of those who are 'protected' from the harsh reality of decision-making and the decision-makers themselves.
>
> (Kerfoot and Knights 1993: 665)

Women's educational leadership was from the start within the state education system limited to administering the feminine – teaching young children and girls and the leadership of women – although still judged against the male norm. The Director of Victorian Education, Frank Tate, referred to Margaret Robertson, the most senior woman at the Melbourne Continuation School in 1907, as possessing the 'qualities necessary to influence the education of girls'. The senior mistress at Ballarat Continuation School was appointed to act as 'leader for women teachers' and to 'care for the girls'. Yet both were known as being strong women, Robertson as having 'style, ability, moral power and withering discipline', and the latter as being 'strict and much loved' (Biddington 1994: 81). To be positioned as a leader, even of women, one had to display male characteristics of strength and discipline, be exceptionally qualified, but to temper one's behaviour with style and love. Frank Tate also argued that 'under the present system of co-education, the making of women eligible for positions in the first class would involve the supervision and control by women of senior boys and the male teachers of the staff. Women are not qualified for such a task' (Biddington 1994: 81). Women's seeming lack of 'natural authority' over boys was secondary to adult male anxiety arising from the perceived unnaturalness of female authority over men.

This seemingly natural association of rationality, masculinity and bureaucratic neutrality was readily challenged by the female presence, as for example, when Julia Flynn, a highly experienced Inspector of Secondary Schools, was actively discriminated against by the Director of Education, Martin Hansen, when seeking promotion to Chief Inspector in 1928. Her appointment was refused by Hansen on the grounds that 'a woman could not do the work' of a Chief Inspector because secondary education was 'preeminently boys' education' and thus required 'male supervision' (Hannan 1975: 3).

the Chief Inspector has to interview parents and councils, discuss all manner of details, even those dealing with sanitary arrangements, holding inquiries into complaints often involving sex matters, and these duties, I am satisfied, a woman should not be called upon to undertake.

(Hannan 1975: 5)

Thus male professionals redefined and appropriated as masculine those skills traditionally viewed as 'female' emotional labour in the family (dealing with social and sexual relationships, the emotional and the affective) once they became relocated in the realm of public. Flynn's case exemplified how 'public personnel practice in Australia was based on the concept that all responsible positions should be a male enclave' (Hannan 1975: 15). It also indicated how merit was readily reinterpreted to maintain their advantage through the 'mobilisation of male bias' as senior male bureaucrats exploited notions of procedural neutrality to justify their complicity in keeping women out of leadership (Burton 1991). By the 1960s, the image of the modern manager of public education bureaucracies embedded in the culture, practices and discourses of education was that of a rational, neutral man exercising legitimate authority in a juridicio-legal manner.

Self-management, the corporate state and strategic masculinism

These discourses linking particular notions of masculinity to neutrality and rationality were to be challenged during the 1970s: first, by changes to the nature of state education policy formation; and second, by the rise of new social movements. State Directors of Education in Australia, prior to the 1960s, had worked 'relatively independently' from their ministers, largely determining educational policy directions and detail. The political disinterest nationally in Australia in education prior to the 1960s was largely because the links between education and economic growth in Australia were more rhetorical than actual in an expanding agricultural and minerals-based economy with full employment until 1974. While government education systems were highly bureaucratic and rule governed, there was an element of a strong public service-oriented ethic in public administration, an ethic that increasingly informed social justice policies in the decades after 1972 (Yeatman 1990). Federal intervention in education during the 1970s was premised on both human capital arguments that education produced economic growth and the belief that education could play a part in reducing social inequality (Dudley and Vidovich 1995).

Entering schools in the 1970s were the first-generation children of the postwar immigrants, largely central European. Yet the mythology of Australian egalitarianism concealed inequalities based on class, gender, race and ethnicity. Education was segmented, by class, with a strong private sector in

Victoria of up to 30 per cent all students; by gender, with numerous single-sex schools; by race, as Aboriginal children were neglected or ignored; and by ethnicity, as there was little provision for students of non-English speaking background. Teaching still provided social mobility for the 'bright' working-class and rural girls of Anglo-Celtic background (see Chapter 3). Indeed, the educational expansion of the 1960s demanded by demographics and increased retention rates had relied upon the part-time, temporary labour of married women.

However the contradictions of modernist expectations and highly discriminatory actions against married women teachers by state employers, together with the increase in qualified female teacher graduates and the rise of the second wave of the women's movement, repoliticized women teachers during the 1960s. It also led to the re-emergence of the sameness/difference debates of the late nineteenth century amongst feminists. Should women compete on the same terms as men by minimizing gender differences or should they argue on the grounds of 'special assistance' as women (Bacchi 1990)? In the context of modern social life being framed by gender-neutral, rational bureaucratic discourses, modern woman's entrance into the workplace in the 1970s, 'the image of women as being naturally maternal and morally superior to men was abandoned as women minimised their mothering role and the characteristics associated with that role' (Bacchi 1990: 75). If women were to succeed in the world of work (and men), they had to overcome their conditioning as women and develop 'male' aggressiveness, assertiveness and independence.

Teaching also acquired professional status during the 1970s, both because women teachers gained equal pay for equal work in 1970 and also because a now highly qualified teacher workforce of postwar baby boomers were prepared to act industrially to secure their status. For over 90 years, women teacher unionists had fought both the male dominated union and the state, sometimes splitting off to form their own unions. When women claimed equal pay, the responses were that women's interests were particularist and against the interests of the state who could not afford equal pay; men were portrayed as the family breadwinners, and the legitimation of teaching as a profession was seen to rest upon the masculinization of teaching. Indeed, male unionists were often complicit with their state employer in mobilizing, or not refuting, these discourses about women's lesser capacities, needs and status. Winning equal pay foregrounded women teachers' underrepresentation in educational leadership and the structural and systemic barriers discriminating against women. In 1970, women in most Australian states could not be appointed as principals of coeducational or boys' schools, were not eligible for the state superannuation scheme, and were listed on separate promotion rolls. Promotion was still predicated on continuity of experience and seniority whereas the majority of women teachers were part-time and temporary (Hughey 1989).

Equal pay also symbolized a changing relationship between women and the state. After 1972, the new social movements (women, students, environmental and peace) had made claims upon the state. A strategy of the newly formed national Women's Electoral Lobby was to install feminists within the new Labor government in specially designated equal opportunity (EO) positions to promote gender equity. This uniquely Australian form of state feminism meant feminist bureaucrats or femocrats officially worked from within the state in the interests of women. After 1975, there was considerable legislative activity promoting equal opportunity based upon the principles of merit, not seniority, at state level. This legislation legitimated and institutionalized discourses of equity throughout the public sector during the 1980s, which in turn, articulated with discourses of equity of other social movements such as multiculturalism (Eisenstein 1996).

The project of corporate federalism instituted by Labor when re-elected in the 1980s was to actively recruit the leaders of the new social movements into the state, a strategy of incorporation replicated by Victorian state Labor governments. Thus educational activists, many of them women, moved into key policymaking positions, matching top-down initiatives with those of grass-roots organizations and unions, so encouraging local ownership of social programs. In Victorian education, a liberal–conservative government in 1974 also responded to the administrative overload of a highly centralized education bureaucracy and to parent and teacher organization claims for greater involvement in school-based decisionmaking by introducing teacher and student representation on school councils. This first shift towards administrative decentralization was followed by a more radical move to participatory decisionmaking in schools under Labor government policies espoused in the Ministerial Papers in Education 1983–85 which promoted school-based decisionmaking, school councils, school review and school-based curriculum development. Earlier federal policies of the schools council promoting localization and participation were echoed within Victoria as education stakeholders (teacher unions, parent organizations, EO practitioners) were 'co-opted' onto local, regional and central educational policymaking committees (Blackmore 1991).

In Victoria, however, as federally, the financial crisis of 1987 meant economic rationalist discourses of efficiency and effectiveness, always present during the 1980s, now openly competed with feminist and multicultural discourses of equity and fairness. In these discourses of economic rationalism, the economic orthodoxy of human capital theory linked education more instrumentally and closely to the economy. Society was 'now recast as the object of politics' and represented as a 'sort of stubbornly resisting sludge, and even as 'an idealised opponent' of the 'economy' (Pusey 1991: 10). Federal corporate managerialism rearticulated down into state public administrations in response to the ongoing legitimation (financial) crisis of the state; the demands of the new social movements for a more responsive state; the rise of the New Right and its demands for reduced public expenditure; and the increased complexity of governance, which led the state to steer through policy (Taylor *et al.* 1997). Corporate managerialism meant devolving responsibility to small subunits to produce flexibility, strong central policy guidelines to coordinate and provide direction to those on the ground, clear processes of review and feedback from periphery to the centre, an emphasis on output not input, and a client focus. Managerialist discourses promoting efficiency and effectiveness took on new force relative to discourses of equity.

The state's response was in terms of *formal* and not *substantive* rationality, with 'the adoption of a rhetoric and measures which are designed to *show* that we have a cost-effective and efficient public sector' although the public sector is unable to take the 'final test of success in the market place' (Yeatman 1990: 5). The effect was to dismantle rule-bound processes and structures and orient all towards output and outcomes, to achieve flexibility by freeing up the state and making the state a player in the open market, and to encourage an ethos of change, although under Labor, still guided by issues of equity. Thus three discourses came to coexist and compete in education during the late 1980s: the social democratic discourse of the period of participatory decisionmaking, the corporate managerialist discourse of the 1980s and the market discourse.

It has been the market and efficiency discourses, however, that have been increasingly privileged as the state has become defensive in the context of global economic volatility with market deregulation (Yeatman 1990: 1–4; Taylor *et al.* 1997: 85). While Labor justified educational restructuring around the principles of managerialism and the market on the grounds of the need to upgrade the national skills base to achieve global competitiveness, Labor was also careful to retain the safety net of the welfare state in a form of regulated deregulation. By contrast, conservative governments, elected in most states and federally after 1995, began dismantling and privatizing the welfare state (education, heath and welfare). Market principles became central to governance, for example, competition policy. These conservative governments took the economic rationalism discourses of Labor to the extreme, aligning the older discourses of localization and democratization with public choice theory and market liberalism, theories predicated upon a level playing field and the view of an atomistic rational individual who makes independent choices to maximize benefits for the self (Pusey 1991).

Throughout the 1980s there was a shift away from the service orientation of public administration (including education) towards an even stronger client focus. While Labor saw ministerial power asserted over their permanent bureaucratic heads through the introduction of 'a new technically-oriented elite' selected externally and on contract (Yeatman 1990; Pusey 1991), by the mid-1990s, the notion of the administrator serving the public had been supplanted by that of the multiskilled manager who serves the minister. This 'ministerialization' of education policy has led to increased emphasis on policies as solutions and on immediate measurable performance outcomes (Lingard 1993). These multiskilled managers, recruited from outside education and moved frequently, were expected to possess generic skills and competencies that enabled them to 'manage' any field of administrative activity. The best attribute of such a manager was a lack of personal commitment to, or experience in, the field of activity they managed, as commitment, experience and expertise represented particularistic, not universal, 'state' interests (of the government in power). The femocrats, as representatives of a wider constituency of women with specialist skills in equity, were obviously in jeopardy. Yeatman (1994: 110) describes this as a shift from the paternalistic welfare state towards that of the contractualist or performative state:

> For paternalism, the state substitutes performativity as the principle which legitimizes both its control functions, and the way in which those functions operate to contain the influence of the horizontally integrated, democratic politics of social movements and their claims on the state. The state is therefore subject to the contradictory dynamics of performativity and democratization. Performativity has the singular virtue of supplying a meta-discourse for public policy. Thus it can subsume and transform substantive democratizing claims within a managerialistic-functionalistic rhetoric.

The performative state is increasingly premised upon contractual exchanges between individuals that become embedded in curriculum and behaviour negotiations between students and teachers, in teacher employment contracts with principals, in performance management contracts between managers and teachers, and in school charter contracts with the ministry, which produce a form of self-regulation of the individual. Their outcomes focus on performativity encourages a process of individuation as teachers and principals work in a 'state of conscious and permanent visibility' resulting in a form of self-surveillance that assures the 'automatic functioning of power' (Bartky 1990: 65). Thus the reregulation of schools and teachers is achieved through curriculum standards frameworks, standardized assessment, and performance management. At the same time the deregulative aspects of the market mean that individual government schools compete with other government and private schools for students and take no responsibility for serving local neighbourhood communities with less sense of a 'public system'. Public schools are corporatized (increasingly reliant for funding upon sponsorships) and privatized (as educational costs and labour are increasingly being shifted to parents).

In this context, people become both the new source of productivity and the focus of control through performance management. While organizational complexity leads to increased executive decisionmaking, it also relies upon worker cooperation achieved through consensus building, mission statements and performance contracts as greedy organizations channel the intellectual and emotional energy of people (Cozer 1974; Drucker 1992). The democratization of line management is dependent upon a notion of professional expertise (implying authority and discretionary power), but the professionalization and democratization of the upper levels of the management does not permeate down to the lower level workers. Thus middle managers (such as school principals) are ambiguously positioned in this democratic fiction. Being labelled as middle managers 'draws them into the rational–technical discourses of management but does not necessarily confer on them the prerogatives of managers' (Yeatman 1990: 24). Here, hierarchy takes on new forms.

> In relation to hierarchy, strategic management both emphasises and de-emphasises differential power and status, simultaneously individualising and collectivising the workforce. On the one hand, removing layers of managerial authority from the chain of command, strategic management generates the appearance of 'flattening' hierarchical structures. Yet on the other, it elevates and reinforces hierarchical distinctions through encouraging career and corporate success by means of individual competition. In attempting to involve all in the collective commitment to the enterprise, this flattening of hierarchy, in effect, relocates managerial control 'at the heart' of the work group, for responsibility and accountability are shifted down to lower hierarchy employees.
>
> (Kerfoot and Knights 1993: 670–71)

In this context, performativity takes precedence over substance (Lyotard 1984; Lash and Urry 1994) as exchange value is added to the product (for example, schools) through image and design, and yet what remains critical to leadership is people management.

This shift from a paternalistic welfare state to a competitive state premised around the market and self-governance produces new images and understandings about leadership. Good leaders need to be entrepreneurial, strong and visionary but also good people managers (Gewirtz et al. 1995; Blackmore et al. 1996). It has meant the remaking of hegemonic masculinity away from the image of the rational bureaucrat to the multiskilled, flexible, service oriented, facilitative and entrepreneurial manager. Whereas old modernist performance principles of the gender-neutral bureaucrat were about delayed gratification and the denial of pleasure for work, which separated preference from fact, human feeling from the intellect, the new performativities of postmodern 'greedy' organizations exploit the pleasure of the win and getting the job done, as well as the intimacy of social relations to achieve organizational goals. Strategic management seeks to exploit diversity (gender, multiculturalism) to channel individual desires, passion and energy for organizational ends. In so doing, however, interpersonal relations are supplanted by depersonalized or contrived forms of intimacy, which produce new forms of self-regulation such as team work. Management thus manipulates intimacy within social relations and reconstitutes it into purposive-rational action, and in so doing reworks gender relations.

Kerfoot and Knights (1993) suggest that paternalistic and bureaucratic masculinities are being partially supplanted by new forms of strategic masculinity. Strategic or competitive masculinity

> equates with reason, logic and rational process; generates and sustains a hierarchy imbued with instrumentalism, careerism, and the language of 'success'; stimulates competition linked to decisive action, 'productivism' and risk taking; and renders sexual and bodily presence manifest through physicality, posture, movement and speech.
>
> (Kerfoot and Knights 1993: 671)

The new strategic management, thus, is 'still privileging men *vis-à-vis* women, ranks some men above others, and maintains as dominant certain forms and practices of masculinity' (Kerfoot and Knights 1993: 672).

New paradoxes thus emerge for women teachers and leaders. The popular discourse of women's styles of leadership – perceived to be more democratic, nurturant, supportive and collegial – gains credibility in this context. Women, traditionally depicted as possessing good people management skills, are seen to be an untapped source of leadership to be exploited. Yet women principals are also located by new discourses about women's inability to be good financial managers or entrepreneurs as well as old discourses about women's irrationality and lack of 'natural' authority. Furthermore, 'equal opportunity in this context comes to be reframed in terms of what it can do for management improvement, not in terms of what it can do to develop the conditions of social justice and democratic citizenship' (Burton 1991: 341). So while the paternalist authority of the household of the nineteenth century was borrowed by the welfare state, and the paternalistic welfare state was destabilized by the politics of voice and difference arising out of feminism and other social movements, the performative state is again reconstituting itself around the social relations of gender.

Continuities and discontinuities

The gendered division of labour premised upon administration as a technology of the masculine and teaching as a 'pedagogy of the feminine' was well founded early in Victorian educational history. While there may have been significant shifts in the relationship between the state, individuals and social movements played out in public and educational administration, discourses of educational leadership continued to reinforce, regenerate and privilege images of masculinity.

Let me now identify a number of continuities and discontinuities in this historical analysis that will resonate throughout the text. First is the strategic importance of the state with regard to feminism, leadership and educational change. To many feminists it is now clear that the state is not a thing, system, or subject but 'a significantly unbounded terrain of powers and techniques, an ensemble of discourses, rules and practices, cohabiting in limited, tension-ridden, often contradictory relation with each other' (Brown 1988: 12; Franzway *et al.* 1989; Watson 1990). These discourses, rules and practices of the state, as a set of relationships, processes and social practices, are disconnected and erratic, and often produce quite contradictory or paradoxical gender effects. The state is not gender-neutral, but a site of discursive struggle in which gender politics is central. The state simultaneously promotes gender equity policies but also actively constructs women as dependent, victims or unproductive. The state is not a uniform ideological apparatus, but a complex network of equally complex histories.

Yet, and this is the second point, the state 'institutionalises hegemonic masculinity' through a 'very active gender process' (Connell 1987: 128–9). Indeed, the state relies upon the changing patterns of gender relations and the reconstitution of masculinity over time. Discourses about masculinity and femininity alter over time and place, however, and have no 'transhistorical essence' (Connell 1995), despite the seeming transcendental continuities of discourses of rationality, masculinity and management. As the new sociology of masculinity points out, masculinity is 'the outcome of socially generated ideas, behaviours and practices surrounding the group named men' (Kerfoot and Knights 1993: 661–2). While the 'psychic realm of business' may be masculine, and 'public representations commonly depict the manager as a rational actor, the non-rational aspects of masculinity are clearly apparent in individual accounts of male managers' (Roper 1994: 20). Few individual men actually fit the image of the rational, logical, hard-nosed and independent leader. Furthermore, hegemonic masculinity is

> very different from the notion of a general 'male sex role' . . . [because] the cultural ideal (or ideals) of masculinity do not need to correspond at all closely to the actual personalities of the majority of men. Indeed the winning of hegemony often involves the creation of models of masculinity which are quite specifically fantasy figures.
>
> (Connell 1987: 185)

Hegemonic masculinist discourses are maintained through negotiation, the incorporation of resistance and counter-hegemonic discourses, and the ongoing repositioning of other modes of masculinity (wimpish masculinity or homosexuality) and all forms of femininity as lesser (Connell 1987, 1995; Segal 1990).

> Hegemonic masculinity is constructed in relation to women and to subordinated masculinities. These other masculinities need not be as clearly

defined – indeed, achieving hegemony may consist precisely in prevent-
ing alternatives gaining cultural definition and recognition as alternatives, confining them to ghettos, to privacy, to unconsciousness.

(Connell 1987: 185)

Although masculinities lag behind the times, masculinism seems to have
'a universal, unchanging quality' – rational, hard and unemotional – across
generations (Segal 1990).

The image of the manager as a rational thinker is evident in a wide
range of writings. Organisation studies have often followed Max Weber
in defining bureaucratic rationality as non-subjective. Taylor's 'scientific manager' manager earned the right to control the production
worker through virtue of his superior powers of reason. Managerial
economics, drawing upon the neo-classical models, assumes that managers are rational men who respond in every efficiently possible way to
market forces.

(Roper 1994: 2)

The gender politics of organizations is fraught with 'irrational' moments,
however. Such is the case of the complicity and collusion between male
unionists and managers to maintain gender inequality that arises out of male
anxiety because the presence of women in the workplace constitutes a threat
to male dominance due to men's ego-investment in waged work outside the
home and family (Cockburn 1991). Paradoxically, male teacher unionists,
no matter how unconsciously, do the ideological labour of the employer in
maintaining the lower status of female workers and, in so doing, serve the
particular interests of *all* males.

At any given moment, gender will reflect the material interests of those
who have power and those who do not. Masculinity therefore does not
exist in isolation from femininity – it will always be an expression of the
current image that men have of themselves in relation to women. And
these images are often contradictory and ambivalent. Masculinity from
this point of view, is always local and subject to change . . . What has
changed is not male power as such, but its form, its presentation, its
packaging. In other words, while it is apparent that styles of masculinity
may alter in relatively short time spans, the substance of male power
does not.

(Brittan 1989: 2–3)

The latter point is significant given backlash discourses claiming men as victims of feminism.

Third, the welfare state as source of legitimacy for and application of
expertise, as well as a labour market for professionals and intellectuals, is
now at risk. The formation of professional identity is highly gendered, and

the recurrent fear of feminization in teaching cannot be disconnected from the 'fear of making males effeminate; the rejection of female authority over men, and women's lack of intellectual ability to educate older boys' (Weiler 1994; Acker, S. 1995). The dilemma for women is that the class structure of the semi-professions and the public sector has not only provided mass jobs for women, but more particularly avenues of social mobility and the authority imparted through expertise, for educated women. Women seeking leadership are therefore caught in the bind of calling upon often competing discourses of professionalism and inequality (Chase 1995). Yet 'organisation man's ability to present himself as a professional first and foremost, [means] his masculine identity is hidden by a cloak of objectivity' (Roper 1994: 2).

Finally, central to feminist strategies to redress their disadvantage in education has been the same/difference dilemma. In western conceptual schema the feminine is usually defined with regard to the male norm – different from or similar to men.

> Feminists use arguments of 'sameness' or 'difference' when political constraints suggest that these are the only means available to improve women's lives. They are influenced in this decision by the available conceptual systems and the paucity of institutional alternatives.
>
> (Bacchi 1990: xi)

First wave feminists after the 1880s were clearly divided as to the strategic value of the 'equal but different' arguments. While the difference position meant women could claim leadership in the female domain in girls' schools, this did little to challenge hegemonic masculinities as the norm in education generally. The mid-twentieth century saw women subsumed as 'the same' under the gender-neutral discourses of administrative rationality and liberal feminism. Feminists appealed to a discourse of 'sameness' (equal pay for equal work) on an egalitarian reading of liberalism. This claim assumed that there were institutional anomalies and did not see the liberal rational individual of the social contract, as many feminists now argue, to be predicated upon unequal gender relations in the family and the public sphere (Pateman 1988). Second wave feminism in the 1970s led to the reassertion of the difference debates, in part due to the rise of sex difference literature of socialization theory, and in part the emphasis of difference nurtured by cultural feminism's maternal ethics of care (see Chapter 2). Both the discourses of sameness and difference have been open to be used against, as well as for, the benefit of women; the former leading to unequal pseudo-inclusion of women, the latter positioning women's experiences, values, expertise, cultures and practices as complementing male norms without changing power relations. The emphasis on difference, in particular that implied by contemporary discourses about women's styles of leadership, portrays women as the problem, and reasserts the dualisms between rationality and emotionality. Yet to ignore difference is to ignore gender as well as race, class and ethnic differences amongst women. The issue for the next decade, therefore, is how feminists will position themselves strategically to achieve gender equity in an era of self-governance and market liberalism in education.

2 Power/knowledge at work in educational administration

Educational administration has been historically constituted as an inter-disciplinary and eclectic body of knowledge and field of practice. The power of the twentieth-century administrative meta-narrative founded on tran-scendental discourses of rationality and science, derives not only from its claim to expert knowledge, but as much from its capacity to maintain social control through normalizing discourses or 'regimes of truth'. To do so means alternative discourses of administration and leadership such as those posed by feminism or critical theory, must be rendered 'marginal', 'invisible' or as 'disqualified knowledges' because they are 'naive knowledge, located low down on the hierarchy, beneath the required level of cognition or scien-tificity'(Foucault 1980a: 82).

In this chapter, I trace the emergence of educational administration as a field of practice and disciplinary technology that has 'othered', subsumed, or ignored 'the feminine'. Feminist research in educational administration has itself, however, indicated the capacity for developing its own discursive truths and disciplinary technologies, particularly those centred around women's styles of leadership. Such discourses have been readily appropri-ated by mainstream management theory (e.g. Aburdene and Naisbett 1992; Karpin Report 1995), partly because of the uneasy relationship between feminist and administrative theory in education arising out of feminism's own origins in Enlightenment thought, and liberalism in particular, a tension most evident in feminist debates about the ethics of care and rationality. Feminists in the field of educational administration have not attended closely enough to the theories of change embedded in particular feminist theoretical paradigms. Focusing upon change leads to a dialogue between theory and practice that can provide feminists with a way of thinking more strategically for postmodern times.

Administrative meta-narratives as disciplinary technologies

As a field of practice seeking a knowledge base since its emergence in the early twentieth century in the USA, educational administration has gained credibility and legitimacy at particular historical moments of crisis and disjuncture by appealing to more powerful discourses – the new sciences (psychology and scientific management) in the 1920s; positivism in the 1950s; neoclassical economics (human capital theory and cost-benefit analysis) in the 1960s; and the market (neo-liberalism and public choice theory) in the 1980s. The metaphors of the military, science, industry, biology and the arts litter the history of thought in the field (Beck and Murphy 1994). Academic and public legitimacy was sought and gained for the field and its practitioners by appealing to the new sciences, such as psychology, on the one hand, and the principles of scientific management on the other.

In the early 1900s, when educational administration was an emergent field of knowledge and professional practice in the USA, education was under threat and criticized by business for its inefficiency. Educational administration adopted key concepts of scientific management: the fragmentation and division of labour into specialisms, the reduction of work to simplistic tasks; and the imposition of hierarchy. In drawing from the scientific management of Frederick Taylor, the emphasis was on control, management as technique, and on an industrial model of organization (Waring 1990). Nikolas Rose (1992: 59) suggests that 'it was part of a wider family of political programs that sought to use scientific knowledge to advance national efficiency through making the most productive use of material and human resources'. So even in the earliest education bureaucracies, there was a marked professional separation between administration and teaching such that 'few now see these occupations anchored in a common history sharing core roles' (Cuban 1990: xiii).

Educational administration also gained credibility by adopting the new science of psychology in the 1920s in its use of personnel management and testing. Psychological knowledge had considerable 'productive' power in the regulation of social positions and identities (Walkerdine 1993: 60–1). As a 'technology of the social', psychology created woman as a separate social category, thus giving 'scientific' weight to arguments about women's unsuitability for leadership and administration (Hollway 1984). Moreover, the 'fair' science of occupational psychology readily accommodated women's increasing acceptability in the workplace with discursive shifts away from 'fitting the right man to the right job' in the 1950s to 'humanizing work' during the 1970s. Throughout such moves, however, 'psychological explanation accounts for the deviations and does not question the normality of the norm: in this instance the Anglo male norm' (Venn 1984: 131).

Such norms did not go uncontested, however. The origins of educational administration as a disciplinary technology were contingent upon particular historical conditions in the late nineteenth and early twentieth centuries – industrialization, the emergence of new nation states, the dominance of political and economic liberalism, the bureaucratization of public life, and the rise of professionalism based on scientific expertise. Each of these phenomena also had emancipatory possibilities for first wave feminism in the 1880s – itself originating out of the same conditions. Early feminism flourished in a period of economic expansion in most western liberal democratic nation states, based on the premise that 'all women have one cause, one movement' (Cott 1987: 3). Despite the different trajectories of modern feminism in specific nation states, as a movement it was characterized by its association with both the rise of trade unionism (equal pay campaigns) as well as the new 'caring' professions (teaching, nursing, welfare). As a product of Enlightenment thought, the issue was equality, 'seeking to extend to women the individualistic premises of the political theory of liberalism' (Cott 1987: 6). This was not without its contradictions. While liberalism provided an avenue of appeal, it also naturalized the gendered dualisms between the public and the private, science and nature, at the historical moment when the new industrial order of late nineteenth-century capitalism, in generating new modes of wage labour and patterns of consumption, established new organizational forms that institutionalized these dualisms (see Chapter 1).

The period from 1920–70, coinciding with the rise of educational administration as a 'modernist science', has also been characterized as one in which feminism was 'dormant'; a time when 'the culture of modernity and urbanity absorbed the messages of feminism and re-presented them' (Cott 1987: 174). Schmuck (1996) lists the factors contributing to the disappearance of a feminist voice during this period:

1 the lack of a public face to the women's movement, which removed any collective impetus;
2 the state's advantaging of men (after successive wars) in gaining access to education, and thus social mobility, while simultaneously actively discouraging women, with the promotion of a cult of femininity relocating women in the home;
3 the urbanization of society and consolidation of schooling, which exacerbated the gender division of labour in education in that men managed and women taught; and
4 the prevalence of the view of leadership as 'scientific management', which technologized leadership.

Despite this attitude, educational administration has continued in its ongoing search for a knowledge base, a search crystallized in the theory movement of the 1950s, which promoted administration as a science. The theory movement called upon highly idealized versions of 'the scientific method' asserted by logical positivism, which offered neutrality, objectivity, generalizability and predictability. While such epistemological claims appealed to education policymakers and administrators seeking system-wide solutions, they were premised upon a distinction between fact and value, a denial of ethics in science, a view that scientific method led to the discovery of knowledge of a 'world out there' separate from self and not culturally and historically produced, and the denigration of experiential knowledge as rampant subjectivity.

This view of science increased man's power over nature, but rendered the subject, the knower, invisible (Alcoff and Potter 1993). Teachers, as students, were, theoretically as well as practically, treated as disembodied objects, not the embodied subjects, without class, gender, race, ethnic or sexual identity (Blount 1994). Educational management, as a research field, actively distanced itself from educational research on curriculum, pedagogy and teachers' work. The powerlessness of the subject, or at least the privileging of structure over agency in power relations, was one product of the dominance of structural functionalism prior to the 1970s, and, in particular, of Talcott Parson's instrumental/expressive distinction of the 1950s. Parsonian sociology came to mean 'other things being equal, men would assume more technical, executive and "judicial roles", women more supportive, integrative and "tension managing roles" ' (Carrigan *et al.* 1987: 39). This gendered dichotomy became deeply entrenched in organizational theory at the same time that organizational theorists treated organizations as gender-neutral. This contradiction was evident in the argument that the intensification of hierarchical authority, the fragmentation of work into specialist tasks, the reliance upon rule orientation, and the reduction of worker autonomy, all characteristics of modern bureaucracies, were justified because of the increasing presence of women in work. Sociologists in 1969 argued:

> Women's stronger competing attachments to their family roles and . . . to their clients make them, less likely than men, to develop colleague reference group orientations. For these reasons, and . . . the general cultural norm that women should defer to men, women are more willing than men to accept the bureaucratic controls imposed upon them in semi-professional organizations, and less likely to seek a genuinely professional status.
>
> (Simpson and Simpson 1969: 199–200)

Systems theory, well into the 1970s, continued to treat organizations as self-adjusting 'natural organisms', which were neutral mechanisms of socialization responding to societal needs. Organizational theory depicted organizations as aggregates of individuals unaffected by power relations or difference (gender, race or class). The organizational problem was the individual (student or teacher) who did not fit. Conflict was an aberration, an organizational malfunction, and therefore to be eliminated. There was little sense of the collective, or of the micropolitics of organizations (for example, unionism). An individual's motivation for accepting organizational goals could be fully explained by organizational factors (satisfactory work situation, good social relations, material rewards, autonomy, security), thereby excluding factors external to the organization (family or political and religious beliefs; Mills and Tancred 1992). Feminists such as Yeakey *et al.* (1986) have asserted that the failure of the theory movement of the 1950s (and one could argue subsequent attempts) to develop a powerful theory of educational administration could be attributed to

1 the theories being derived from other disciplines and not rooted in school experience;
2 the employment of particular social science methods and concepts of positivism, unaffected by the epistemological debates within social science; and
3 the uncritical borrowing (of Parsonian structural functionalism) from sociology.

Even early neo-Marxist reproduction theory and the new sociology of teachers' work of the 1970s, tended to characterize teachers as the passive dupes of their socialization, deficient, even dumb, resistant to change, overly concerned with family and relationships, and without a sense of social issues or broad overview (Biklen 1993; Acker 1996). Women teachers in particular were depicted as making the wrong individual choices, which worked against their careers and capacity to become leaders. Teachers were neither real workers nor real managers (Biklen 1993). They were powerless with regard to management, and despite their claims to expertise, they were not 'real' professionals. This sociological construction of teaching sees, on the one hand, altruism, child-centredness and care as a 'problem' of women teachers to be discouraged; and on the other hand, teacher activism and unionism as the enactment of self-interest, and therefore equally problematical (Weiler 1994; Acker 1996). Thus the ongoing construction of teaching as a pedagogy of the feminine was empirically and theoretically justified.

The conceptual framework of socialization theory in the 1970s continued to reproduce stereotypic images of existing gender relations – that male and female were relatively static categories into which individuals were inducted. Thus the trait, attribute and contingency theories of the leadership literature of the 1970s produced what were stereotypically male characteristics of leadership – strong individualism, aggression and independence. Women, measured against such criteria, were portrayed as psychological failures, lacking the innate attributes, acquired skills, or aspirations for leadership. In sex-role socialization theory, women were caught in the bind of not fitting their prescribed gender role if they assumed too 'masculine' characteristics and of being 'too feminine' if they did not. The paradox was that a gendered division of labour was actively contested, negotiated and rejuvenated under the guise of the gender-neutrality of modernist science and rationality (Connell 1987). Meanwhile, the theoretical discourse of 'blaming' women was naturalized by the continuing absence, even decline, of significant numbers of women in formal leadership roles during the 1970s in the USA and most western liberal states in a time of contracting education systems.

Paradigm wars and subjugated discourses

Prior to the 1960s, in contrast to the USA, educational administration was neither a well defined field of theory or practice in Australia, the UK or New Zealand, where the career move from teacher to principal was premised upon seniority and experience rather than specialist administrative knowledge or qualifications (Grace 1995). The growing complexity of educational governance, the increase in the number of more qualified teachers, together with the politicization of education with the demands of new social movements, gave impetus to the formation of educational administration as a field of practice and discipline in Australia, as elsewhere. During the 1960s, due to the influence of the academy, ethnocentric, but seemingly generic, discourses of American management theory were appropriated and imported to compete with local discourses about educational leadership and administration (Grace 1995). By the 1980s, the tendency for policy borrowing across nation states meant that

> fashionable theories of education management that accompanied marketization, devolution and local financial management in education . . . [had] shifted the paternalistic English [and Australian] culture of gifted amateurism and academic leadership towards a very different mode.
> (Ozga and Walker 1995: 35)

This mode was one of authority premised upon managerialist hierarchy and specialisms.

Not surprisingly, it was from the margins that challenges to the dominance of positivism in educational administrative theory, and all its cultural baggage, originated in the early 1970s. The challenge came from the perspective of the new sociology of knowledge and critical theory from Australia (Bates 1994) and New Zealand (Codd 1992), and liberal humanism from Canada (Hodgkinson 1991; Greenfield and Ribbins 1993; Young 1993). Even the humanist impulses that supplanted the value neutrality and means-end dichotomy of positivism in the 1980s tended to reduce to new universalizing 'truths' about *man the administrator*, best represented by the work on leadership and values of Christopher Hodgkinson (1991). By contrast, critical theory, as feminism, argued that the narrow focus upon the technical, the operational, and the measurable in educational administration, without regard to new sociological or political science theory, meant little engagement with the power relations surrounding gender, race or class.

While second wave feminist theory fuelled postpositivist/postmodernist/ postcolonial theoretical trajectories during the 1980s, gender was still treated as a 'variable' within the paradigm wars in educational administration, rather than an organizing category. Women suffered a form of 'pseudo-inclusion' in educational administration texts, in the token paragraph, chapter or special edition of a journal discussing the 'peculiar problems' of women in leadership roles in education. By implication, men continued to be 'the norm' for leadership. Women were still cast as the problem, but now for their deficiency, in the context of the education market, in the new leadership skills of rational financial management or aggressive entrepreneurship. Once again, in a time of economic crisis and public administrative reform, educational administrators turned to discourses of business management. Ozga and Walker (1995: 35) comment on this tendency:

> Most conventional education management theory is parasitic on ideas from business and industry, where major themes in social science are present only in diluted form. It is not part of the debates in social science which connect such ideas to questions about the nature and purpose of society and to political, social and economic factors that influence such debates. As a consequence, education management theory does not engage with the issues raised by the heavily gendered nature of the division of labour between managers and managed in the education labour force, nor does it address fundamental issues of control and power in education work, except in very superficial accounts of how best to lead or to manage in the workforce.

As a disciplinary technology, educational administration has remained relatively quarantined from the more critical impulses of the new social movements, although always susceptible to business pressures, usually reacting to external pressures by looking inward to produce better mechanisms of control, rather than proactively working outward on the basis of educational principles to inform social change. Throughout the twentieth century, leadership has been continuously reinvented as *the* solution to political and management problems, rather than the means to democratically negotiated educational ends, through the effective schools literature of the 1970s, the 'visionary leadership of strong corporate cultures' of the 1980s, and now 'best practice' in the 1990s. Thus 'the vast, repetitive and intellectually stultifying literature on leadership recycles idealised masculine virtues of decisiveness, incisiveness and strength' (Ozga and Walker 1995: 37).

The disciplinary technology of educational administration displays considerable regenerative capacities. Its ongoing reconstitution is not a conscious

conspiratorial act, but more the effect of an ongoing set of discursive practices favouring particular interests centred around fundamental theoretical
binaries (rationality/emotionality) and the gendered division of labour
between administration/teaching. Together, these work against any fundamental change in gender/power relations and lead to research paradigms that
perpetuate business interests and repress ethical or social justice considerations. Now in the late twentieth century, in a period of restructuring, the
proliferation of knowledges and technologies, masculinist administrative discourses of rationality and efficiency are being reconstituted around postmodern discourses of change, performativity, self-management and the
market, to produce new 'economic' truths about choice and competitive
social relations.

Administrative discourses, however, as all discourses, produce only what
Donna Haraway (1988) calls 'partial truths' or 'situated knowledges'.
Feminists point out that claims that certain knowledge is 'objective' collapse
because of the absence of women's experience and the refusal to accept the
partiality of powerful knowledge. The notion of the partiality of knowledge
equally rejects the view that all knowledge is masculinist or phallocentric, or
that 'women's only alternatives are to speak in a masculine voice, construct
a new language, or be silent' (Sawicki 1991: 1). Indeed, all discourses,
including feminist discourses, can be read, within limits, openly and subversively and can also produce truth regimes. For that reason, feminist discourses about leadership must also be considered for their political
implications by exploring both their regressive and progressive tendencies.

Re-viewing the 'problem' of women and leadership

Feminist discourses equally have the propensity to reactive and proactive
responses to change; of displaying theoretical moribundity and political
naivety; of possessing repressive and normalizing tendencies. As discourses
they are also productive in the constitution of 'the feminist' and 'the female'
subject. The next section briefly reviews feminist thinking about women,
leadership and educational change. While recognizing that all discourses are
necessarily partial, I suggest that it is informative to consider which particular feminisms have been called upon to disrupt the technologies of gender at
work in educational administration, and to what effect.

Feminist research has brought women's voice into, and troubled, the field
of educational administration by challenging the dominance of positivist
epistemologies and narrow views of science. While the different feminisms
(socialist, liberal, radical, cultural, poststructuralist, postcolonial, black,
eco-feminism; Tong 1989) still disagree upon how gender inequality is
defined, and how gender equality can be achieved, they can be said to share,
as a common political project, the understandings that 'the concept of

gender is socially constructed'; 'that females and their experiences have been excluded from the development of knowledge'; and that 'feminism calls for a change in the balance of power relationships politically, structurally and interpersonally' (Schmuck 1996: 345).

Furthermore, feminist thought has also undergone significant shifts. Early feminism in the 1970s saw a western universalizing consensus-seeking feminism framed by the modernist impulse that focused upon an agreed cause of women's oppression (patriarchy, capitalism or the home–work divide), the unproblematic nature of this oppression, and the emphasis on structural explanations (Barrett and Phillips 1992). Feminist strategies in the 1970s largely fell at the 'equality' end of the equal–difference continuum, with, for example, liberal feminism's notion of androgynous leaders in response to sex-role theory. Strategies in the 1980s were at the 'difference' end, exemplified by cultural feminism's celebration of 'being female'. Meanwhile the destabilizing tendencies of postmodernist feminism arising out of black, postcolonial and lesbian feminisms' challenges to the hegemony of white heterosexual middle-class western feminism has fractured any universal category of 'woman' in the 1990s, leading to a new identity politics (Collins 1991; Spivak 1993).

The multiplicity of feminist voices by the 1990s, with all their competing analyses and views about the origins of oppression and nature of change, has produced significant conceptual shifts in feminism (Tong 1989). First, there is the recognition of how race, gender and class work in often contradictory ways in particular contexts. Second, there is a more positive view of the intransigence of sex differences which emphasizes morality and care as a positive form of gender identity, away from the quasi-androgynous view of 'I just want be a person'. Third, the postmodern turn of the late 1980s now links feminism into non-feminist strands of contemporary social, political and cultural theory. Central to this shift is the postmodern critique of Enlightenment thought and 'its notion of the powerful unitary self-conscious political subject, its belief in rationality and progress, in the possibility of grand schemes for reform' (Barrett and Phillips 1992: 5).

These shifts have not been reflected to the same extent in educational administration. Certainly, there have been shifts of meaning about how women and educational leadership have been 'problematized', although the contributing factors are not seen to have significantly changed over two decades. These factors include women's underrepresentation in formal authority; a lack of role models; biases in recruitment and promotion practices; the composition of selection committees; the nature of job progressions and successions; the different job titles and status for equivalent work; the unequal sex-segmented distribution of extracurricular work; separate recreational activities; age; domestic responsibilities; and women's isolation on the job (Adkinson 1981; Yeakey *et al.* 1986; Victorian Department of Education 1996).

What is different now are the theories called upon to explain these phenomena, the greater awareness of the intransigence of individuals and institutions when confronted with gender equity reform, and the strategies proposed to remedy it. For example, sex-role socialization theory and psychological factors that dominated explanations for women's failure to attain leadership in the 1970s have now been displaced by more agential theories of action. Constructivist perspectives no longer individualize the problem of underrepresentation, but look to wider contextual and organizational factors, such as organizational cultures, and how they impinge on women's 'choices'. In turn, women's 'choices', in not applying for leadership, previously described as disguising their ability and abdicating from competition, have been reread by cultural feminists as being as much the rejection of, and resistance, to male values (Adler *et al.* 1993). 'New' feminist psychology suggests that women's 'fear of success' is as much the 'avoidance of visibility' under the male gaze, the result of discriminatory practices, and an awareness of the isolation of being the token woman (Hollway 1984). Women's lack of career planning or 'intrinsic' work motivation is now equally well explained by life histories tracing women's dual familial/work responsibilities (Biklen 1993; Acker 1996).

A range of different theoretical and strategic positions now coexist and overlap within the literature on women and leadership. Each of these discursive 'positions' mobilizes different logics and gender change strategies. Gender equity policies initially drew from liberal feminist discourses about individual rights and gender-neutral merit, but with limited success. In part, this was because they stressed rule-governing, top-down relationships, which meant working within the tolerance levels of men in power. In part, they did not challenge mainstream organizational theory, which treated organizations and structures as gender-neutral. Rather, they appealed to some universal humanism 'out there' while maintaining as central the notion of the 'autonomous rational individual' (Tong 1989: 3). The logic was that removing structural and procedural barriers meant 'a critical mass of women' would, through their merit alone, gain access to formal power. Discrimination itself was irrational, and could be averted procedurally. The gender equity strategies arising from this position focused upon changing individual women, not changing cultures or structures. Such strategies included workshops and training to improve women's skills in c.v. writing, conflict management, interviews, change management, assertiveness and financial management; the development of male practices of networking, career planning, acquisition of a range of administrative experiences in acting positions; and role modelling, mentoring as well as women's advocacy groups (Schmuck 1996: 349). Individual women, once informed of their choices, would seize the chance to take up leadership.

Cultural feminism arose out of, and in antithesis, to liberal feminism (Tong 1989). Liberal feminism presumed that men and women were essentially the same and defined the problem as one of equal access to, and success in, neutral structures and processes. Cultural feminism's constructivist perspective saw organizations and knowledge, and therefore notions of merit and skill, as historically constructed to privilege men. In seeking to revalue women's experience, cultural feminism has particularly informed educational administration through the moral theory of Carol Gilligan (1982), the ethics of care with the work of Nel Noddings (1992), and women's ways of seeing and knowing (Belenky *et al.* 1986). Whereas liberal feminism was premised upon a politics of access and success, largely from a gender stratification perspective, cultural feminism's constructivist perspective led to a focus upon how meanings frame decisions and actions as articulated through particular power relations in organizations. This facilitated a shift in feminist analysis in leadership away from individuals and structures to context and values (e.g. Ferguson 1984; Marshall and Anderson 1995; Still 1995). It also offered greater explanatory power for women's underrepresentation because it focused upon the exclusionary practices of hegemonic masculinist cultures and leadership; the seeming complicitness of subjugated groups in their own oppression; as well as providing an understanding of counter-hegemonic cultures and agency through notions of subjugated knowledges (Blackmore 1993; Court 1993).

The feminist tradition of an ethics of care informing this paradigm derived from object relations theory, a strand of psychoanalytic theory developed from Nancy Chodorow's *The Reproduction of Mothering* (1978) and philosophical work on maternal thinking. Feminist psychoanalysis argues that gender identity formation is not premised upon the presence or absence of the phallus, but upon parental relationships. Therefore shared parental responsibilities for child rearing could produce masculinities that value care. The strategies this position took sought to change gender identity formation through more equitable sharing of parenting and, in schools, through their organization, administrative practices and value priorities, to recognize the interpersonal and value caring relations as a significant part of educational work (Noddings 1992; Beck 1994). Such a position would advocate women-only professional development courses and networking in order to develop more consultative and collegial leadership practices as viable alternatives to dominant approaches to schooling. Cultural feminists thus provided an ethical alternative to the dominant hegemony, arguing that the world can be different. It named competitive individualism, socially constructed views of merit and skill, hierarchical and authoritarian structures, aggressive and rights oriented behaviours as masculinist and problematic, although masculinity itself was not the central issue. While controversial, cultural feminism is valuable in distinguishing between behaviours prescribed for women (as in liberal feminism) and activities arising out of women's lives (the experiential). The assumption was that women would become empowered and agential through the community of women and shared values, and once in power, wider cultural shifts would eventuate.

Neither liberal nor cultural feminism explicitly provides sophisticated ways of theorizing the complexities of cultural change, however. Liberal feminism assumes a benign view of culture, as a monolithic entity with a high level of consensus in values, actions and beliefs, as depicted in mainstream management notions of corporate culture. Corporate culture treats culture instrumentally, as a manipulable, coherent unitary and unifying resource, which can be shaped towards organizational ends. It treats workers as passive recipients of shared value systems. It invokes a top-down view of initiating change and a technicist view of people management. Whereas liberal feminism focuses upon changing organizations through individual effort, cultural feminism sees culture as a powerful tool due to a more collective sense of agency. Cultural feminism draws upon notions of women's voice as a subversive subculture in mainstream organizations (e.g. Ferguson 1984), and seeks a more 'woman centred' approach. Ultimately, however, it also treats culture as cohesive, homogenous and consensus oriented, although privileging women's over men's cultures. Neither actually challenges the dualisms embedded in organizational discourses connecting rationality to masculinity and leadership, and depicting emotionality as being irrational.

Feminism, humanism and the postmodern moment: when rationality meets emotionality

Feminism's more recent flirtation with postmodernism also has its dilemmas. While postmodernism rejects, as do more radical feminisms, the epistemological foundationalism and meta-narratives of science and humanism, thus challenging male/female binaries embedded in Enlightenment science, feminism is itself 'intimately tied to the emancipatory impulse of the Enlightenment' as a product of liberalism. 'Liberalism and Marxism will allow women into the public space of politics, but only if they renounce the "feminine" values that excluded them from this realm in the first place' (Hekman 1990: 188). This dilemma surfaces in the seeming desire of some feminists to reconcile the ethics of care discourse of Gilligan and Noddings with the liberal humanist discourses of justice dominant in educational administration (Sergiovanni 1992). In seeking to achieve this end, there is a failure to recognize the basic rationality/emotionality binary embedded in liberal humanism that is the basis for the exclusion of women's experience. Key writers in the liberal humanist tradition in educational administration have not included women on an equal footing in the universalizing meta-narrative of 'man', although they speak broadly in terms of social justice and equity without self-reflection on their whiteness and maleness. Some are explicitly sexist in both their use of language and their theoretical assumption of the universality of male experience (e.g. Hodgkinson 1991).

The seduction of feminists by the ethics of care has also diverted attention away from the issue of rationality. The meta-discourse of rationality in educational administration has permeated through epistemological discourses that link rationality to one truth; philosophical discourses that associate rationality with abstract moral hierarchies; psychological discourses that equate rationality with particular male norms of behaviour; physiological discourses that perceive rationality and authority as embodied in the male body; and economic discourses that define rationality as gender-neutral atomistic individuals making choices to maximize their benefits. All position rationality in opposition to emotionality (and by default care).

The Enlightenment myth of rationality is closely bound to idealized notions of governance – more particularly Weber's bureaucratic ideal of rule-governed organizations premised around technical competence and formal authority – which excluded the personal, the sexual and the feminine from the rational, and presumed that emotion was morally lesser (Bologh 1990). When extrapolated, the rational/emotional dualism defined the cognitive and intellectual as the only form of legitimate and objective knowledge. By implication, the experiential was subjective; passion and feeling were 'irrational' and linked to a negative, feminine view of the world', and, as a value-laden concept, 'disruptive, illogical, biased and weak' (Putnam and Mumby 1993: 40). Emotion was a deviation from that which is 'sensible or intelligent', 'linked to the expressive arenas of life not to the instrumental goal orientation that drives organisations' (Putnam and Mumby 1993: 36). In the 1990s, new modes of educational self-management premised upon market principles are reproducing the same rational/emotional dichotomy through public choice theory, which treats individual decisions in the marketplace as instrumental, unemotional, self-maximizing, and therefore 'rational'.

The differing feminist positions on rationality have produced unusual alliances between liberal and Marxist feminists who accept the notion of rationality and seek women's inclusion, and radical feminists, who reify women's irrationality. In the latter case, a masculinist epistemology is replaced with a feminist one 'exalting the virtues of female nature, nurturing, relatedness and community as replacing male values of domination, rationality and abstraction' (Hekman 1990: 5). Neither really challenges dominant notions of rationality. Feminist postmodernist philosophical critiques differ in that their critique of the 'rational subject' and liberalism sees rationality as not just being a question of truth but also our conception of a good person (McNay 1992: 2).

Whereas modernism looks for the conditions of right reason, postmodernism's search for the discursive economies of the different versions of the right reason that we have inherited . . . They desacrilize reason, they do not reject it.

(Yeatman 1994: viii)

A poststructuralist deconstructivist reading of modernist master-narratives of rationality, while paying attention to their political effects, can reconstitute what we mean and understand as authority and reason in ways that do not depict authority as premised upon a mode of reason in opposition to emotion, or justice in opposition to care. Such an approach, which views emotion and reason, justice and care, as integral to each other, creates possibilities to develop feminist discourses of leadership that interrogate male/female dualisms, that offer substantive ethical positions, but that can also provide an ongoing analysis of their political effects. Likewise, however, narratives of care need to be scrutinized.

Women's ways of leading

The ethics of care has provided a powerful discourse for women, collectively and individually, because it offers an alternative image of organization and leadership premised upon ethical and moral positions for educational administrators, which revalues women's experiences; it recognizes that schools should serve the public and private needs of all individuals; it emphasizes the moral aspect of education in terms of personal relationships and civic responsibility and not just the public needs of men; it fosters caring attitudes in children (and administrators) by prizing kindness, compassion, and commitment; and it seeks to organize schooling around long-term social relationships, not differentiating disciplinary boundaries that serve the economy or an élite (Beck 1994; Noddings 1992; Martin 1994). The ethics of care deals with the substantive and not formal, procedural aspects of leadership and administration, thereby restoring some balance to a field increasingly bereft in these aspects.

There is now considerable research on women in leadership informed by cultural feminism in the USA (Shakeshaft 1987; Chase 1995; Grogan 1996), the UK (Al-Khalifa 1989; Adler *et al.* 1993; Ozga 1993b; Hall 1996), Australia (Blackmore 1993, 1994; Limerick and Lingard 1995), New Zealand (Strachan 1993; Court 1995), Canada (Young 1992) and Israel (Chen and Addi 1993) which focuses upon the sameness amongst women in their ways of seeing, knowing, organizing and leading. Ozga (1993b: 11) synthesizes this research:

> Women's leadership styles are less hierarchical and more democratic. Women, for example, run more closely knit schools than do men, and communicate better with teachers. They use different, less dominating body language and different language and procedures. Women appear more flexible and sensitive, and often more successful . . . women spend less time on deskwork than men, visit more classrooms, keep up to date on curricular issues, spend more time with their peers and sponsor other

women. Their language is more hesitant and tentative, their agendas more informal and flexible, and there is less distance from subordinates . . . Women emphasize cohesiveness. They are much less individualistic and spend time on fostering an integrative culture and climate . . . women cope more readily with 'routine stress' and defuse conflict. They do not engage in displays of anger as control mechanisms and hence may be judged as weak . . . Group activities are much more highly valued by women than men.

This popular discourse about women's leadership being flexible, democratic, valuing openness, trust and compassion, 'humane and efficient' is seemingly convergent with 'new' and softer management discourses that focus upon good people management as the new source of productivity in postmodern organizations.

In the process of its popularization, however, the logic of the 'women's ways of leading' discourse treats women as a homogeneous group without differences in race/class/gender or in beliefs. It effectively conflates 'being female' into 'being feminist' in what Chantal Mohanty calls the 'feminist osmosis thesis':

Being female is thus seen as *naturally* related to being feminist, where the experience of being female transforms women into feminists through osmosis. Feminism is not defined as a highly contested political terrain; it is the mere effect of being female.

(Mohanty 1992: 77)

The conflation of women's experience into feminism produces limited versions of what the different feminism(s) might bring to leadership because it collapses the distinction between leadership as practiced by women in general and feminist women in particular. The osmosis thesis is fed by the reluctance of feminists, as a gesture of sisterhood, not to criticize women in leadership. Such solidarity is often misplaced, as it ignores substantive value differences and has significant political repercussions.

Such a discourse produces a new regime of truth that needs to be interrogated. Its discursive dominance undermines strategic thinking about theorizing change in gender relations by distracting attention away from the gender/power relations embedded in organizational life, values, structures and processes; away from the differences between women (race, class, gender), and the differences between feminisms; and away from masculinity. In education, this discourse is often read as asserting that women principals are *inevitably* more caring, collaborative, communicative, consultative, communitarian, consensus-oriented and student- and curriculum-focused. It is a discourse, obviously, in which feminist educators have a significant investment. Yet it in its popularization, the substantive political and moral feminist position derived from the ethics of care is reduced to a view of care as just a matter of technique or style that can be readily acquired without any substantive shift in values or attitudes (Weiner 1995b).

As a 'transformative' discourse revaluing femaleness, the ethics of care is, many feminists suggest, too readily reducible to essentialism and to biological and psychological explanations attributable to the gender of the individual and not the characteristics of the context or the job. This 'transformative essentialist' discourse, in appealing to notions of women's moral superiority and concern for relationality, fails to address how feminist discourses themselves can be constraining and disempowering in that they create their own meta-narratives or universal truths. In particular, the 'discursive formation of action around notions of gender equity theory, policy and practice inscribe 'women's ways' and other similarly preservationist liberal pluralisms as new 'regimes of truth' in educational policy' (Bryson and de Castells 1993: 341–2), as is the case of the discourse about 'women's styles of leadership'. The ethics of care therefore is potentially troublesome for developing a feminist politics of educational leadership.

Theorizing change

The discourse of 'women's style of leadership' is dangerous in that first, it has the potential to produce a meta-narrative universalizing the category of women, a strategically dangerous position for feminists. Presenting women as a homogeneous category recycles the modernist storyline that women, because of their differences, even in leadership, merely complement men. The feminist ethics of care is readily misread in the process of its appropriation and popularization, often leading to reverse sexism by privileging 'feminine' values of nurturance and care over 'masculine' values and behaviours by idealizing women's preferences for democratic organization (Eisenstein 1996). Wendy Brown (1988: 189) cogently argues: 'Simple reversals' substituting 'feminine values' for masculine ones in the public sphere are inappropriate, because viewing the mother–child relationship as central to human relationships merely supplants conflict and competition with nurturance. Female values have not been shaped for public purposes nor under conditions of freedom, but often under conditions of 'overprotectiveness, masochism or fear of autonomy' (Brown 1988: 190). Nor is the family the only model of relationality. This reversal ultimately reduces to the position that men and women are irreconcilably different, fixing rather than making fluid the category of gender, thus reducing the possibilities for changing the social relations of gender. Politically, there is fine line between cultural feminists' arguments about women's culture and the 'new conservative feminism', which reifies traditional familial roles.

Second, the problem is that discourses about women's styles of leadership, in reifying care, can position women as self-sacrificing, and are prone to idealize women's oppression. The 'strong' woman leader discourse implies that 'When people face oppressive conditions, they often develop strengths and attributes that many in our culture admire. Women may have developed qualities like caring and compassion as survival responses to society wide sexual oppression' (Ferguson 1984: 92–9; Blount 1994). Furthermore, as Karen Green (1995: 150) points out, 'by itself, an ethic of care, is not necessarily feminist. It becomes feminist when incorporated into a theory of the good society which attempts to bring about the good of women as well as the good of men'. The ethic of care's adequacy as a moral theory may derive out of women's experience, but is not confined to women, although the ethics of care has always been associated with a male fear of effeminacy (Noddings 1992).

Third, the focus on how women talk and work in groups reifies their language practices as something that is 'naturally' female and not constituted through the social practices of the contexts that shape what they are doing. Is, for example, women's style of leading an attribute of the organizational role of a primary school principal in the pedagogically driven context of the primary school, or of a gender that emphasizes a culture of care? (Schmuck 1996: 353; S. Acker 1995). Deborah Cameron (1995) rejects the mythologies about women's and men's talk being necessarily different, arguing that women's turn-taking and listening capacities are not products of their gender per se, but arise because men and women do things differently in different 'communities of practice'. Language is a product of the things we do, and how we do them, and communities of practice shape the language patterns. That women may be concerned about intimacy and connectedness, while men are concerned about status and power, is true only to the extent that contexts make certain gendered forms of communication acceptable and not others.

Educational bureaucracies are very different communities of practice to school staffrooms, EO units or parent voluntary bodies. Women tend to describe similar work activities to men in very different ways, with men calling upon formal work-related language and women on a pragmatic life skills approach; the former is valued and rewarded in the organization, the latter is not (Poynton 1993). Many women do not name their initiatives and actions as leadership, but see them as 'just getting things done'. Men, more familiar with the reward systems of paid work or the language of leadership, define what they do in organizational terms, whereas women refer to it as a process and interaction rather than a one-off action, for example, 'I made a decision' (Sheppard 1992). This is particularly evident in the ways in which men and women promote themselves in curricula vitae.

Status and connection strategies exist simultaneously in all groups, regardless of gender. Women may overtly organize themselves in ways that attend to connectedness and the group – turn taking and shared leadership – but status does not disappear. Gendered subjectivity is constituted out of a range of discursive practices in specific organizational sites informed by particular sets of gender power relations. 'Men do not control meaning at all; rather, women elect to use modes of expression men can understand because that is the best way to make men listen' (Deborah Cameron quoted in Sawicki 1991: 2). These language ploys work against women in administrative contexts, however, because they deny them a language with which they are comfortable but which is valued organizationally.

Fourth, focusing on women's styles of leadership retains the focus upon women, and diverts attention away from the politics of workplaces and labour process research on teachers' work or administration, an important consideration given the radical restructuring of teachers' and principals' work. Teaching is where women have largely been located and where feminist political activity has occurred. Judith Glazer (1991: 337) suggests that

> feminist theory building and testing are more pervasive in the literature on teaching than administration, which continues to adhere to theories of leadership and organization that discourage collaborative models of leadership and reinforce patterns of male dominance–female subordination.

Nor does this focus question the values of the new work order of postmodern times, which requires such relentless personal sacrifice to work.

Fifth, the discourse about women's styles of leadership does not attend enough to the range of political differences amongst women. Many women administrators eschew any notion of discrimination, while others point to it as central to their experience; some women are more politically committed to gender equity, while others do not see gender reform as their responsibility. Many women 'principals are not advocates for sex equity', and 'many women principals had adopted the prevailing culture of school administrators despite their personal experiences with discrimination . . . they had assimilated themselves into old models of leadership' (Schmuck 1996: 350). There are women who are controlling, and women who are facilitating, and women who are both. Women do not suddenly assume masculinist behaviours as leaders; leadership is learnt over a long period of time, and behaviours do not change unless conditions force that change. There is also no reason why merit, itself a culturally constructed concept which historically has served some men's interests and not others, will not serve the same purpose for some women and not others (Burton 1991; Young 1990).

Finally, the dominance of feminist discourses of caring and sharing sets up new universalizing norms. Such discourses expect women to be exemplary in controlling their negative emotions of anger and frustration in their desire to be caring. The convergence between child-centred/person-centred professional discourses and discourses of a caring leadership reifies care for children and colleagues in a way that can become a guilt trap for women teachers in that they put the interests of others (students and colleagues) first and their own welfare second (S. Acker 1995). Care is both the responsibility of women, and also their downfall. The issue here is whether the world is seen to fall into the carers and the cared for, those who 'prefer' democratic practice and those who see no need for such practices.

Women therefore waver between being either 'overfeminized' (playing on their feminine wiles and being weak) or 'underfeminized' (taking on male characteristics and being too strong; Riley 1988), positions categorized along the emotionality/rationality divide. Either position offers little potential for women or men to change, because they do not, as Eva Cox (1996: 91) argues, fundamentally challenge the 'macho decisionmaking structure' that typifies leadership as individualistic, autonomous, dominant, rational, aggressive and entrepreneurial. 'While challenging the dominance of masculine norms, they have left untouched the abstract oppositions of masculinity and femininity upon which these norms rely' (Johnson 1990: 23). The challenge, therefore, is for feminists in educational administration to develop a form of relational ethics, *as well as* a form of democratic practice and community, which interrogates such binaries.

Few feminists in the field have taken Lyn Davies's (1990) position that the focus on leadership by western feminists itself has thwarted educational change, and that one must consider the overall structuring and restructuring of educational work focusing upon cross-cultural and cross-national differences, as well as gender differences, to better understand women's positioning and how discourses of gender, equity and efficiency worked out differently for women in specific contexts. The underrepresentation of women in educational administration and the feminization of education is largely, Davies points out, a western phenomenon, due to issues of class and economic development. Yet theories that look as educational administration through labour process theories of work are neglected, not only because socialist feminism is out of favour in postcommunist postmodern times, but because of the theoretical separation of educational administration from industrial relations, teachers' work, and social justice. Theories focusing upon management as educational work and postcolonial feminist theory may offer greater theoretical possibilities in a globalized restructured workplace. As yet, however, feminist leadership discourses remained too contained within the discursive parameters set by the disciplinary field of mainstream management, and are thus ultimately constrained in doing strategic work for gender equity reform.

3 Gendered lives: becoming educators, feminists and leaders

Feminist research has been characterized by first, its rejection of the desirability and possibility of value free research; second, by its emphasis on 'lived experience and the significance of everyday life'; and third, by its political commitment to produce change (Weiler 1988: 59). A feminist politics is a necessary condition of feminist research. In any such research, the representation of self emerges as an issue in the messy nexus of research, theory and feminist practice. Feminist poststructuralism also demands that the positionality of the author is made transparent. Authorial representation can regress into a confessional/self-indulgent mode, however, privileging the voice of the author over that of the research 'subjects'. So my history interrupts this text selectively at points of familiarity between my story and the storylines of those 'interviewed', as the open-ended conversations with teachers and principals often slipped between autobiography/ biography, conversation, debate and therapy (Stanley 1993). This chapter gives voice to the women who were teachers, principals and bureaucrats in the Victorian state education system from 1989–96. These women's voices provide a critical counter-point to the meta-narratives of the previous chapters. Their stories are the product of interview, observation, workshops and focus groups with teachers and administrators in two major research projects: one analysing the cultures of educational bureaucracies as experienced by female administrators; the other exploring both perceptions about women and leadership and the reception of gender equity reform for women teachers.

To gain a sense of multiple ways in which subjectivity is actively constituted through experience, a number of methods of data collection were pursued: open-ended interviews styled as conversations with individual women; focus groups of equal opportunities (EO) practitioners, principals and teachers; and writing professional journals. Multiple interviews with some principals meant I could disrupt the coherence of the storytelling genre of the interview. One interview would begin with the questions: Tell me about your daily work. What do you do, how do you do it? In the second interview, we would together deconstruct their representation of themselves as leaders in the text of their curriculum vitae. The third interview took a life history approach: how did they come to be where they are now; what were the critical points? Throughout I interjected with their own voices from the other interviews, reminding and contradicting, thus leading to new insights.

Another strategy was to create focus groups consisting of women already in leadership, leadership aspirants and non-aspirants. I used discussion starters, such as maps of the disabling and enabling factors for women seeking leadership, to provoke wide-ranging but intense discussions that fleshed out the different discursive positions about women and leadership. In workshops, I focused upon women writing: 'When did you first think of yourself as a leader? What did you feel at the time? How did you 'construct' yourself as a leader? What are the silences here? This exercise was derivative of Frigga Haug's (1987) memory work, which argues that we actively participate in the formation of memories about our past experience and that memory is important to the construction of the self (Crawford *et al.* 1992). Getting women, individually and collectively, to talk about their work and personal lives, how they came to be teachers, feminists, 'leaders' or just interested in gender equity produced densely intertextual narratives. As individual life narratives, they overlapped and meshed to produce 'subjective and collective meanings of women and men as categories of identity which have been constructed' (Scott 1986: 6).

If the self is largely, but not only, a cultural and linguistic 'fiction' constituted through historical ideologies of selfhood and the processes of our storytelling, then the interview has those same elements of self-dramatization and performance that do not occur with the written text and in which the interviewer is an active participant. This recognizes the dynamic nature of the interview as

> an act of collaboration between two people . . . It is autobiographical in the sense that both subjects make decisions about their presentation of self for their own purposes. [The notion of auto/biography] disputes that biography and autobiography have different genres so as to undercut the divisions between self/other, public/private, and immediacy/memory [which are ever present].
>
> (Stanley 1993: 42)

As a participant (questioner and listener) in the interviews and writer of this text, I found the stories of the women familiar but different (Hamilton 1990). It is in the familiar, however, that we need to look 'in order to understand how professional women make sense of their contradictory experiences of power and subjection' (Chase 1995: x) and how these women 'draw and struggle with various cultural discourses – networks of meanings

– about individual achievement and inequality' (Chase 1995: x–xi). I learnt to listen more closely to how women narrated their experiences of how culture and narrative shape experience and to my own responses and questions.

> We need to hear what the women implied, suggested, and started to say but didn't. We need to interpret their pauses, and when it happens, their unwillingness or inability to respond . . . we need to allow women to explore their 'unwomanly' feelings and behaviours.
>
> (Anderson and Jack 1991: 17)

'Women tend to filter out where experience does not fit dominant meanings', and 'mute their thoughts and feelings when they try to describe their lives in the familiar and publicly acceptable terms of prevailing concepts' (Anderson and Jack 1991: 11). This 'muted channel of women's subjectivity' was particularly evident in how these women constituted themselves as leaders, all claiming to prefer and practice 'women's styles' of leadership, commonly characterized as being caring, consultative and student-centred. To do otherwise was to put their womanhood (and claims to leadership) in jeopardy.

I also listened to how the stories were told – some with anger, some as familiar stories told before, others more tentatively, as if articulating something for the first time – but all with a sense of confession or therapy. Many women and men, once the tape recorder was turned off, thanked me for the interview because it assisted them to clarify their values, acted as a form of reassessment of their 'place', and actions, at work and home, as well as led to them to reflect upon their own leadership or aspirations. It was also comforting to share common experiences, but particularly for the principals in a time of radical and stressful educational restructuring. For principals, the interview provided a space to release emotion and tension to talk to a relatively disinterested but knowledgeable participant. There was also 'an abundance of laughter and joking. They were humorous anecdotes and personal narratives, some of them self deprecating. The jokes seemed to reinforce communal bonds' (Minister 1991: 33). They were jokes for women in private – 'jokes which do not have the normal put down punch line'.

Yet the tendency to use the reading or writing of women's narratives as a means of promoting community and affirming the premise that the personal, the political and the professional are one also needs to be questioned. There is no utopian terrain upon which women's biographies exist. The danger is that the life narrative genre, with its recursive production of 'woman', can produce a normative definition of subjectivity and a particular female subject out of exemplary accounts of women's experiences in leadership if the discussion is left at the level of women's experience disconnected from a broader sense of gender politics and context.

The matter of experience

'The status of "female" or "woman/women's" experience has always been a central concern in feminist discourse' (Mohanty 1992: 76). Feminist critiques of mainstream social theory began with the premise that it ignored, pseudo-included or distorted women's experience. Experience has often been juxtaposed as subjective in opposition to other more 'objective' forms of knowledge (e.g. sciences). Many women, when interviewed queried: 'This is only my subjective experience, so how can this help your research?' This comment exemplifies dominant understandings about subjective/objective binaries positioning 'experience' in opposition to 'objective research'.

Feminism's appeal to women's experience to counter transcendental claims of male objectivity leads to the question: what is a truer account than the subject's own account?

> [Many feminists] take as self-evident the identities of those whose experience is being documented and thus naturalize their difference. They locate resistance outside its discursive construction, and reify agency as an inherent attribute of individuals, thus decontextualizing it. When experience is taken as the origin of knowledge, the vision of the individual subject . . . becomes the bedrock of evidence upon which explanation is built. Questions about the constructed nature of experience, about how subjects are constituted as different in the first place, about how one's vision is structured – about language (or discourse) and history – are left aside.
>
> (Scott 1992: 25)

This foundationalist approach treats experience as outside the discourse and making of meaning without any analysis of the inner workings and logics of systems or their historicity. Experience is treated as either that grounding of the subjective witness as 'immediate, true and authentic', or as social conditions, institutions, forms of belief and perceptions, the 'real' things outside to which people react, that is, the subjective/objective divide (Scott 1992: 25). A feminist politics starting from either position does not see identity as a contested terrain, the site of multiple and conflicting claims.

Feminist poststructuralism, with its emphasis on language, meaning, culture and subjectivity argues that language constitutes identity as a particular kind of subject. Language is not the mere reflection of experience, and experience is textually mediated. Such a view denaturalizes the experiences of women so that all categories are contested, contextual and contingent. Language, by naming experience, is powerful because it can promote the realization of shared understanding or 'subjugated knowledge' (Ferguson 1984). The naming of sexual harassment in the early 1970s, for example, meant a social interaction most women had experienced as individuals was given a new and more critical meaning because it connected to other feminist discourses about sexual domination and power, and more recently to legalistic discourses of EO and 'best practice' management discourses.

Thinking about experience in this manner leads us to think how women educators' stories (interviews) both shape and are shaped by particular cultural and historical discourses about education, leadership, and inequality. Their stories indicated the contingent and fragile nature of the formation of gendered identity, the fluidity and open-endedness of narrative practice. There was no obvious fixed end product of the individual, rather a constant awareness that self was constituted, that it was tenuous and therefore could be readily destabilized in particular contexts. There was no constant 'I' that was the centre. Their responses reflected the

> state of current understandings of 'women'; embedded in a vast web of description covering public politics, rhetorics, feminisms, forms of sexualization or contempt; and, behind these, larger and slower subsidings of gendered categories which in part include the sedimented forms of previous characterizations.
>
> (Riley 1988: 6)

Women's construction of their life stories was part of how they made meaning of their lives *now* and not merely an unproblematic rendition of a previously lived reality back *then*. Experience is constantly redefined by pre-existing discourses, both patriarchal *and* feminist. Women's experiences as leaders in the 1990s are shaped by a wider range of discourses about women and leadership, feminism and femininity, education and inequality, professionalism and mothering.

> Western culture's metanarratives about women – as communicated through literature, popular culture, the natural and social sciences – emphasize women's selflessness, orientation to and development through others, and preoccupation with family and domestic affairs.
>
> (Chase 1995: 8)

Understanding the narrative practices that constitute gender identity formation helps us better understand what constrains women's and men's self-understandings and informs their capacity for change. Women's life stories are simultaneously 'culturally intelligible' and 'unique' or 'particular' to the individual (Middleton 1992). By focusing upon the similarity amongst women through biography and autobiography, feminists have produced new collective truths which, in turn, frame other women's stories. Most women spoke of women's styles of leadership in their interview. They drew upon this feminist discourse unproblematically, spoken as a truth about all women's experiences because it provided a language to explain, and a legitimacy for, many women's experiences of leadership.

Becoming educators, feminists and leaders

The generation of teachers now seeking and gaining leadership positions in the context of the radical restructuring of education in the 1990s were the schoolgirls of the 1950s. The 1950s was the peak period of modernization, one full of promise and potential for Australian cultural and national identity formation and unprecedented prosperity 'which applauded the heroic image of a conquering, pioneering, austere masculinity – the modern individual in a particular guise – but scorned the world of domesticity and everyday life of modern suburbia as not a fit place for men' (Johnson 1993: 51). It was an era of conservatism, comfort and consensus – stability and normality – located between the first half-century of class, hardship, empire, nationalism and the cultural diversity, quality of life issues, protest movements and liberations of the 1960s. While official educational texts spoke of integrating the individual gender-, class- and race-neutral individual into a unified democratic society, public education systems produced differentiating practices. Vocational/academic educational pathways formed within schools around gender, ethnicity, race and class as more working-class students stayed on in school due to rising class aspirations in a period of economic growth. It was a dominantly Anglo cultural milieu, untouched by the increasing presence of non-English speaking European immigrant children and ongoing absence of Aboriginal children (Blackmore 1997b).

In recalling their schooling, women spoke of their positioning as female in a taken-for-granted way indicative of the gender-neutral ways in which girls' choices were then constructed:

> I taught because that is what girls did in my year.
>
> (Bernadette)

Their stories indicated the ideological force of dominant discourses of liberal meritocracy, child-centred learning and ideologies of motherhood. The decision to become a teacher, spoken of abstractly as a 'choice', was clearly shaped by cultural understandings about their gendered options.

> In our time, girls either chose to become teachers, nurses or office workers. If you could not get any of these, you could always serve in Myers or Coles retail stores.
>
> (Bernadette)

There was a 'certain naturalness' about becoming teachers: 'What else could I do?' Few said: 'I refused to do that'. Becoming a teacher was not seen to be a *gendered* choice, however, because it provided a form of social mobility and status not available to less academically successful girls. For teachers, class rather than gender was foregrounded.

> I think all the women I went to school with are now nurses or teachers.
> It was an avenue of social mobility.
>
> (Fran)

Academic achievers, male and female, but particularly 'bright' rural and
working-class girls, were drawn into teaching by teaching studentships that
funded their university education. Being a good student (and female) was
'naturally' conflated into being a teacher.

> We were the second year of the Higher School Certificate (Year 12) at
> the tough working-class Pascoe Vale Girls, the Pacco Moll House, to
> have done HSC. Myself and another girl were the first to get into uni-
> versity. I had that opportunity due to a girls' education and a liberal
> (probably we would now say feminist) English teacher in Form 4 who
> talked about female rights and child care in 1970! I always excelled in
> school without really trying and in sports, as they encouraged all girls
> in sport. I always wanted to be a maths teacher from primary school. It
> was a natural progression into teaching . . . particularly being a female.
> I got a studentship.
>
> (Betty)

Teaching was the most 'suitable' occupation for educated women, and
many girls absorbed that message. For some, like myself with both parents
and an older brother being teachers, it was also a family tradition. Teaching
was something I always wanted to do, like Pam, now a principal:

> I was the product of teaching parents, whose father was a principal and
> whose stories at home were of salvation or success. I was brought up in
> a value system that would be characterized from progressive to left-
> wing to just socially aware. I was an academic achiever and childhood
> burdens were lightly taken. No blockers in career, just in timing. I came
> from the vintage of university scholarships in a meritocratic system
> with teaching studentships . . . there were a multiplicity of enforcing
> factors which led me into teaching.

Class and ethnic background, parental aspirations, particular school
environments (for example, girls' schools and convents), school experiences
in academic and sporting leadership and even particular teachers were the mix
that shaped girls' sense of self. One assistant principal, Sandra, commented:

> I have always been too pushy, up front and assertive . . . I was a leader
> whether it was a sporting team or in debating. It came from the tra-
> ditional working-class values of parents of the 1950s.

Without exception, the women interviewed and now in formal leadership
positions, spoke of strong familial support and encouragement to achieve
educationally. Mafalda was a child of 2 when her parents emigrated from

Italy to Australia 'to make money and go back home'. She was one of the few women of non-Anglo background who were principals, in this instance in a primary school renowned for its multiculturalism (only 20 per cent of the school population was of Anglo background). Her father's valuing of education (and there being no boys) meant 'he refused to let me leave school' although peer and cultural pressures meant I wanted to 'do what other girls did' and get a job. Likewise, Bernadette accommodated familial aspirations:

> I liked maths and science at school. I had people in my family encouraging me to do architecture but no, I wanted to do primary teaching. But I acquiesced to them and went to uni.

Due to their success in a highly meritocratic and élitist male-dominated academic system, they did not necessarily identify themselves as disadvantaged due to gender.

> I went to a normal country HS and it was more the class thing rather than the gender thing which was important. I was advantaged because I was middle-class. In a country town it was gendered in terms of sport . . . yet there were lots of facilities for girls.
>
> (Colleen)

Although not acknowledging the implicit masculinity in the images of success, they were treated differentially as women (Johnson 1993). Carolyn Steedman suggests that the sex-neutral language of the 1950s and 1960s did not render all women as invisible.

> Many women, living through the years of the 'sex neutral' 'he' refused, when they heard or used the pronoun to imagine man. They thought rather of a genderless 'human being' or 'person'. Some of them, with much struggle, actually managed to image themselves in the category of the genderless human being.
>
> (Steedman, quoted in Johnson 1993: 9)

The image was of an androgynous leader and manager. Yet gender was unexpectedly foregrounded in specific contexts and place; it intervened at particular moments in a disjointed and arbitrary fashion for these girls, most often around disciplining the body, the female body being subject to strict uniform regimes monitoring the wearing of hats, gloves, length of skirt, type of shoe and colour of stocking:

> We emulated the private school model even though we were very rough girls.
>
> (Betty)

Feminists viewed their strong sensibility about social justice arising out of their earlier class, ethnic and religious experience, their familial value systems and, later, union and feminist activism.

My mother would have been a feminist of her time. I went to a single-sex Catholic girls' school where girls could do anything they wanted. In some ways it was very narrow and also very empowering . . . I did science largely because it was expected of me . . . dux of school and school captain. My passion was English, the family won in that I stuck at science.

Such experiences left them, as one convent graduate wryly commented,

open to becoming activists in education due to a sense of guilt, a desire for social justice, and a sense of feeling capable of changing things.

(Bev)

The women's movement later provided these women a capacity to articulate and focus these desires in a more libratory way, although still tinged with a sense of victimhood. Feminism in the 1960s was largely an intellectual, not mass, movement. Feminist discourses at that time depicted women as either the passive receptors of a culture that manipulated women such that their desires were limited to being a 'woman', or the self-determining and autonomous individual central to the emergence of second wave feminism, that of the developmental psychologists, who saw women as choosing, as being interdependent, connected and relational, and thus assuming some authentic self (Johnson 1993).

As highly trained teacher graduates in the 1960s, the professional work identity of these women was constantly undermined by 'naturalized' gender inequalities:

I mean we were on three-quarter pay of what men got. But again that was accepted.

(Sarah)

'I didn't know that it was restrictive then. I suppose there are others things in your life. I didn't feel restricted.

(Ann)

The generic meaning of universal man went unquestioned.

At an obvious level, educational literature, for instance, frequently used the pronoun 'he'; or talked in terms of 'men'; at another level, it gave legitimacy also to notions of individual competitiveness and objective, rational thought which historically have been designated as masculine capacities and placed in opposition to characteristics such as cooperative and nurturing capacities designated as feminine. But neither of these points can be used to claim that young women found themselves *necessarily* excluded. To suggest that they do is to assume that young women are conscious of themselves at all times and in all places as gendered selves first and foremost.

(Johnson 1993: 8)

Other responses were denial of discrimination or rapid politicization (Marshall 1993). When women teachers did rage against the universal 'he' they faced, like my mother in the late 1950s, overt structural and cultural prejudices that defined her work, although equal to that of her male colleagues, as lesser because she was female. She also possessed fewer legal and citizenship rights than men. My mother, having returned to full-time secondary teaching after 10 years caring for me and my older brother, gained promotion in 1960. Her claim for transport costs from the Department of Education was rejected on the grounds that my father, on transfer, owned the family possessions. After a successful appeal to the Teachers Tribunal, which showed her strength against the odds, my mother was invited to stand for election to the male-dominated executive of Victorian Secondary Teachers Association. There she became a leading activist for improved teacher conditions of work and equal pay for women throughout the 1960s and one of the first female principals in coeducational secondary schools in the 1970s.

Having grown up as a girl in the 1950s and educated in the 1960s, the issue for my generation of women teachers by the 1970s was more one of identity than structural and legal boundaries (Johnson 1993: 1). My generation was, unlike my mother's, able to continue teaching after marriage and children, whereas 'mothers who worked' in the 1960s were positioned as deviant. This sense of difference was internalized by many women who felt guilty and inadequate, deemed to be behaving inappropriately.

> The most disempowering thing was when people said, 'You should be at a home with the child'. My husband appeased my guilt: ' Do what you want to do'. And I did.
>
> (Sandra)

Gaining equal pay in 1970 disrupted the myth that women teachers did something 'different' in schools, a view that excluded them from *being seen to be* in positions of authority and responsibility. One female principal, Colleen, laughingly recalled:

> I can still remember equal pay for equal work coming in and the hostility of many of the men saying things to us such as, 'Now you will have to take assembly'. Like this was going to be a horrific thing that no women would be able to get up in front of a group of children and take an assembly!

I unproblematically accepted equal pay for women teachers as the norm for women when I commenced teaching in 1970. An academic achiever, I had always wanted to be a teacher, and, as my brother, received parental encouragement of my aspirations. But being a woman is a 'state which fluctuates for the individual' so that there are always 'different densities of being sexed in operation' (Riley 1988: 6). My first experience of structural discrimination was not based on gender. The Education Department withdrew my teacher studentship (a wage provided to support student teachers in training) on the grounds of my 'disability', given that I had one leg affected by poliomyelitis as a child. Although later re-employed by the department (on reduced super-annuation benefits) once qualified in maths and history and teacher training, it was marriage a year later which fully disqualified me from the lucrative superannuation scheme available to all men and single women. I could not abstract my experience of being a woman from being labelled as married, middle-class and indeed 'disabled'.

Change agents

As one of the baby boomer generation of highly qualified teachers in the radical activism of the 1970s, unionism and professionalism were synonymous. In Victoria, the unions were the primary source of innovative ideas for teachers in a paternalistic, conservative, top-heavy, highly centralized educational bureaucracy. Union issues focused upon professionalism and work conditions, manifest in union resistance to school inspectors, external assessment, and demands for school-based peer evaluation, decisionmaking and curriculum development. Collegiality arising out of grass-roots union activism encouraged critical reflective professional practice (Weiner 1995a). While I found myself being sponsored into leadership positions (Year 11 level coordinator of 200 students) in my third year of my career by a benignly paternalistic male principal, I did not think of myself as a leader. I was puzzled and irritated when fellow teachers jokingly referred to me as 'one of the administration'. I was anti-authority, because administration was at that time of the anti-Vietnam war movement seen to be paternalistic, authoritarian and, in education, constraining teacher professionality. The paternalism of principals in a highly centralized bureaucracy either impeded innovative change or did not actively encourage it. Change initiatives tended to be bottom-up as teachers initiated new forms of curriculum (general studies), school organization (mini-schools) and assessment practices (negotiated). Being innovative was what made a good teacher, but innovation or change was not associated with formal leadership. Teacher innovation framed itself in opposition to the bureaucracy, in a language of social justice and practice rather than a language of leadership.

Often an elected staff representative in the union, the staff association, and on school council, I still had little sense of being a change agent or a leader. I was just a teacher fighting for a better education for students around issues of curriculum and assessment, improved professional standards and working conditions for teachers. Pam, now a principal, also recalls:

> I learnt from working in the unions about how to be a leader as branch president . . . At Preston I led an anti-grading campaign and 26 teachers

were taken to the Teachers' Tribunal and charged and fined . . . Yet it
was a relatively secure position, and I still didn't see myself as doing
anything except being and becoming a better teacher.

This capacity to imagine ourselves as reformers or activists was validated
by wider discourses about education as a site of social change promoted
through federal government policy imperatives after 1972, although gender
was not foremost in social justice issues until 1975. The women's movement
then made explicit what to many had been implicit, by foregrounding gender
and providing a range of ways of thinking about our capacity to act and
strategize for change, and by developing a sense of collectivity around a
common feminist political project.

The women's movement was a fairly obvious way to go for women of
my age. I really do believe that there were real gender inequalities, but
I was personally less aware.

(Colleen)

Many gender equity activists and feminists referred to the significance of
feminism in their consciousness-raising as activists in education and the
community:

One day I read the *Female Eunuch* . . . and I thought . . . shit . . . that
was me. Hurtsville in the late 70s, a male-dominated and very radical
union school. There was not a lot of feminist politics. It was only when
I got the words and articulation through EO that I realized.

(Mary)

I was brought up considering social justice issues (particularly of race)
since early childhood. My parents tried consciously to treat me and
brother equally. I was also sent to an all-girls' boarding school, a highly
academic Catholic convent. Then I read the *Female Eunuch*. Now all
those things which I thought were my personal problem I realized were
many women's feelings.

(Clare)

Their experience was that the organization of schools clearly marked
them as women through the differential rewards system and the seniority
principle that worked to benefit men (Sampson 1986). Entrée into formal
leadership roles for most women principals well into the 1990s was contingent upon benevolent paternalism, being tapped on the shoulder, and being
in the right place at the right time. Being recognized early in their career,
as for me, established many women's leadership credibility, but most often
female expertise was restricted to 'administering the feminine' and not general school administration.

I was the dreaded Senior Mistress, later Girls' Coordinator. My role as
decided by the boys in the staff was girls' discipline while they made all

the decisions. My life was spent in the girls' toilets catching smokers and measuring girls' skirt lengths.

(Jean)

Their perceived capacities for leadership were shaped by subtle gendered biases that favoured particular experiences and subject areas: science and maths over humanities, finance over curriculum. Science teachers, largely male, were inevitably the timetablers (Sampson 1986).

> You came out of college and went into a large school as infant teacher; the men came out and were sent immediately to rural areas as head teacher. I was lucky – I got Grade 6 straight away. That gave me some status. But the view that women were unable to teach older boys persisted . . . the District Inspector said: 'You could teach Grade 6 boys maths.' Not that I could teach Grade 6 girls, but Grade 6 boys! Unbelievable!
>
> (Trish)

EO policies during the 1980s created new opportunity structures for women teachers. Government policies and industrial agreements in Victorian schools after 1982 required the appointment of EO coordinators in all government schools and on all committees. Gender equity reform became a path for advancement and learning institutional politics for many junior female teachers, but EO work was fraught with tensions.

> My male principal encouraged me to go into EO as this was an area where attitudes had to change. At the beginning it was a hard task because you had the antagonism of both staff and students in a traditional boys-only technical school . . . It was very political then. Now it is policy and is legitimate. I learnt a lot.
>
> (Amanda)

Julie was a junior teacher representative on a local principal selection committee:

> It was a pleasant collaborative committee. When it came to the actual choice it was a locked decision – males went for the male applicant and females for the female. I felt it was the first time that I had to really assert myself. I normally consult, negotiate and conciliate. I had to write down points and argue. We did not give in and we got a female principal who I thought was the best easily.

Involvement in EO facilitated learning the game of administration.

> The good side is that, even if it is token, EO membership on so many committees means you as an EO representative get to know the process and [be] immersed into decisionmaking.
>
> (Helen)

EO policy provided a language and legitimacy for EO representatives, one that could change behaviours, not attitudes. A principal, Amanda, commented:

> I think EO policies have been very helpful. In the early days they caused a lot of antagonism, because men felt threatened seeing their territory recede . . . The EO position had always been taken by women because it was too 'soft' and not a male thing to do. That is changing.

For younger female teachers, EO provided them with a sense of agency. Sarah, an EO coordinator and relatively junior, said,

> I had to counsel a few older male teachers about the way they were referring to younger women because it was against the law. It was really empowering because I was able to do it in a non-confrontational way and appeal to the policies . . . and it was easier for them. I actually think it also gained me a lot of their respect.

On the other hand, there was no guarantee that due process would produce equitable outcomes. Indeed, token women on committees were well aware that they were often perceived to be complicit in any decisions that worked against women's interests. Fair procedures were not enough, as Anna commented, unless made transparent:

> The old time operators know how to avoid due process, particularly since EO representation is on all committees. They'll make sure that new members on the committee have no idea of the process – it's tucked away in the handbook where no one sees it.

EO provided administrative and leadership experience to many women relatively early in their careers because it required them to develop and implement policy and initiate change in the particularly disruptive field of gender relations. Most were conscious of the various subversive activities and resistances that undermined their work, and the need to work with staff with whom they had little in common to produce change.

Feminist teachers took on supervisory and disciplinary roles with regard to gender in schools. While they were denigrated, teased and derided for their passion in EO, they were also successful change agents (McLeod 1995; Kenway *et al.* 1997). Ella spoke of how she came to a school which had a high EO profile.

> What was happening in classrooms was quite contradictory to policies in equal opportunity. Yet the staff kept saying, 'Yeah we know all about it, we have being doing this for years'. So I chose to stand back and watch, to create a situation where I could actually work with staff, mix and mingle, and watched their attitudes change over 12 months.

At the same time, EO could mean death to one's career as EO was not valued equally with similar administrative tasks until it became a paid position. Many younger feminist teachers consciously spread their activities:

> I keep up in other areas, maintain my interest in science, do professional development in other camps.
>
> (Sarah)

> For me it has been good in career terms because I have done things across the curriculum, and gained good recognition for that. But I don't just work on gender inclusiveness – also race and disability. I try and get everyone involved and said to the principal – 'you support EO' so this is your job to encourage it. But I also would not go to my next school and just say I've been an EO coordinator. I would talk about it in curriculum and administrative terms.
>
> (Ella)

Being political was part of the job, and gender equity reformers learnt to appropriate the dominant discourses to achieve their ends in order to get things done.

'Just getting things done'

Many women did not see themselves as leaders until well into their 40s and were surprised when they found others saw them that way. None of the women interviewed imagined themselves to be principals of schools when they entered teaching. More typically, it was a male principal who said. 'You can do that – why not apply?' They depicted their career histories as being based on luck, not merit, being in the right place at the right time rather than indicative of their capacities of leadership. Many applied for promotion out of anger and frustration when they saw less qualified and capable men rapidly move up the school hierarchy and thought 'I can do better than that'.

> Seeing all those incompetent people becoming senior teachers or assistant principals or even principals, mainly men. I know I am more efficient, organized and with an idea about what is good in education. But a man doesn't have to prove himself, where a woman has to do doubly better.
>
> (Dorothy)

The daily grind and frustration of male-dominated school cultures and professional relationships led many to become gender aware and active:

> The ways the males perceive the world, their domination of the administration. Because you are female you are treated as little girls.
>
> (Anna)

They constantly struggled between the seeming contradiction of being female and being leaders. Dominant images of leadership meant rejecting their femininity.

> I had some good male role models and some real doozies, male and female. But it is only when you get a good female model you say, I can do that and still not lose my female attributes.
>
> (Lesley)

Women described what they did as 'just getting things done', good teaching, and not leadership. Many women redefined what they did as leadership once they had access to the institutionalized discourses and system-wide information formerly restricted to the 'boys' network'. As with postgraduate study, these different communities of practice provided them with a language of the abstract, an overview and a capacity for critical analysis; a way to name what they did in organizational terms.

> The regional position gave me the chance to see if I could communicate with strangers. I had a strong sense that I was only powerful and effective when relationships were built up and when I was secure in these relationships . . . My career wasn't important in my mind. In regional office I learnt to manage upwards.
>
> (Philia)

Most women did not think in terms of career paths, usually changing jobs out of impulse, passion, boredom or because their partner shifted. Without clear career aspirations or expectations, their professional identities were tied to their capacity to do things well, being professional and not to particular jobs or career expectations. For many women, taking on formal positions produced a constant state of insecurity and sense of fragility. Leadership was perceived to require doing things differently, as different from teaching and previous change work. Whereas leadership is often constructed as heroic work, 'teaching has suffered because of its reputation as a haven for ordinary and unambitious people' (Biklen 1993: 11). Women read these contradictions and 'discomfort' as 'not coping' rather than normal.

> I never really questioned that I was a good teacher. I was very happy, secure and rather comfortable in my job. My current spouse and principal pushed me to apply for promotion . . . In the coordinator's job I was run off my feet. I learnt so much but thought I'd have to drop it. I told the principal, 'I know you know I am not coping'. He was amazed and helped me work through that lack of confidence.
>
> (Dorothy)

The balancing act of the triple shift

It is now well documented how women's work histories differ from men's in that they are marked by discontinuity, lack of planning, diversity of paid work and voluntary experiences, shifts between part-time and full-time employment – largely organizing around others – due to most women working the 'triple shift' of paid work, and unpaid domestic and community work. June, an acting primary principal, pointed out,

> there are different moments in your life. At some point, there is a space for you. I focused upon my children, then assisted my husband setting up a business. I taught throughout – enjoying doing the nine to four shift. Then when everyone else was OK, I thought, what about me, what do I want? It was in my 40s when I decided I wanted to become a principal.

The pattern continues to be that most female principals are single or without childcare or domestic responsibility (Victorian Department of Education 1996). Younger women teachers are working more, with shorter breaks for child-rearing, but with little redistribution of the domestic labour or childcare, with lack of workplace childcare and 'the need to train our bloody men to do half the work' as major barriers to their promotion possibilities. Janice's ambivalence was typical:

> My husband doesn't have that opportunity to move and I feel that I am in a situation where I have to decide between family and career, because I come from an Italian background and I'm the mother of another family in another sense . . . I know I want children and I would have to stop work or leave them with my mother. I also want to be able to work part-time and have children, but not to have to do a fantastic balancing act.

Women teachers who did prioritize family responsibilities were often viewed by their fellow members of staff, male and female, as uncommitted, disinterested and apathetic, because they were not actively involved in school committees – 'the nine to fourers'. These women were made to feel guilty and apologetic when indeed often they were just worn out. Women principals with dependent children were positioned differently from men. Sandra observed,

> Our female VP has two children at primary school . . . They actually come up to school sometimes, which is interesting. Men in that position do not have that ultimate responsibility and would tend not to do that. She was seen to be either not coping or exploiting her advantaged position.

Sandra voiced the contradiction for many women:

We in gender equity are seeking to develop more nurturing and socially aware children and yet still undertake the work at home.

It was an ongoing internal struggle between the 'I' and the 'we'.

If you look at my children's generation, there's a whole different way of living in the world. It's very much 'I' centred, whereas I think grew up in a world which was very much being beholding and subservient to other people. You know, you're here to serve, you're a wife, you're a mother, you're this, you're that. It takes a long time to cast that off. It took a pretty stormy period in my life to say, 'Ultimately everybody's responsible for themselves'.

(Judy)

Gender and generation

There were clear generational differences in the storylines of these women. Women teachers in their 20s and 30s had different histories and investments in feminism than the baby boomer generation. One consequence of feminism is that many now aspire early in their careers for leadership. Most were educated during the 1970s, growing upon the context where discourses of EO circulated in the media, schools, universities and in public policy. Many came to teaching with the assumption that gender equity was in place. They were gender aware, with partners in relationships that were openly lesbian or de facto. Some lived with 'sensitive new age guys' (SNAGS). These younger women saw themselves as active agents and powerful enough to produce change. They consciously drew upon a range of discourses about career opportunities, life choices and feminism. They were also politically astute, and aware of the strategies required to construct themselves as 'leaders': to record and document their work, to write good curricula vitae, to work strategically and across a range of tasks so as to get both breadth and depth in their experience. They drew upon the common-sense knowledge circulating in schools about feminist practice, leadership styles, and professional development and acted upon them. They took up postgraduate courses to improve qualifications, professional development activities and opportunities in acting positions. They tapped into networks. EO provided many young female teachers with empowering organizational knowledge:

I am getting in to know how you do things. I am on the welfare committee, I'm in the resource group, I have to do reports to staff meetings. I can look at three-quarters of the staff who have never done that. There is no other way I could get this if I weren't in EO.

(Sarah)

Ironically, these well-prepared and motivated women now work in schools where the legitimacy of EO is being actively undermined. In the context of the radical conservatism of the 1990s, equity discourses are being marginalized and equity structures dismantled:

> When the state EO commissioner was given the boot by this government, I walked into school next day and the staff were talking budgets. The budget person walks across and says to me, 'We won't need an EO budget next will we?' (and he laughed).
>
> (Ella)

In any budget decision, equity was the first to go.

> The EO position was the first under scrutiny . . . You have to decide whether you are going to keep on fighting for it all the time . . . They couldn't wait to get rid of EO now the decision was left up to the school as a local priority in policy and not government mandated policy.
>
> (Anna)

Even the Advanced Skills Teacher (AST) and Leading Teacher categories, which offered career paths for teachers, thus encouraging them to stay in the classroom and not move into administration, held little promise. Amanda commented:

> I've noticed that most of the women in senior positions don't have children . . . not that they have grown up but that they don't have them at all or any other sort of commitment. And that worries me about the AST positions if I take family leave and try to get back in.

The rhetoric of gender-neutral discourses of procedure, performance indicators and the structures and practices camouflaged more hierarchical relationships with fewer opportunities in a performance-oriented profession.

> A few years ago I thought about a career path . . . now everything has closed down . . . there is no mobility.
>
> (Belinda)

Or 'the doors are shutting' as 'the issue is just keeping your job each year' (Ann). Many commented on how they had not applied for assessment (required for promotion) in their schools because 'they didn't like the people or the values of the administration' and 'did not see their chances as great in such a macho competitive culture'. Leading teachers now worked in a highly competitive environment that required teachers to be seen to perform outside as well as inside the classroom, increasing not decreasing the demands of time and energy for those seeking promotion.

It is still a boys' game in that the goal posts have again been shifted or raised.

(Belinda)

I don't think that we have flexibility in teaching anymore. You go gung-ho and forget family responsibilities and go for career.

(Joyce)

Others saw the language of competitive individualism as antithetical to the collective impulses of feminism and education and did not wish to play the game. They expressed disillusionment, and frustration that their skills and knowledge were being ignored, even devalued.

I really enjoy teaching but find the whole notion of a career increasingly disempowering with all the cuts. There are so many fantastic female classroom teachers – male too – but you don't get recognition for being a fantastic classroom teacher.

(Tanya)

The opportunity structures of the more democratically organized schools in the 1980s were fast disappearing in the competitive culture of the 1990s. Instead, the intensification of teachers' work made teaching, least of all leadership, increasingly difficult for women. Clare voiced the view expressed by many: 'Being a principal is not the be all and end all'.

Most women were 'easy and eager' narrators in the telling of their work and life histories. Interdependencies, relationships and responsibilities were integral to these stories. Familial responsibilities were never far away from work, blurring home/work boundaries.

I think a lot of women choose to have a balance in their life. Some look at principals and the hours a lot of people work – they think: 'Is that what I want?'

(Cherry)

Quality of life, pleasure and work satisfaction were important, and achievement as defined not by status or authority, but about passion and improvement.

I think that it is important that you keep growing and enjoying your work ... I mean I am 44 ... I don't have to be a principal to feel empowered and responsible for myself. I love the job of teaching.

(Bella)

Talking about their professional work led them into a 'settled, discursive realm' in which they could, in the main, construct themselves as 'accomplished, successful and powerful individuals' (Chase 1995: 45–6). For some, gender was not foregrounded, and often denied as a factor in their careers and professional attitudes, indicating 'women's primary commitment to professional work in itself' (Chase 1995: 178). For others, there was an increasing tension between their feminist politics and dominant perceptions of professionalism in leadership.

Being strong

There are now in the 1990s many competing discourses surrounding women and leadership. These discourses are complex and contradictory, products of old and new times, although all reduce to the belief that 'it takes an extraordinary woman to do what an ordinary man does'. As one male manager, David, commented:

> Women tend to be located as principals in schools to which 'traditional white males won't aspire' because that is where the opportunities are. Thus some women get an opportunity. But 'women in general' don't. Beating the traditional would mean a woman getting a prestigious middle-class suburban state school which emulates private schools. To do that . . . requires an outstanding person, not just a good person. That extra dimension is not asked of her male colleagues.

The discursive construction of women as leaders in the 1990s emphasizes the woman leader as 'being strong' (morally and ethically) in the face of adversity, discrimination, resistance, taunting and teasing while maintaining her good nature and 'niceness' along the way, never showing the dark emotional side of anger, just passion and courage (Mirza 1993). This popularized superwoman image expects women to be successful mothers, wives, daughters, leaders and community workers, powerful on all fronts as well as good role models, mentors and advocates for other women at work, all without complaint and recognition of the personal costs, although harshly criticized if they put family before job or exit from the chilly climate of male dominated management (Cox 1996: 93–4).[1] For those who choose leadership over love, particularly if they are overtly feminist (as feminism outside a heterosexual relationship is often read to mean lesbianism), there is less sympathy as they have both seniority and mobility.

Women are now being positioned in the gender scripts of new management discourses as the new source of leadership talent, as change agents in 'new' postmodern times, because of their caring and sharing propensities and their communicative and organizational skills (Beck 1994; Marshall *et al.* 1996). As 'outsiders inside' women managers are cognizant of the values, practices and workings of management, but outside the male networks and dominant organizational cultures, and therefore have less investment in the status quo (Yeatman 1994; Cox 1996; Eisenstein 1996). Their power is derived from their difference, out of the shared cultural experience and attributes of being female, out of women's shared ways of seeing, being and doing. It is a difference, however, valued only to the extent that it serves organizationally defined goals.

At the same time there is the gender script of professional success, the gender-neutral 'I', built upon the notion that 'my success is due to hard work and merit and sheer professionalism alone'. This is the ultimate expression of the freely operating individual, who makes choices, and who, through her capacities as a person, not a woman, 'makes it'. It is an image favourable in the competitive culture of the education market. Chase (1995: 187) found that women in leadership 'embrace their professional competencies and success and develop a primary commitment to their professional work'. She concludes that 'a narrative of the successful, ambitious woman has achieved a certain substance'. Women are positioned as either without gender, or having the wrong gender. Gender is still a problem for and of women. Both these discursive positions are ultimately alienating for many women aspiring to, and enacting leadership, because they demand too much, because they often portray women as flat templates of real life without the flesh, the angst, the emotions and beliefs that are the makeup of being female, being feminist, and indeed full constituted humans.

Note

1 My spell-check insists on inserting superman for superwoman.

Part II

DISRUPTIVE VOICES

4 Gender equity policy in the 1990s: a moment of disjuncture?

Shifting frames of gender equity policy

The 1990s have been a watershed for equal opportunity (EO) policy generally and equal employment opportunity (EEO) policies for women in particular (Eisenstein 1996). The past decade has witnessed significant transformations in the nature of the state in western liberal democracies in the context of the conjuncture of global discourses of economic restructuring and New Right ideologies. Contracting public sector expenditures and economic restructuring have coincided with the period of greatest EO legislative and policy activity (including equal employment opportunity/affirmative action, anti-discriminatory and sexual harassment legislation), partially explaining the marginal increases in the representation of women in leadership in many western democracies during the 1980s.[1] Radically different relationships between the state, education and the individual in the 1990s now challenge Australian feminists' previous 'use' of the state to strategically intervene into gender politics (Sawer 1991). The dilemma for Australian 'state feminism' lies in its historical reliance upon state paternalism. Will the strategies of the past two decades work in the next? This second section of the text focuses upon these themes. In this chapter, I trace recent shifts in the policy paradigms and assumptions underpinning gender equity policies. The following chapter provides instances of how Australian 'femocrats' have worked in and through the state in order to achieve gender equity reform. The third focuses upon different forms of resistance to gender reform change. This Australian 'case' raises issues for gender equity policy formation in other western liberal democracies because it signals the need for new strategies in how feminists and feminism as a social movement relate to, and make claims, upon the state.

Women have long had a contradictory relationship with the state, a point of contention amongst feminist theorists (Franzway *et al.* 1989; Connell 1990; Watson 1990). On the one hand, the state, as a set of diverse and often contradictory practices, discourses and structures, enforces anti-discrimination and affirmative action laws (for example, Title IX in the USA, Affirmative Action Act and Equal Opportunity legislation in Australia, Sex Discrimination Act in the UK) and is a major employer of women in the public sector (education, health, welfare). On the other hand, the state fails to provide adequate childcare provision to make fully equal participation in work possible, or delegates gender equity to male bureaucrats with an investment in existing arrangements (Cockburn 1991).

Feminist academics have sought to theorize the state in order to inform their strategic engagement with the state as a social movement seeking to produce gender equity reform (Arnot and Weiler 1993). Radical feminists have tended to position 'the state' as a unitary and repressive institution which either embodies a class interest or *a* sexual politics. Liberal feminists see the imperfections of the state able to be rectified by extending to women the same rights and privileges as their male counterparts. Australian and Scandinavian feminists, due to their particularly active engagement with strong welfare states, tend to see the state as a site of contestation over gender, class and race relations and not just a unitary or monolithic entity, as not totally repressive of women, but also as an agency of, and for, social change (Franzway *et al.* 1989; Watson 1990). Feminists now

> see the state as a social process and not just a legal category or set of institutions. Processes of mobilisation, institutionalisation, the negotiation of hegemony between social groups, are all central to the character of the state. [There] is the renewed recognition of the state as a social force in its own right, and not just the vehicle of outside interests. The state may legitimately be seen as the initiator of important dynamics and as a place where interests are constituted as well as balanced.
>
> (Franzway *et al.* 1989: 33)

The state actively engages in the production and reproduction of gender relations, simultaneously transforming and institutionalizing gender power arrangements, defining and renegotiating the shifting boundaries between the public and the private, and, in the 1990s, increasingly mediating market, familial and education relations. Yet the state is culturally 'marked as masculine', although it does not always, or necessarily, produce a conventional view of masculinity or femininity nor serve male interests (Connell 1987).

The conjuncture of economic and cultural globalization with particularly conservative ideologies is transforming the nature of the modern state. Yeatman (1993) depicts the shift since the 1980s as one from a welfare state, where the state actively intervened in the market for the public good, to a contractualist or performative state, where the state mediates the market only to control its excesses. Public administrative reform premised upon managerialism and the market has converted citizens into clients of the state (Ferguson 1984). A growing sense of national financial insecurity in globalized economies has led politicians to assume greater power over the bureaucracy and policy production in what is termed the ministerialization of policy (Taylor *et al.* 1997). Due to the growing complexity of government, however, the performative state seeks through policy only to steer rather than row, to coordinate rather than administer on a daily basis. Instead, responsibility for daily administration is devolved down to smaller units on the ground. Policy priorities are maintained through tight accountability systems of the margins which provide feedback to the centre, a form of centralized decentralization in which the centralizing tendencies are stronger than the decentralizing tendencies.

The paradox is that at the historical moment that women would seem to be 'acceptable' to public administration because of their so-called 'people management' skills, there has been a shift in Australian state orientation towards management and market principles based on choice and efficiency. Gender equity is increasingly framed within the economically driven argument that women are a 'wasted resource of leadership', thus confusing past feminist claims based on special needs and equal rights. Despite new management discourses highlighting the 'soft' management skills, as in the Karpin Report on management education (1995), public sector reform has closely identified with the 'technical features of effective and financially accountable line command' rather than its human resource management side, 'a shift of values symbolised by the supplanting of the terms of "public administration" by those of "management" ' (Yeatman 1990: 5).

Educational restructuring globally has sought to improve national productivity by linking education to the economy more closely with the vocationalization of liberal education and introduction of national curricula. Yet social justice and gender equity are markedly absent in education reform policies in most western countries, such as 'America 2000' or the Education Reform Acts in England (Sadker and Sadker 1988; Stromquist 1992; Arnot and Weiler 1993) .

> The reform books and commissioned reports . . . clearly indicate that the past decade of legislation, new scholarship on women, research and action for sex equity in schools has gone unheeded. Gender is not a relevant category in analysis of excellence in schools. When gender was considered, it appeared to merely embellish the traditional – and male – portrait of the school . . . The goal of excellence does not even have the female student in mind.
>
> (Schmuck 1996: 348)

Gender equity for women is mentioned only in terms of how it improves student outcomes or national productivity. Yet evidence is mounting that recent 'reforms' have increased inequalities on the basis of class, gender and race (Blackmore 1994; Gordon 1994a; Whitty 1997).

How EO policy is conceptualized and received is shaped by shifting social, political and economic agendas. While the state in the 1980s has been largely depicted as welfarist, protectionist, even 'maternal', in most western liberal capitalist societies, the 1990s indicated a selectively interventionist, more radically conservative competitive state informed by particular economic orthodoxies (economic rationalism and human capital theory), a state seeking financial stringency, reluctant to intervene in the 'free' market, but happy to intervene on moral agendas (Giddens 1995). The changing nature of the state (structurally and ideologically) in the context of globalization, has significant implications for women and their strategic engagement with 'the state' in terms of women's citizenship claims, although with significant national differences.

An international perspective on gender equity policy

Despite the shared rhetoric amongst the feminisms about education as the means for promoting social change, gender reform strategies have varied considerably across western nation states. This is largely due to differences in federal/state political structures, industrial relations systems, levels of union activism and labour market structures, as well as cultural differences in terms of the emphasis upon different institutions as avenues of social change (for example, the courts in the USA and the public sector in Australia). Prior to 1975, most western educational reform policies focused upon class rather than gender inequality. Even after 1975, strong state policy on gender equity was largely restricted to Australia, New Zealand and Sweden (Watson 1988; Wernesson 1989; Yates 1993), with weaker top-down policy intervention in the USA, England and Canada (Arnot 1991, 1993; Stromquist 1992; Coulter 1996).

Most countries have been reluctant to legislate in the same way for equity for women (such as quotas) as they have for girls or race (for example, desegregation) (Marshall 1993). Even where there has been widespread acceptance of the discourse of EO, feminist agendas have not permeated through mainstream policy processes. The pattern of gender reform in the 1980s is marked by symbolic policy statements, voluntary implementation, and delegation of responsibility for gender equity to marginalized women's units with few resources or monitoring powers (Watson 1988). Gender equity educational *policies* in most western states have tended to be framed by liberal feminism and constrained by the level of political (and male) tolerance to change. The focus of liberal feminism has been to change individual women and girls to be more like men and boys (for example, getting more girls into male-dominated areas of science and maths and more women into leadership) on the assumption that a 'critical feminist mass' (30–40 per cent) in male domains would produce a cultural shift to 'gender inclusivity' (Arnot

1993; Weiner 1995a; Kenway *et al.* 1997). Beyond this, there are significant national variations.

Arnot depicts four types of initiatives in gender reform in the UK (also present in Australia): teacher initiated change, action research with external researchers, teacher contact and communication networks; and teacher union initiatives arising out of the women's movement and the gender politics of schools (Arnot 1987; Weiler 1988; Kenway *et al.* 1997). In the UK, Canada and New Zealand, while legislative initiatives and policy were the consequence of lobbying by the women's movement in political parties, trade unions and organizations, fundamental change relied upon grass-roots activity with only weak governmental, relatively benign support (Weiner 1995a, Coulter 1996). Feminist teachers, individually and collectively, often without formal power, used multiple strategies of writing reports for school-based policy, developing pilot curriculum projects, gaining funding for research projects, lobbying ministers, demanding non-sexist processes of promotion and selection, networking amongst women teachers, developing publications and materials (Watson 1988; Gaskell and McLaren 1991; Middleton 1992; Weiner 1995a).

In England, as the USA, race discrimination legislation provided precedents for later claims by women, but there was no central enforcement agency. Race and sex discrimination relied upon the local 'partnerships' between local education authorities, which were particularly active in Labour electorates, the Department of Education and Science, and teachers (largely through unions) to embrace race and sex discrimination legislation, although education was exempt from the law in many instances. The assumption was that 'sex discrimination would dissolve with increased knowledge of the issues, rational discussion and limited coercion. It was premised upon proscription not prescription, it was reactive not proactive, and defined equality of opportunity as equal treatment' (Arnot 1987: 316; 1993). By the mid-1980s, it was accepted that it was indifference, hostility and lack of political will and not lack of information that led to non-action. By 1987 there was no explicit policy statement on equal opportunities of either girls or women, no comparable committees of inquiry into gender as there were into race. Thatcherism dismantled these local alliances, disenfranchised teachers and attacked progressivist education. EO was positioned simultaneously as a failure and irrelevant.

In the USA, gender equity reform has largely been through coercive legislation seeking to remove sexually discriminatory practices and targeting women in educational leadership under threat of withdrawal of federal funds. Nelly Stromquist (1992) argues that implementation has been limited because the legislation was minimalist, narrowly interpreted by the judiciary, had insufficient enforcement mechanisms, limited and reduced funding over time for related legislation, and low levels of research funding in a decentralized system of governance. As elsewhere, it lacked coercive force and monitoring mechanisms and relied upon voluntary action by the states, organizations and individuals.

> In the countries where there have been longer periods of social-demo-cratic government and stronger trade unions there is far less pay-differ-ential and occupational segregation (both vertical and horizontal) between women and men, and far greater expansion of welfare services . . . Despite the existence of the largest and most vociferous feminist movement in the world, US women have seen the least overall change in the relative disadvantages of their sex compared to other Western democracies.
>
> (Segal 1990: 90–1)

While Canada, Sweden, the UK and New Zealand shared with Australia radical and socialist feminist traditions that worked for change through grass-roots activities and the unions, Canada's provincial orientation under-mined the emergence of strong national gender policies evident in Australia or Sweden, although with a strong state bureaucratic role increasingly influ-enced by market liberalism and managerialism. There were moments of proactive intervention, however, as in 1989 the Minister of Education in Ontario legislated for a goal of 50 per cent of supervisory positions occupied by women by the year 2000 (similar to the goal set in Sweden). Both Can-adian and Swedish initiatives have been lost, and indeed past equity legis-lation is under threat, under conservative governments which argue that there is no systemic inequality for women or other 'minority' groups (Coul-ter 1996). Canadian feminists in general view the state as 'containing' rather than 'empowering', encouraging a more strongly non-governmental profes-sionalised women's movement lobby than in Australia. As in Australia, Can-adian emphasis was on wage justice (unions) and not social justice (as in Sweden; Sawer 1994).

Overall, gender equity policy formation and implementation in the USA, UK and Canada has been more fragmented, localized, subject to the whim of different administrations, contingent upon economic good times, and under-resourced without the legitimating state support evident in Australia, New Zealand and Scandinavia (Poiner and Wills 1990; Stromquist 1992; Arnot 1993). Sweden's success lies with developing women's economic indepen-dence (with average women's wages now 95 per cent of average men's wages), treating racial, class and sexual inequality under a social democratic idea of fairness and equality, focusing on responsibilities as well as rights in the expec-tation that both genders would benefit (Wernersson 1989). Common to all is the ongoing underrepresentation of women in leadership positions, particu-larly at executive level and the growing influence of market liberalism, man-agerialism and devolution (Bell and Chase 1993; Court 1993; Limerick and Lingard 1995; Victorian Department of Education 1996).

'State' feminism and gender reform policy in Australia

While Australian feminism shares the same liberal feminist origins, it differs significantly from the American, for example, with its strong sense of collective action and egalitarianism, its school rather than university focus, and the presence of the 'femocracy' openly working for gender reform *within* the state (Eisenstein 1996). Australian feminist teachers, have like their English and Canadian counterparts been a powerful force as grass-roots activists, but in combination with strong top-down state initiatives giving greater impetus to gender equity reform (Weiler 1988; Acker 1996; Kenway *et al.* 1997).

'State' feminism has developed more in some nation states (e.g. Scandinavia, Australia, New Zealand) than others (UK, USA, Canada), although there is a trend in western nations for women as a social group to become more reliant on the paternalistic state and less on individual men (Hernes 1987). Australia has a tradition of strong state welfarist intervention to 'protect' women and children, for example, factory laws, basic family wage. The Australian 'femocracy' arose out of the deliberate strategy by the Women's Electoral Lobby in 1972, on the election of the first federal Labor government for over 20 years, to position feminists within state bureaucracies (femocrats) as Women's Advisers to the state premiers and the Prime Minister supported by Equal Opportunity Units (Burton 1991; Poiner and Wills 1990).[2] Governmental receptiveness was a reaction to the 'legitimation crisis' of the state signalled by the upsurge of 'new social movements' (student, women's, gay rights, civil rights, environmental and consumer movements) demanding greater participation in decisions that affected them. The 1970s experienced a renaissance of citizenship and democratic values. Leaders of social movements were recruited into the public administration where they developed their citizenship and representative claims from within the state. 'There they became the architects of the new types of policies which fostered the democratisation of public administration such as equal opportunity in public employment' (Yeatman 1990: 50). This incorporation of dissident voices was characteristic of the neocorporatist policy approach of federal and Victorian state Labor governments (Lingard 1993).

Consequently, through an uneasy alliance with the male dominated Labor Party and unions at state and federal levels, gender equity reform has been institutionalized through the Australian public sector. The raft of affirmative action legislation, policies and action plans for women and girls during the 1980s produced 'popular' discourses about equal opportunity and feminism within the public sector and the press (Eisenstein 1996). The Labor party/union alliance, through a series of economic accords after 1983, led to minimalization of wage claims upon the state in return for other work-based benefits such as childcare. Whereas the earlier strategic pushes were for anti-discriminatory legislation and affirmative action (AA), access to work and education, equal pay for equal work, the late 1980s sees a realization of the difficulties associated with extending the notion of discriminatory policies to arguments about group disadvantage, particularly those around casual part-time employment, retrenchment and work benefits (for example training, superannuation).[3] Institutional rules and practices became the issue. It was accepted that while there was no conscious policy or conspiracy of exclusion of women from promotion or leadership, discrimination arose out systemic discrimination operating through institutional processes and practices, perceptions about women's skills and the valuing of skills. Thus feminist unionists sought to reconceptualize the award restructuring being undertaken after 1987 to produce workplace reform as 'affirmative restructuring' (Affirmative Action Agency 1994). Yet many saw the shift to enterprise bargaining, in moving away from centralized to decentralized wage systems, as weakening the capacity of the state to 'protect' women workers (Zetlin and Whitehouse 1996). The focus of EO policies shifted by the late 1980s onto systemic discrimination, which sought to 'remove unintentional barriers to women's employment, be they attitudinal or structural', to women's promotional opportunities and to embed notions of equity and enfranchisement into state policy production and industrial relation workplace agreements, thereby promoting regulation in the context of industrial deregulation (Franzway *et al.* 1989: 90).

The extent to which the discursive shifts from corporate federalism to market liberalism have resonated in state gender politics has varied. Some states have historically been more amenable to gender equity reform (e.g. Victoria and SA) than others (Queensland and NSW). In Victoria under Labor governments after 1982, EO policies and industrial relations agreements expected schools to appoint EO coordinators, who also were placed on local principal selection, staff promotion committees, and school-based administrative and curriculum committees. Schools, regional offices and ministries were expected to write policy statements, establish EO committees, formulate sexual harassment policies, adopt plans and procedures for appointments, allocate administrative and organizational tasks fairly, include women on decisionmaking committees, examine job allocations, have women representing the institution in community forums, examine all documentation for sexist language, review job selection processes and undertake evaluations. Yet this process of institutionalization was both erratic and uneven.

In 1986, a State Board of Education report stated that women's underrepresentation in leadership was because 'many employers still believed that there were differences in work performance, abilities and staying power between men and women' and young male teachers continued to be 'encouraged and groomed for leadership' (State Board of Education, Victoria 1986: 6; Sampson 1986, 1987). Three year Action Plans modelled on the public sector plans were initiated. The first Victorian Action Plan (1986) focused upon awareness, commitment and implementation of equal opportunity policies; recruitment, selection and promotion on merit; staff training and development programs to address the needs of women; designing career structures and opportunities amenable to women's career paths; and improved working conditions (hours of work, family leave, parental leave for sick children, extended sick leave, child care). Its overall aim was the identification and removal of discriminatory practices and redress of past discrimination. Its main effect was to create an awareness of equal opportunity within the system. The second Action Plan (1989–92) introduced the notion of desired outcomes in principal class and promotion positions. It effectively improved the application and appointment rates of women to senior positions.[4] These plans established processes and lines of responsibility, reporting back to the centre about implementation and effects, and built networks between and within the central bureaucracy, regions and schools.

The key principles of the representational politics of gender equity during the 1980s were

1 clear criteria, processes and procedures in recruitment; selection and promotion based on merit;
2 gender balance on decisionmaking committees;
3 removal of all sexist language from educational and administrative material;
4 school-based committees trained in EO;
5 job searches to encourage women applicants; and
6 information feedback to policymakers to inform policy and staff development.

While rejecting quotas, the unwritten practice tended to be that the woman be appointed when selection committees chose between a female and male with equivalent qualifications, experiences and capacities. Strategic interventions included, in Victoria, a ministerial memo requiring all local principal selection committees to interview *all* women applicants (given that women's c.v.s tended not to reflect ability). In Western Australia, a requirement was for schools to have one female deputy principal wherever two deputy principals existed. Although challenged in 1993, the legal decision agreed that having women in senior administrative positions benefited the community, as otherwise narrow views of women's position in society are reinforced.

Yet the persistent underlying assumption of EO was that women were disadvantaged because they were deficient – not only did they lack administrative, financial and supervisory skills but they also lacked job commitment, assertiveness, leadership aspirations, career plans, confidence, risk taking tendencies, networks and a sense of opportunism. Most gender strategies focused upon getting women to upgrade their skills through professional development programs, to train women in writing c.v.s and interview procedures; to improve their self-esteem through self-presentation skills, conflict resolution and assertiveness training; to encourage them to develop career plans; to acquire leadership skills through job rotation and assuming acting positions; to network and be mentored, and to 'shadow' managers. While these policies put gender on the political, and indeed management, agenda, its take-up was erratic and its effects underresearched.

Another assumption underpinning the EEO policies of the 1980s was the thesis that all women seeking leadership have a similar if not equal commitment to equal opportunity. Therefore it was seen to be a sufficient condition for cultural change merely to increase the female presence which, by weight alone, would shift decisions more in favour of women, that is the 'critical mass' theory. EO was sometimes built into job statements, but, as in the case of the Advanced Skills Teacher, no evidence of commitment was required, only knowledge of EO and a stated commitment to policies. There was neither coercion or incentive for schools to undertake these measures, their success relying upon feminist activism in schools. The emphasis was upon clarity and transparency of procedure and processes.

Out of step? Efficiency vs equity

As elsewhere, the financial (and legitimation) crisis of the state after the 1987 crash led to an increasing tension between equity and efficiency. This tension was resolved by Labor governments mediating New Right demands for small government and social movement demands for participatory bureaucracies through corporate managerialism (Blackmore 1989; Lingard 1993). One mechanism to resolve the tension was to devolve responsibility for determining priorities down the line to the local unit (democratization) or 'faxing the crisis down the line' (Watkins 1993). From 1987, public sector reform was premised upon three principles of effectiveness, efficiency and equity, although equity was included as the best use of 'people resources' rather than on human rights principles (Yeatman 1990). Public sector corporate management, in adopting 'best business practice of restructuring', also sought to mainstream and downstream gender equity. While most gender equity reformers saw the mainstreaming of gender equity as a long-term objective, the devolving of responsibility to smaller units and individual managers was seen to be premature as there had not been the cultural change necessary to produce the necessary level of receptivity amongst predominantly male managers to take on these new responsibilities in an informed way. Equity became the responsibility of individuals with little understanding of good equity practices. Indeed, many had a high level of investment in the existing system (Burton 1991: 58).

Another mechanism of the union/labour alliance of 1987 was to promote 'affirmative restructuring' by negotiating an Advanced Skills Teacher (AST) career path designed, in part, to establish alternative career paths within teaching parallel to administration, encouraging women into leadership. By 1992, Victorian teachers had also gained significant improvement in working conditions with a seven-year family leave (without pay) without loss of position, paternal leave for two weeks on full pay at the birth of a child, and permanent part-time positions. It was also increasingly evident, however, that while gender equity policies removed structural impediments, that indirect discrimination embedded in organizational practices, images and cultures were equally powerful in excluding women from leadership – often called the 'glass ceiling' or 'chilly climate'. Thus the third Action Plan for 1992–94 focused on promotion to leadership positions such as the AST and higher duties as well as the principal class positions in schools. The second focus was to develop more family-friendly workplaces. The third focus encouraged EO committees to be active in collective bargaining at the institutional level in the decentralized industrial relations environment.

Pre-1992, the uneven success of EO in Victoria, as in other states, was marked by distinct regional differences. Clusters of women in leadership tended to coincide with supportive regional managers, designated EO positions and in small rural or culturally and socioeconomically diverse schools. Despite the variance across schools, regions and states, a shift in attitude was evident:

> When I started teaching 15 years ago, if a woman applied there was some surprise. Then they would go for female designated type jobs. And then only one or two. Now there is an expectation that women are capable and can do the job as well as if not better than males . . . The action plans for women ruffled a few feathers on both sides at first, but people have learnt and are going with it. It is still fundamentally on merit and what the individual can do.
>
> (David, manager)

> The action plan for women forced women, not just men, to confront things . . . I needed forcing to do things. I wouldn't have gone on the principal selection panel if I hadn't been pushed so as to meet gender balance guidelines out of the union membership. I was really glad afterwards – an incredible learning experience for me. I will do it again.
>
> (Helen)

By the late 1980s the representational politics of the femocracy was out of step with the economistic approach of corporate management which emphasized lean and mean management structures. Women located in senior management or casual employment tended to be most vulnerable in times of organizational restructuring. The Joint Committee of Public Accounts of the Australian Parliament (1992: 24–5) cited the disadvantages of devolution generally as being 'a loss of consistency and equity' resulting in 'fears of redundancy and reskilling', while noting the increase in temporary and part-time employees was largely female. The Labor government's commitment to inducting women into educational leadership was being tested. The strategic dilemma for femocrats was whether to call upon equity principles, or, given the shifting context of public policy, on the principle of efficiency. The latter prevailed because it appealed to both the 'rationality of bureaucracy' and to the 'productivity of the private sector' (Franzway *et al.* 1989: 91–2). While the marginalization of women's lobby groups commenced under Federal Labor governments, the election of neoconservative governments at state and federal level during the early 1990s not only accelerated the privatization and marketization of education but also initiated the dismantling of the welfare state and the disenfranchisement of teachers (on the grounds of union capture) from education policymaking.

Diluting gender: from EO to diversity

Under the radical conservatism of the newly elected state Kennett government in 1992 and neotraditional conservatism of the Howard federal government (1996), the underrepresentation of women in leadership has been reconceptualized as a problem of individual choice, sidelining the collectivist (and unionist) tradition of Australian state feminism.[5] The resources of the EO infrastructure at the state and federal level have been significantly reduced in status, nature and size, undermining the remaining femocrats' capacities to work effectively, while retaining their symbolic presence.[6] The ministerialization of policy has further eroded the relative independence of bureaucracies as well as the position of femocrats and equity units within the bureaucracy (Lingard 1995). Most femocrats have exited the state and federal bureaucracies under pressure, leading to significant loss of the institutional history of 'state' feminism.

In Victoria, the central EO unit was replaced by a Merit and Equity Unit restricted to monitoring of recruitment and selection procedures without a policy role. A Ministerial Review of Employment Equity for Women Teachers (1996) sitting throughout 1994–95, oversaw the radical restructuring of Victorian education.[7] This restructuring introduced new teacher career structures, self-managing schools, school charters, performance management, redefinition of school council roles, teacher appraisal, curriculum standards frameworks and standardized testing in primary and secondary schools. At the time that women were fleeing the chilly climate at the centre, with women in executive positions reducing from 18 per cent in 1990 to 16 per cent in 1996 (Victorian Department of Education 1996: 13), a much publicized Women in Leadership Program was funded by the Victorian Department of School Education to encourage women to apply for over 600 principal class positions made vacant by the spill of jobs, amalgamations and closures and the taking of lucrative voluntary redundancy packages by many male principals. Interviews with male and female managers in the bureaucracy undertaken throughout this period indicated a significant shift in the ways gender equity was defined, how policy was produced and the possibilities and problems arising from this for women. A male regional manager commented:

> I think there is a fertile ground for women who have taken themselves seriously and their careers, their aspirations, in the current state of play in education. Opportunities have been made available to them in this region because there has been a high turnover of largely senior male staff in schools . . . Mind you in another region with older more traditional teacher workforces and lower turnover there have been fewer opportunities.

The new government tapped into the large pool of well-prepared, experienced, eager and capable women teachers enthused by a decade of equal opportunity policies and practice. Change became the norm, with over 70 per cent of all principals in 1996 appointed after 1993.

The Ministerial Review of Employment Equity for Women (1994–96) signalled significant departures from former policy paradigms. First, in the context of a newly devolved governance of education under Schools of the Future policies, the review focused upon head office managers, regional managers, and principals as agents of change, not teachers or EO units. It sought to integrate equity into individual principal performance management contracts and school charters, seeking a commitment from those in power as 'strong and visible action and support from all managers and leaders in education' was a necessary condition for making environments more conducive for women (Victorian Department of Education 1996: 4). The intention was to make the monitoring or performativity mechanisms (performance management, school charters, reviews and outcomes etc.) of the accountability frameworks of self-managing schools work for gender equity by mainstreaming. An EO manager commented:

> I try and make equity other people's responsibility as I cannot do it all. My responsibility is to the women of Victoria. I try to get people to feel the need themselves, and if necessary embarrassment, to the point that, as in performance contracts, it is paying off. It is a much better use of resources to have the departmental heads do the work even if they get the credit.

The lack of transparency of performance management plans, negotiated between individuals (for example, principals and managers without parent or teacher input) facilitated tacit agreements about values or priorities, and gender equity was not high on the list.

Second, the review's emphasis was on changing organizational cultures without naming them as 'masculinist' or as 'advantaging men', although most women teachers referred to being 'put off by the boys' culture' in administration. Pragmatically, the review did not wish to alienate the powerful men needed to legitimate the review's report. It sought to be user-friendly, using non-alienating language and targeting individual managers, emphasizing measurable outcomes and assuming neutrality of processes and procedures. The message, however, was that the unwritten practice of affirmative action (appointing a woman when all things were equal) was now rejected.

Third, there was a significant shift in language away from direct, indirect and systemic discrimination to that of 'managing diversity', reflecting public sector and new management influences such as the federal Government Working Party on Management (Karpin Report 1995) which portrayed the manager of the twenty-first century as being female and of non-Anglo background. The review (Victorian Department of Education 1996: 3) defined diversity as 'a range of individual attributes and skills people bring to their work. It covers the dimensions of gender, race, culture, age and disability and includes merit and equity requirements'. Good management became an end in itself and not the means to achieve social justice. One manager saw Karpin as shifting the frame of gender equity away from

> woman as victim to woman as client, and therefore a plus for gender equity. Women can no longer be ignored. We now see this in managers' willingness to have targets in their performance planning about doing things for women and they make reference to it.
>
> (Miranda)

Romaine believed Karpin made the unspeakable possible.

> Gender equity has not been talked about amongst senior managers because it is an uncomfortable issue. Now Karpin has put it on the agenda . . . we have fierce arguments at executive level about women in leadership programs, what shape they should take, and about diversity, and whether we ought to have targets. They have given time where previously they ignored it.

The successive replacement of the language of affirmative action, social justice and equal opportunity by that of diversity signified a reconceptualization of gender inequality, however.

> The Karpin report certainly indicated the importance of diversity in senior management in corporations and public sector as an important ingredient in making change in organizations. You have to have courageous CEOs . . . But Karpin is about productivity and success so the ground has shifted. It is not about equity and social justice and EEO.
>
> (Justine, EO manager)

While the concept of diversity originated in the social movements of the 1960s out of an egalitarian impetus, managing diversity, by contrast, is a management response to structural and cultural change in the desire to maintain productivity (Morrison 1992). The discourse of diversity has various readings. One reading treats all difference as of equal status, but 'the assumption that sex or racial differences are no more important than individual differences as baldness or extroversion is insulting to those who have encountered discrimination in their lives' (Morrison 1992: 6). Another reading of diversity is the assimilation of difference, which anticipates diversity (as a problem) will ultimately disappear. A third pluralist view is premised upon the assumption that an equitable representation of diverse groups in organizations will produce the necessary cultural shifts to produce more inclusive environments. Finally the multicultural approach seeks to increase consciousness and appreciation of difference associated with the heritage, values and interests of all social groups (leadership diversity; Morrison 1992).

The review argued that the 'talents and competencies of women will be acknowledged and utilized to a much greater extent' (Victorian Department of Education 1996: 26), following on from the public service *Merit, Equity and Managing Diversity Guidelines*:

> Excellence in people management is demonstrated where merit and equity is optimally balanced and integral to corporate values and actions. Merit improves efficiency and effectiveness through fair and open competition to select the best available person for the job. Equity is based on a 'fair go' and helps maximise the potential for all employees to contribute to achieving corporate goals.
>
> (Office of the Public Service Commissioner 1994: 2)

Thus managing diversity was conceptualized as exploiting individual differences for corporate ends; not about managing *for* diversity, nor treating diversity as a benefit and expression of the richness of society. Once again, it 'conveys the image of white men at the top regulating their employees' affairs from afar' whereas 'leadership diversity' means sharing control with people who are 'different' (Morrison 1992: 9).

The ministerial review's focus upon leadership, best practice in managing people, visibility of women leaders, and professional development for female leadership aspirants, worked within the ideological boundaries of a conservative government whose policies were informed by market liberalism and 'strong', 'hard' leadership models (embodied in the leadership style of the Victiorian State Premier, Jeff Kennett) in a reassertion of hierarchical relationships between teachers and principals. The technologization of leadership is further brought about by more instrumentalist forms of professional development and mechanistic approaches to principal accreditation, focusing upon leadership competencies, task-oriented approaches, benchmarking, and skill checklists in short-term training sessions, rather than more holistic, value driven, reflective and potentially more inclusive leadership practices in longer leadership education programs. While claiming value neutrality, such shifts from leadership education to training impart certain messages to gender equity policymakers about how to work with and through the state.

> The main trick I use is to identify the common currency and what is important to key managers and link equity strategy into that currency. So my strategy has been to talk about leadership vision for schools, the reform program of Schools of the Future, performance management, organization, and link it to our diverse customer base – the students, the parents, their aspirations. So I try to make links back into student outcomes and performance outcomes of schools. I try to talk their language and link it back to productivity.
>
> (Ellen)

Reconceptualizing justice by the New Right as 'individual choice within the marketplace' has provided space for radical conservatives to co-opt feminist agendas while simultaneously justifying (in the national interest) the feminization of a more flexible teacher workforce. A high level bureaucrat commented on his departure from public service:

> The strangest thing is that the meaning of the words has changed. We used to know what 'equity' meant. It meant looking after the less well-off. Now it means not hampering business. Social justice was a phrase we used to use in submissions all the time. Now you never hear it.
>
> (*The Australian*, 27–8 February 1995: 5)

Reconceptualizing equity for women as individual choice means inequitable power relations are now naturalized as market forces at work. This exemplifies the power of the discourse of choice in constraining emancipatory practices generally, and the unpredictability and tenuousness of gender equity reform in particular. Subtle discursive shifts have occurred with the introduction of new vocabularies of choice and the market resulting from the colonization of education by accounting, advertising, management, therapeutic and marketing discourses. These frame equity quite differently. The managing diversity discourse, in gesturing to the 'multiculturalism' of Australian society, does not problematize the lack of women of Aboriginal or non-Anglo background in leadership positions (Cox 1995). Instead, its advocacy of the mainstreaming and downstreaming of gender equity has led the EO principles and practice formulated over a decade to become more diffused, confused and ultimately diluted – a process described by one equity manager as akin to 'pouring a bottle of concentrated ink into a river'.

Strategic change: the power of, and problem with, policy

Gender equity policymakers now confront a series of strategic dilemmas in the late 1990s. First, the 1980s' emphasis on transparency and procedural justice did not necessarily produce more equitable outcomes because the issues and appeals were not about substantive debates about just outcomes.

Second, the EEO focus upon merit legitimated the assumption that merit is a neutral and unambiguous term rather than an unstable, changing cultural product of a particular set of social (and power) relationships tending to favour those already in power (Burton 1993). To jettison the principle of merit as the cornerstone, however, is to open up EEO to the subjective, political and highly personal relationships of gender politics which puts EEO strategy at risk.

> In consequence, the equal opportunity strategy abstracts from the social context in a radical way, and tends to miss much of the potential (e.g. for solidarity and collective action) in the lives of disadvantaged groups with whom it deals. This leaves it in a relatively weak position to deal with the political conundrum created, when in challenging the gender distribution of 'merit' it engages in the politicisation of the concept whose objectivity is its own tactical base. Opponents of affirmative action well recognise this conundrum.
>
> (Franzway *et al*. 1989: 100)

Third, there was strong policy under the Action Plans for women teachers in the 1980s, but relatively weak systems of sanction/reward because of the fear that central control reduced professional and local autonomy on the ground. Now the centralized-decentralism of self-managing schools is strongly interventionist in monitoring in such areas as performance pay, charters, curriculum and testing, but weak in areas of equity.

Fourth, gender equity policies have focused upon changing individual women to be more like men on the assumption that a critical mass would produce cultural change (Arnot and Weiler 1993; Kenway *et al*. 1994; Weiner 1995a). The impetus was less to change the system, organizational values, leadership models or indeed men. It left the benchmark male unsullied. It meant a privileged group of women have gained access to the same positions as an élite class of men. While legitimating particular equity claims and change processes, EO policy has failed to address the more amorphous, culturally embedded aspects of gender power relations, and to 'appreciate the dynamic complexity of the problems facing various disadvantaged social groups. Central to this dynamic are questions of attitudes, interests and values and the power to advance and uphold them' (Poiner and Wills 1990: 100; Sinclair 1994).

While EO legislation is 'a necessary but not sufficient condition' for gender equity, EO policy has successfully produced an active discourse that provides a language of reform to practitioners (Limerick and Lingard 1995: 2). David, a manager, believed that

> There is now a fertile environment produced by the whole feminist movement, the legislative framework, and the legitimacy it gives to people's attitudes and aspirations which requires those who make the decisions to reappraise their traditional values . . . there has been a cultural shift . . . the legislation doesn't actually change anything itself . . . It locks it in so that it is harder to regress, or so I thought, as there is some regression occurring now with the backlash.

Gender equity workers were also conscious of the limitations of top-down policy to produce radical change:

> You need someone to drive it, someone on the ground who is willing to push the policy . . . the practical stuff about how to do it.
>
> (Romaine)

> I don't think policy changes anyone's hearts and minds. In some instance, it changes behaviours. But it is not the policy itself, more the framework the policy gives. It has to be followed up by on the ground initiatives at the coalface . . . policy does not change cultures, practice does. The change in cultures and institutions is actually about having women in there and doing well and changing the culture from within.
>
> (Justine)

Policies, while open-ended texts, still shape, frame and legitimate particular readings. The new EO strategies with their choice-oriented discourses about women and leadership are more open to highly individualistic readings. They imply that women should learn the institutional ropes, plan and pursue a career path, network, mentor, practice succession building and fix the technical 'weaknesses' in women's applications for promotion by supplanting the 'we' with the 'I' in interviews and curricula vitae. The tendency in this context is increasingly for women to work together for their own individual advancement. David again:

> This [government] cares about women as long as they are individuals, not as groups. I mean the current ideology is the cult of the individual, not the cult of social consciousness or of a socially cohesive mass.

It is increasingly difficult in this context for women to be overtly committed to EO, or to do the necessary grass-roots advocacy for gender equity work, as organizational loyalty and adherence to the minister's wishes are the grounds upon which potential leadership is judged.

The shift in the education debate since the 1970s in most western capitalist democracies signifies a move away from education as a sense of collective social responsibility with the desire to democratize knowledge towards a view of education as a national enterprise concerned about output, excellence and the competitive edge. It is a highly technical view imbued with notions of managerial rationality and tinged with anti-statism. Yet the inherent contradictions of liberalism between individualism and the government imperatives of planning and monitoring will continue to be played out in gender equity reform (Middleton 1992). Equal opportunity policies have long revealed the difficulty of 'resolving the tensions between demands for local autonomy and centralisation, between laissez faire and interventionist policies, between grassroots and top-down initiatives' (Arnot 1987: 326). The issue for the next decade in Australia is how the new educational settlement of the 1990s in the context of the new contractualism redefines the relationship between the performative state, education and the individual, and, in turn, how gender equity policy will be effectively 'delivered' in self-managing schools.

Notes

1 While Australian legislation is called affirmative action, there are no quota systems as in the USA. In Victoria, from 1991–95 female principal class appointments increased from 18 per cent to 31 per cent although 70 per cent are teachers. Women held 75 per cent of senior Advanced Skills Teacher positions in primary schools but only 39 per cent in secondary ones (Ministerial Review 1996: 12–13). In Queensland, men were 12 times more likely to be principals than women in 1990 compared to nine times in 1996, although men were only one-third of teachers (Limerick 1991). In WA, female principal appointments increased from 38 to 66 from 1992–94. In SA, appointment on merit and not seniority increased female principalships by 10 per cent in 1991 to 37 per cent of principal class positions.

   In 1993, over half UK male primary teachers and one-sixth female primary teachers were heads or deputies; over 10 per cent of male secondary teachers are heads compared to 4.6 per cent of females although there are equal numbers of male and female secondary teachers (NUT 1993 unpublished).

2 Anna Yeatman (1990: 61) argues all women in upper and middle level professional/management positions are femocrats regardless of whether in Equal Opportunity Units or designated women's issues positions, since they enjoy a privileged position being materially independent of men, and yet with the shared gender class position with other women due to their relative disadvantage with their male peers.

3 *Sex discrimination* is discrimination on the basis of gender; *direct discrimination* is intentional (unequal pay for equal work); and *indirect discrimination* is action that appears to have the same effect on everyone but which disadvantages one group more than another, for example overtime; *positive discrimination* means giving preferential treatment to a group who have experienced disadvantage; and *systemic discrimination* occurs when a complex set of policies, practices, unwritten and written rules and attitudes disadvantage a substantially larger number of

one group more than another, such as sexual harassment or promotion based on seniority not merit (State Board of Education, Victoria 1986: 21). By 1992 Action Plans emphasized *gender balance* (at least 50 per cent women) and *merit* (job selection on ability, knowledge and skills in fair and open competition).

4 The appointment rates to principal class positions increased from 13.5 to 40.11 per cent and in secondary schools from 18.9 to 34.48 per cent. By 1992, the women constituted 17.6 per cent in primary and 13.9 per cent in secondary principal positions and 41.3 per cent and 22 per cent assistant principal positions (Action Plan 1992–94).

5 I distinguish between the radical conservatism of the Victorian state Kennett government premised upon market liberalism in which women are seen to be the new source of leadership and the neoconservatism of the federal Howard government reverting to traditional notions of the nuclear family and women's roles.

6 The proactive Victorian EO Commissioner was replaced after one year of conservative government. The Federal Office of Status of Women and Commission for Equal Opportunity and Human Rights lost 40 per cent of its budget in 1997 under Howard and specialist commissioners in gender, race and disability have been replaced by a reduced number of generalist human rights commissioners in 1998.

7 I was a member of this review as the tertiary sector representative and for my expertise on women and leadership.

5 Working inside a system not of your own making

Outsiders inside

Women managers working in male-dominated bureaucracies, insiders with institutional power and authority but outside the 'male culture', are positioned in highly contradictory ways. Dorothy Smith argues from women's standpoint: 'We note the discrepancies and feel the strangeness as we come to work inside the discourse that is not of our own making' (1990: 2). This chapter explores how female managers or bureaucrats, some of them feminists (femocrats), engaged with the often contradictory processes of policy production in the Victorian education bureaucracy, focusing in particular on the gendered discursive practices surrounding policy generation rather than policy implementation (Taylor *et al.* 1997). Through interviews with two cohorts of female managers in the central educational bureaucracy, one cohort in 1989 and a second in 1995, I explore how the shift from a more progressive to a more conservative educational politics, in conjunction with the recurrent radical restructuring from a centralized towards a devolved system with more 'lean and mean' administrative structures, impacted on the gender politics of policy work in Victorian state education. The analysis begins in the context of the corporate federalism of Labor governments at state and federal levels in 1989 and ends with conservative/liberal national coalitions at state and federal levels in 1996.[1] The contrast highlights the changing relationships in the communities of practice between policymakers – educationalists, representatives of social movements, feminists and public sector managers – and the women's movement, unions, teachers, practitioners, and within the bureaucracy itself between feminist bureaucrats or femocrats, and politicians. As a case study, it signifies how new relationships between the state and individual due to public sector administrative reform and neoconservative politics impact on the nature of policy production and its potential for change.

In 1989, women only held 12 of the 167 high level administrative positions in the Victorian Ministry of Education. In the interviews with seven of these women, I explored through life and career histories how they came to be bureaucrats and what they understood to be the work practices that inhibited and enabled them to produce change in schools. The proportion of women bureaucrats had reduced by 1995. Due to frequent managerial restructurings and the ministerializaton of policy, many femocrats fled the increasingly chilly climate of central administration. The second set of interviews, with a different cohort of six bureaucrats, focused more upon the production of gender equity policy. The women in both interview cohorts tended to be located in policy development areas of parent participation, student disadvantage, EO, professional development, change management or curriculum – the 'soft' areas of the bureaucracy – simultaneously part of the mainstream of everyday bureaucratic life and yet marginalized. What was significant was the social justice orientation of many of these women. Their life histories indicated these women had a background in voluntary community work with working-class and Aboriginal children, parent and teacher organizations, feminism and their professional reform activities in teacher unions, subject associations and professional development. Despite this, all women interviewed were of the mainstream – Anglo, middle-class, and Christian. Indeed, it was their whiteness and middle-classness that made them acceptable to the overall homogeneity of white male-dominated bureaucracies (Eisenstein 1996; Cox 1996).

Most of the women in 1989 felt some ambivalence about becoming a bureaucrat, least of all a femocrat. While 'being female and being feminist placed femocrats outside of the mainstream' (Eisenstein 1996: 132), their more radical sisters considered the femocrats were 'co-opted' and 'traitors to the cause'. They, as their advocates, saw femocrats as doing the 'good work' of feminism by seeking to change the system from within, to make it more equitable and empowering for practitioners and women in particular by influencing policy at the centre. Their previous experiences as feminists, unionists, teacher and parent activists, had led them to perceive of bureaucracies as largely disabling structures. Yet their leadership experience in various other organizational contexts had led them to understand that administration was about people not things. Bureaucracies could change as well as produce change.

The second study indicated a growing unease amongst women in the bureaucracy, particularly those femocrats committed to the traditional Labor policies of social justice. While their disquiet had began with Labor's move to corporate managerialism after 1987, the neoconservatism of state (after 1992) and federal (after 1995) coalition governments presented the contradictions more starkly. Under Labor, 'the sting [was] that their individual power [was] derived from their location within the state, but their access to that location depended on the collective power of the women's movement' (Franzway *et al.* 1989: 160). 'Official feminists' under Labor were 'marked women' – ideologically and formally – in that they had an extrabureaucratic 'mission' to the constituency of women.

If it is possible to speak about feminist work as constituting one's professional qualification, about feminist commitments as belonging in one's resume, then it is possible to articulate the struggle for equality and one's professional work.

(Chase 1995: 189–90)

Feminist bureaucrats were increasingly on dangerous ground, however, as conservative governments curtailed their advocacy role by prioritizing loyalty to government policy and upward to ministers, over other loyalties to feminism or even the client, and by encouraging individual competitiveness over collective responsibility as the public administrative ethic was supplanted by a bottom line of corporate efficiency and client service.

Yet the language used by many of the women administrators in both cohorts to describe the processes of policy production contrasted starkly with the managerialist language which treated policy texts as static, non-debatable and instrumental. These women spoke of policy as a living text, a non-linear, interactive and ongoing discursive process, a dialogic process between policymakers and practitioners. Policy addressed real problems with real people. Policy to them was a communicative or discursive practice that constantly changed the relations between constraint and agency. As texts, individual policies privilege some messages more than others. Two communities of practice shaped the dialogic relationships that informed the process of policy production – one centred on the relationships between policymakers within the bureaucracy, the other centred around the bureaucrats relationships with practitioner–clients.

Policy: problem solving or problem setting

All the women interviewees referred to the lack of open policy debate within the bureaucracy, a silence arising from an emphasis on formal and not substantive rationality in the older bureaucratic as well as new managerialist discourses. Formal rationality emphasized policy as problem solving and 'crisis management'; substantive rationality emphasized problem setting and improving practice. Two agendas were in constant tension: the system priorities of 'administrivia' driven by demands for quick statements in response to perceived political (not educational) crises and the performance orientation of accountability; and their personal priorities to promote real change in practice in the field in which they were appointed, whether it be parent–school relations, change management, social justice or professional development (substantive rationality).

I am continually frustrated by the way the place is actually constructed and operates to consume all our time. It is very difficult. There is no pressure to do what this section was established for in the first place . . .

By trying to give substantive answers to superficial queries you actually
get drawn into a different bureaucratic argument.

(Bev 1989)

This is a Weberian distinction being made between formal rationality, as
legitimated by the legality of general rules and dealing with technical matters, and substantive rationality that addresses values and the benefits gained
by particular individuals. The former leads to a search for norms or standards that can be equated to general need (performance indicators or benchmarks) against which policy can be judged and which guides the allocation
of resources, although such norms are abstracted from particular settings,
institutions and individuals' lives (Bologh 1990; Yeatman 1990). This
formal/substantive distinction embedded in an idealized notion of the 'neutral bureaucracy' was also evident in the cost-efficiency driven managerialism of the late 1980s. It also reduced all decisions to technical decisions, thus
devaluing the human element. Yet the person–process public orientated
administration of the 1970s did consider how policy affected social and
political relationships whereas the economic rationalist ideologies underpinning the new managerialism treated policy as a means to an end in producing new efficiencies. Efficiency was the basic principle of operation, not
service. Furthermore, while policy has always performed a symbolic func-
tion in the bureaucratic welfare state, policy in the performative or market
state was as much about 'being seen to perform' as actually changing practice. A 'good' policy was that which solved short-term political problems
such as managing a crisis. In both, the underlying assumption was that
policy texts, once written, were unproblematically received. This meant any
failure to produce the intended outcomes was attributed to implementation
problems (with practitioners and clients) not one of misconceived policy.

Policy, Susan commented, was 'produced as if from within a vacuum after
reading a few books and with no consultation with those who know the field
or the target population'. This view of policy as product not process permeated the daily practice of policy formation. In the era of the multiskilled
manager who was seen to possess generic skills transferable across any area,
a common practice was for the first drafts of any policy to be written by
someone outside the field. The draft, once written, was then circulated for
consultation to 'interest groups' or specialists, that is, those with substantive
knowledge or experience. Much expertise, energy and time was wasted
remedying, or marginally altering, what was often a fundamentally flawed
text. Policies were thus written with political/management agendas prioritized, uninformed by substantive knowledge or understanding of key issues
in the field of practice. Sometimes major reports were rewritten by 'writers'
(often consultants) who had never attended any of the numerous meetings
or consultations leading to particular policy statements. This practice, it was
argued in the new client focus of managerialist discourse, made policy texts

more accessible to the 'novice' reader. Meanwhile the implementers of policy, the practitioners, were constructed as overworked, ill-informed, suspicious, resistant or just plain lazy. Knowledge in this process was treated as information and culturally (politically) neutral; writing policy was treated as technique; and the policies or reports were seen to be discrete informational texts rather than cultural products of considerable contestation and negotiation.

This logic of policy production based upon formal rationality had significant and potentially dangerous effects in how it positioned those femocrats largely concentrated in social justice, community, curriculum and professional development areas. First, critics were excluded from the ultimate decisionmaking as they were more often cast as 'whingers' or 'oppositional' because they were always revising policy texts, or complaining about lack of consultancy. Through this process, senior male bureaucrats were able to define what was relevant and valued by casting 'those women' as obstructionist, idealist, and offering unviable responses. Second, debate amongst those appointed and active in the substantive policy field was further hindered by an 'ideology of procedures' which sought to persuade those in the bureaucracy that the policy process was 'just' as well as efficient. Hence the emphasis on procedural justice through consultation and consensus. In practice, however, such processes merely mobilized particular biases. Although there were numerous occasions set aside for meetings and consultation to produce goal consensus, these were dominated by top-down one-way communication where managers were informed of, and not informing of, the agenda and priorities. As Kathy Ferguson suggests, 'consensus' in such a context does not mean mutually agreed upon decisions in which the parties had some say in defining. Rather, consensus is about the 'manufacturing of consent', 'a shorthand term for the enforcement of the official definition of reality' (Ferguson 1984: 103).

When such a culture joins the rational-technical with the line command of corporate management controls, it leads to 'highly normative and prescriptive directions for policies and programs'. These become 'ideological slogans' rather than value orientations carefully thought through and reflected upon in terms of their practical complexities for daily life (Yeatman 1990: 17). These slogans in turn feed into the overriding norm of cost-efficiency and all attempts to revert to more consultative and open practices of decisionmaking are denigrated as unrealistic. Bev recalls how her attempts to promote debate or reflection meant 'a lot of people see me as oppositional, others see me as a dinosaur left over from the 70s who hadn't realized the world has changed'. Feminists, previously positioned as radical change agents, were positioned as being resistant to change. Furthermore, managerialism revived the old antithesis between democratic and hierarchical models of bureaucracy which depicted democratic styles of leadership as dysfunctional. This was exceptionally problematic for feminist women who were expected to practice collaborative styles of management. Unable to argue against procedural justice as it was the basis of their own equity strategies, they were often seen to be complicit in unjust decisions.

Finally, the myth of formal rationality as a mode of thinking means patriarchy still resides unchallenged in the perceived 'objectivity of these structures' (Franzway *et al.* 1989: 29). Formal rationality, by turning substantive moral and political issues into technical and procedural ones, and through its structural form of fragmentation and specialization of tasks, territoriality and hierarchy, naturalized the gendered division of labour and all its associated binaries between rationality and emotionality. The dominant technical-rational approach meant that

> what was a very masculinist patriarchal environment was seen by most merely as bureaucratic practice. The whole thing about taking the personal out. Most contact here is impersonal through memorandum and by seniority. Avoids all versions of conflict, hides problems, and no information sharing. As a manager you are supposed to 'get your rocks [sic] off' because you are powerful.
>
> (Julie)

One could be passionate about power, but not about equality. Allegiance or loyalties other than the organization (e.g. family or feminism) were irrational. Stressing the nature of women's *dis*advantage in such a situation through affirmative action to recognition of women's interests was constructed as a special pleading to the male norm. Thus 'the privilege of maleness gains its ascendancy through the virtue of the normative standard which mediates and accords not only value, not only relevance, but also material and empirically verifiable advantage' (Eveline 1994: 11).

Formal rationality was exemplified in the multiskilled bureaucrat. Managers were frequently transferred across many areas (education, health, transport etc.) in order to acquire generic skills in management, and therefore possessed only superficial knowledge of each policy field. The image of the 'good multiskilled manager' excluded any substantive commitment to any field of practice or beliefs, such as social justice.

> That is a real dilemma in bureaucracies. As some people really believe that you ought not be committed to anything. To be a good bureaucrat to many requires you to be neutral and content free . . . It is the kind of thing you have to weigh up – your personal commitment. I don't think many people come into education without some sort of commitment. There are a lot of people in other departments who are true bureaucrats in that the content of what they do isn't the important thing. It is the papers you can produce and whatever it is you do to show you are delivering on something. And I think often with not much understanding of the people you are delivering to. That commitment is an important

part of how I see what I do. I couldn't enjoy it with superficial sort of responses.

(Jenny)

Feminists, with their passion for particular human values, democratic principles and social equity so central to their personal, professional and work identity, were marginalized by these discursive practices.

I find that most of the time when I am in a meeting I am responsible for women's issues, migrant issues and democracy, as well as being the expert on history of system change . . . I must keep this up because it is part of my background, my experience, my life . . . While a lot of guys see it as important . . . they do not seem to worry about it as a person. They abstract the issues. But I can't disconnect and fragment myself into different compartments – here I am the woman, and here I'm the bureaucrat, and here I am the anti-racist. They are all things I deeply care about, not just issues . . . I don't tear myself to pieces, but it does affect me . . . I think about them with feeling. They are not just issues.

(Julie)

Feminism provided a framework and principles for judgement for many of these femocrats, but the identification of women with equity had ramifications for the process of policy production, for why some policies were legitimated, taken up and others were marginalized, undefended or dropped. Many felt that they were participating in a 'dialogue of deafness', where people talked past each other, particularly about equity, rather than a dialogue of openness.

These administrative practices had gained dominance by 1995. The new managerialism did not challenge the older bureaucratic emphases on formal rationality that portrayed policy production as technique, a neutral and objective process, rather than the product of contestation over different value positions. It did however supplant any sense of service to the public to servicing the individual client. Any commitment to a position (e.g. equity) other than the agreed-upon end of cost-efficiency and effectiveness, implied a 'vested or particularistic' interest, and was therefore dismissed as 'ideological'. Gender equity policies therefore were on tenuous ground, given their origins in notions of systemic disadvantage and the women's movement. Yet such policies still had important symbolic purposes in the performative state which claimed to service a more diverse clientele. Their symbolic use was maintained by redefining and selective inclusion or exclusion of particular terms. Thus equal opportunity units become merit and equity units, and social justice disappeared from all policy texts. Policies thereby, through such redefinition, illustrate the capacity to produce new regimes of truth and self-regulating behaviours by shifting meaning through a process of seemingly consensual social relationships. So the message of gender equity policies in the 1980s, of the democratic failure to represent women equally in leadership, has given way the message of the 1990s, which speaks of inducting individual women into management to improve corporate efficiency. Paradoxically, state bureaucracies, in seeking certainty in an era of uncertainty, have produced highly modernist responses (hierarchical, individualized, fragmented, technical, impersonal, instrumental, non-reflexive, unilateral) to postmodernist demands (flexibility, change, emotional management, teamwork, listening, nurturing, interpersonal competence, coping with value conflicts, gaining self-knowledge, embracing error), the former leading to conformity to bureaucratic norms rather than innovative bureaucratic leadership.

Citizen or client?

The dialogic relationship between bureaucrat and practitioner (or client) was also transformed with the shift away from the service orientation of the welfare state to the client orientation of the performative state after 1990. Whereas conventional top-down impositional models distinguished between policymaker and practitioner, many of the femocrats argued that policy would not touch upon the practise of those in schools if those in positions of authority claimed to possess privileged knowledge or expertise. Bev argued that

> I have a different view of leadership other than that of instructing schools. We will only get changes and better education because people see the wisdom of what is said. That is not well understood in the bureaucracy.

Cynthia concurred:

> The relationship with schools is important for me to know what I am saying is relevant. What I am trying to do is to be useful in improving society . . . and I can do this by visiting schools.

Asked what was a major problem with being in the bureaucracy, Kerry replied unhesitatingly:

> The impediment is the distance I am from schools. It is all very well for me to be sitting up here with thoughts of change and curriculum structures. My view of educational reform is that you haven't got it until the teacher walks into the classroom and shuts the door and enacts it in the process of teaching. That is educational reform.

Policy was only good policy when it improved educational practice and not just because it was a strategic solution to an abstract social problem. Effective policy meant interaction between the policymakers, self-criticism and reflection and critical dialogue with practitioners. Julie saw policy-making as

> getting forums together in ways which make it possible for people to criticize and evaluate policy as it is being formulated and how it relates to different kinds of practices. Making sense of policy and practice.

Their assumptions, now recognized by educational change theory, was that fundamental change occurred when those most affected had a sense of ownership about the change process and outcomes (Fullan 1993; Hargreaves 1994). In a participatory bureaucracy the bureaucrat was accountable to the citizen and policy is evaluated by those it affects.

By 1995, any bureaucrat who presumed bureaucrats and politicians could share 'co-authorship of state policy and action' (Pusey 1991: 166) with community and client and indicate some sensitivity to value conflicts, ethics and integrity, increasingly worked outside, if not against, the new orthodoxy of the marketized social policy formation of the performative state. Feminist educators could no longer tap into 1970s human relations organizational theory seeking to 'decentralise, humanise and "dereify" administration and thus recast management and service delivery as socially interactive processes' (Pusey 1991: 166). Policy, in the new contractual relationship between the individual bureaucrat (provider) and citizen (client), became a response to client needs as determined by the policymaker through market research; evaluated against so-called 'objective' measures determined by the state; and rendered accountable only to the government, not the consumer. The provider (manager) rather than the citizen was repositioned as expert in defining and prescribing human need in the national interest, casting the citizen into the role of the 'second sex' as passive and dependent (Yeatman 1990: 23; Ferguson 1984). This technocratic positivist approach 'first, gives primacy to the economy; second, to the political order; and finally, to the social order' (Pusey 1991: 10). The very subject of politics, the citizen, was thus reconstructed as a client to be serviced, not served, not an active participant in the policy process.

This shift from citizen to client signalled the ideological dominance of economic rationalist ideologies, one consequence of the external recruitment of a technical intelligentsia into the federal bureaucracy in the 1980s. The corporate policy model of managerialism reimposed a pre-1970s top-down view of policy texts as static and closed and managing policy as an implementation problem. This 'technocratic positivist' approach to policy sought to depoliticize educational reform in the name of flexibility, responsiveness and effectiveness. In removing any possibility of substantive debate about a particular policy issue within the bureaucracy, a debate which necessarily calls upon experience, recognition of various ideological positions, corporate memory and policy history, the political administrative system distances itself from 'both the intellectual and "ordinary" culture, and so from participation, from interpretations of need, and from many of the normal and supposedly normative prerogatives and entitlements of citizenship in a liberal social democracy' (Pusey 1991: 12). This inability to discuss the normative dimensions of policy as a reallocation of values, raised issues for feminist bureaucrats, now silenced as representatives of, and advocates for, women.

Work practices and the politics of differentiated sexuality

The discourses of formal rationality centring around efficiency, effectiveness and managerialist procedures promoted particular work practices which the femocrats associated in both cohorts with a hegemonic masculinity characterized by rampant individualism, competitiveness, authority and technical competence. Gender subjectivity was central to the construction of work practices (Casey 1995).

> Apart from most of the managers and senior bureaucrats being male there is also the ruthless competitive male way of operating. A major consequence of the dominance of such a group was closure of any debate or marginalization on issues outside their agenda.
>
> (Bev 1989)

The gendered structuring of organizational life framed, although not in a deterministic way, what was said, when and how it was said, how things were done, what was valued, what issues stayed on agendas, as well as the distribution of resources. While few male managers recognized gender as a problem, all the female managers agreed that 'by and large men's opinions still seem to count for more'. This masculinist hegemony maintained dominance through branding most femininities (and some masculinities) as oppositional to the rational logic of procedures. Individuals moving outside the logic of procedures or questioning processes were positioned as obstructionist or not a good manager. Jenny recalled one meeting:

> It was on the agenda that the women were to speak. When they finally did, I commented quietly that it took one and a quarter hours for the first woman to speak . . . the manager took offence and drew attention to it. He later told me I had spoken out of turn. Unbelievable. It would never happen at a school. People were outraged, yet felt fairly powerless as a group despite the fact that half the branch were women, amongst them the two EO officers.

To draw attention openly and publicly to the gendered nature of seemingly neutral bureaucratic practices, which allowed the manager to exploit differential gender power relations, was dangerous. Jenny's stance not only threatened the rule governing formal rationality but also the gender regime and particular masculine identities premised upon authority.

Entering into the game of the politics of discourse also meant self-regulation. Each woman felt partially enculturated into masculinist cultures and behaviours in that they learnt 'when to speak and when not to speak, to conserve one's energy for important issues' (Bev). Some consciously chose to 'play harder' than others.

> It means that if I am going to relate to male managers then I have to speak their language. It doesn't mean that I have to become a man . . . It is just an approach.
>
> (Kerry)

These linguistic games were manifestations of the individualizing tendencies of bureaucratic life:

> Even feminists who have a long history in the movement and women's issues only survive by using bureaucratic practices.
>
> (Susan)

They produced significant tensions for feminists in practice. Anti-feminist discourses were readily used as a form of control. Being labelled 'feminist' was problematic because of the stereotypic image of 'rabid and ranting butch women in jeans and T-shirts' (Julie). Such labels led to marginalization or denigration – of being seen to be too radical by some colleagues and too complicit by others.

> The price of being an assertive female . . . is seen to be a critic by my senior colleagues and therefore suspect . . . In my own area I think it is celebrated and acclaimed. By some, I'm seen to be too much of a restraining influence, playing the game more than I should.
>
> (Susan 1989)

Yet Susan was seen to be a source of potential conflict and 'disruptiveness' by her male colleagues:

> They saw me as being capable of raising uncomfortable questions. They suggested it was not worth it or that it would get me into trouble being seen to criticize.

Women internalized these messages in a form of self-management – choosing when to speak, to whom and how – constantly seeking not to undermine their credibility and the capacity to work strategically on their priorities.

> In negotiations on an issue in a committee I often argue and compromise a lot over the little issues, really quite marginal, but making certain that important issues get through quietly.
>
> (Susan 1989)

While expected to speak for all women when asked, the response to an individual woman to raise gender as an issue was to individualize the problem –

'That might be your experience but I am sure that is not the case for all women'. Women speaking out were frequently constructed, either consciously or unconsciously, as 'the nagging female', 'that silly bitch', or 'that feminist'. Some learnt to use their femininity to their advantage:

> I get away with displaying my feelings in a type of reverse sexism because I am a woman. It is helpful and important to not just treat people as 'positions' . . . I am committed to building some type of shared understanding about what we are doing.
>
> (Julie 1989)

She learnt to strategically exploit her discursive positioning as a female. Her capacity to be strategic arose from her understanding of how the organization worked, her capacity to exploit powerful discourses about femininity and masculinity which produced the gendered cultural scripts of leadership that allowed her to show emotion but also 'get things done' in a different, more collaborative and communicative way. Being female was both problematic and powerful.

Silence or voice: strategic issues

As state workers, these female administrators were faced with competing demands arising out of conflicts of interest between social classes or interest groups of their clients, the 'logic of policy production' based on 'bureaucratic rules, purposive action and consensus formation', and collegial loyalty amongst femocrats (Franzway 1986: 52). On the one hand, they were discursively united, as femocrats, not only because of their different approach to policy but also because of the threat of their femaleness. To disrupt masculinist discourse of bureaucratic rationality by questioning procedures or calling for debate, their femaleness, as much as their point of view, was foregrounded (Hearn *et al.* 1995). Differences with male colleagues arose as much over approaches to practice not substance.

> I think there is a powerful group – the male mafia – who see me as a threat. They deliberately marginalize me as they are not open to issues. Powerful people here . . . always knowing what the answer is . . . My style is open, theirs is closed; mine is talking through issues with people, confronting issues and finding resolution; theirs is organizing how to get their way. These are two broadly different styles. I certainly do not support this although I agree with many of them on agendas. I don't believe in adopting them as 'right' answers but rather working with people until they are ready to adopt them. The essence of devolution is that it is better for people to make decisions locally. That puts a

leadership requirement on the Ministry in terms of stimulating material
. . . but not making the word and telling people to do it.

(Julie 1989)

Conceptualizing leadership from a feminist perspective, that is working
with, rather than over, others, was marginalized or silenced. It produced the
notion of a 'politics of discourse', the politics that had the power to create
reality by shaping alternative meaning (Yeatman 1990). Because discourses
of economic rationalism 'interpenetrated' agendas however, at all levels of
the bureaucracy and in all aspects of policy production, discourses of equity
or alternative modes of leadership were readily displaced or practiced in discrete units (e.g. EO) or lower down the hierarchy where the power was not.
To counter the orthodoxy of economic rationalism and management by
objectives was too risky. Furthermore, the femocrats' less prescriptive
approach to policy in the context of more ministerial control and prescription of education policy, an approach framed by particular economic and
political ideological imperatives, meant their struggle over substantive issues
became quite contentious (Hearn *et al.* 1990; Taylor 1991).

On the other hand, as white middle-class women, they were discursively
constructed as different from each other and their constituents by class, race
and ethnic background. This positioning thus undermined their capacity to
speak in one voice for other women, given that there was no longer a single
standard of justice even amongst feminists. Indeed, the proliferation of
social justice policies in the 1980s was one response by the state to the complexity of governance resulting from a 'plurality and fragmentation of voices
which seek to be heard' (Yeatman 1990: 154–5). Representatives of the new
social movements were therefore wary of any 'essentialist conception of
their identity', as female experience alone did not lead to any essential
agreed upon 'oppositional women's culture'. Yet most of the feminists
amongst them spoke of the discursive power derived from the notion of the
collectivity of women, even if tenuous and fluid, which provided a key criterion upon which they could make judgements – what will this do for
women? (Eisenstein 1996). The issue was how, as part of the symbolic male
order of the state, to avoid remaining tangential to mainstream policies
while conscious that full (even if unequal) integration into the state could
'blunt' their impetus by being caught up in its 'solution strategies' (Franzway
1986: 53).

In balancing strategically between silence/co-optation and voice/disruption,
the femocrats developed 'bureaucratic tendencies'. One strategy was to channel energy, resources and time towards worthwhile policies by distinguishing
between 'maintenance' 'change work' when determining staff priorities.

The maintenance work . . . doesn't necessarily work towards change
as special projects or activities do. We created smaller teams, led by

different people, to work on change initiatives regularly two days a week. We found the maintenance stuff dragged us away.

(Bev)

A second strategy was, as done by Jenny, to judge each item that crossed her desk, considering whether to respond in a superficial manner when the end product is known, or to take it seriously. Another strategy to get feminist agendas considered when feminist discourses were so readily marginalized as lacking in moral legitimacy, was to link equal employment opportunity policies and teacher career path restructuring to discourses about improving educational leadership in self-managing schools 'because it was better utilization of the pool of leadership talent' (Kerry). A fourth strategy was to tap into powerful hegemonic discourses of the 'hard' management areas, justifying equity on the basis of efficiency and effectiveness not fairness. While short-term gains were small, long-term aims were never forgotten. Gender equity claims were also 'safely contained' within the parameters of male tolerance, although change did occur through the small shifts involved in the process of co-option or assimilation of resistant discourses. Bev was conscious of this dilemma:

> Co-option is when you are taken over by other people's purposes or causes and not be able to commit yourself to what you wanted to do in the bureaucracy. It is whether you get put onto someone else's agenda. Co-option is when you are seen to legitimate those agendas because of your previous position of leadership in the movement.

Yet Julie argued against the view that 'power within bureaucracies is not change-making power' (Ferguson 1984: 203). Bureaucracies, as part of everyday life, had the capacity to operate in different ways, and were capable of producing change as well as reproducing inequality.

Radical conservatism and the manufacturing of consent

While policies for educational self-management had propensity for professional autonomy and participation as well as prescription, control and accountability, the discursive space in which female bureaucrats worked was further restricted with the election of a conservative/liberal government in 1992. This took the form of structural backlash marked by many senior women managers 'voluntarily separating' from the bureaucracy, in part due to the 'chilly climate' (Still 1995); in part due to reduced opportunities as redeployment rules relocated senior male staff into jobs for which experienced women had been 'waiting in the aisles'; and in part as middle management was 'hollowed out' as curriculum and professional development (areas where women were largely located) were devolved to schools. So-called 'rational' processes of organizational restructuring provided possibilities for embedded systemic and value biases to be mobilized by men in decision-making positions. These biases put into play in terms of how merit and skill were redefined, what was open to change, and the covert rules and pro-cesses, leading to the reassertion of discourses of 'hard core' over 'strategic' masculinity.

One feature of the restructured gender regime was the dismantling of EO structures. Long-term gender equity reformers were replaced by 'multi-skilled' managers without experience in either education or social justice policy development.

> Well the guidelines are just merit and equity and employment. There is nothing about affirmative action. There is no real commitment. They are downsizing the central office and regional offices. The women are the ones being forced to take the departure packages and being declared in excess in school and the ones who will lose their jobs in central office as they jostle for positions. With teaching backgrounds, they are easily deployed . . . If a woman has to work and doesn't have a public sector job, she opts for the classroom at a reduced salary, and ends up in the pool of excess teachers who move around lots of schools. Finally, they give up and leave teaching.
>
> (Romaine, EO 1996)

This structural backlash was accompanied by a cultural backlash symbol-ized by a linguistic shift away from the rights-oriented language of equal opportunity and gender to the more 'value-neutral terms' of merit and equity. Words such as social justice and democratic decisionmaking were expunged from policy texts (e.g. school charters), reversing earlier tenden-cies to develop more broadly inclusive definitions. Merit and equity struc-tures, regulations and policies refocused upon gender-neutral criteria, seeking only to redress procedural anomalies experienced by individual women. This discursive shift sent a message to the system that EO was on hold, if not endangered.

> In this context, with EO being dismantled, many male principals feel that it is OK to say that we don't have to listen anymore to that EO shit . . . we can do and say what we like.
>
> (Dana 1996)

Thus EO policies, as all policies, 'posit a restructuring, redistribution and disruption of power relations, so that different people can and cannot do things . . . policy texts enter rather than simply change power relations' (Ball 1994: 20).

At the same time, the government invested considerable media attention on women and leadership, targeting resources to specialist programs encouraging women into leadership. Through good image management, the government sought to capture the constituency of women. In the performative state, EO policies now act as both symbolic solutions to diversity issues and indicators of their good performance. Their existence simultaneously portrays the government as a radical change agent and good financial manager. At the same time, however, the structural backlash led to the remasculinization of the central administration with policy and finance (male-dominated areas) consolidated at the hard core and the soft areas of person management, curriculum and professional development (female-dominated) devolved to schools. At the centre,

> continuous downsizings and restructurings meant jobs are thrown open every six months. Women who have signed contracts are again having to compete. This destroys our networks and causes women to compete against each other to survive.
>
> (Dana 1996)

The production of policy was increasingly conducted by a ministerially-driven executive mode of government, which privileged hard core masculinity premised upon strong leadership, and competitive individualism. The representational politics of the previous decade were replaced by individualized contractual relations, thus changing the nature of the communities of practice in which women policymakers worked. Women in management could no longer speak for the constituency of women, only as individuals.

The conservatives were also able to tap symbolically into managerialist orthodoxy, the legacy of Labor's corporate federalism, to mainstream and downstream equity. This meant individual managers in schools were expected to take full responsibility for equity. Yet equity was not central to the policies of devolution to self-managing schools.

> There is no clarity about what is meant by merit and equity, and there is no longer a regional focus. It is all being left up to the schools where it relies upon individual people and principals and their particular version of EO.
>
> (Justine 1996)

Principals were now dependent upon their own networks and private consultancy firms for professional development, hindered by constrained budgets. Equity was absent from the core aspects of principal professional development courses – financial management, industrial relations and human resource management – and given low priority in the frameworks shaping principals' and schools' accountability back to the centre.

While undermining the legitimacy of previous equity and feminist discourses, the new discourses of the market and accountability did provide limited windows of opportunity. The performative state's concern for accountability meant that the same measures monitoring outcomes could also make individual managers and schools more accountable for gender equity. Women managers seeking to embed equity into management practices therefore tapped into the language of accountability:

> While they are changing a number of things in HRM [Human Resource Management] and accountability, we do the equity thing. We say: let us help you shape policies to include the gender focus. Now we have merit and equity in managers' performance plans . . . and into principal performance pay. We also want regional figures so that it is linked to regional managers' performance.
>
> (Laurel 1996)

The shift to ministerial control of policymaking, while emphasizing the hard core leadership modes of executive management and market liberalism, also led to an increased uncertainty as policy formation became dependent upon personalities.

> The ground was constantly shifting – there were huge walls of silence one minute and then we rolled something through without even knowing what had led to the change.
>
> (Romaine)

This phenomenon exacerbated the precariousness of gender reform and the reliance of gender equity reformers upon male patronage. Strategically, it meant

> knowing who are the stakeholders and whose support you need to get the policy into practice. We work with those people throughout the development processes to make sure that not only you make them implement it but that it is something they want to implement.
>
> (Romaine)

In a context in which equity and social justice have little legitimacy, all initiatives had to link equity to governmental objectives and priorities while gesturing to ministerial eccentricities.

> It is about reading the political – reading the climate and political signs – the broad policy within which the government is working. Then you can hang your own area of concern on. Look for the impetus for change and bringing those at top level. Steer it through personally at all stages by knowing who is on your side.
>
> (Laurel)

Managing them gently

Dissent was closely managed through the policy production process in gender equity, although contingent on personalities, timing (e.g. pending elections) and process. The shift from the more representational to executive politics meant that teacher unions were excluded from policy production while senior male managers were now included. Female bureaucrats focused more upon managing upward rather than down or outward, constantly practising self-censorship over language that may be construed as 'ideological' or 'over the top', fearful of alienating executive management.

> We kept the Minister and management aware of the changes . . . so no surprises. Providing regular reports to those responsible for its implementation means that the checks and balances are worked out and we do not confront a monumental wall when complete. We gentled them through, incorporating their suggestions on the way.
>
> (Laurel)

As all 'good girls', the issue was never to confront patriarchal power. Certain areas were too difficult and dangerous to mention. As Dana, an EO manager, comments:

> There are things that they don't want to look at. If you actually presented real data – it appalls and threatens people. People are into denial about gender. If you actually get too close to the problem – without even defining it from a feminist position – they back off from doing anything. They'll look at extreme verbal abuse, and say, 'Yes I recognize that', and do nothing.

While male managers were gentled towards gender equity, feminist dissident voices were likewise gentled towards consensus. The discourse amongst gender equity reformers was of political pragmatism, 'not putting up too radical policies as they will not get through'. Certain individuals in this community of practice of gender equity policy reformers, due to their employment status and capacity to utilize the dominant language discourses of government policy and management, were seen to be more legitimate than others. Certain forms of research were given more official credibility than others – those that were more practical and less theoretical – privileging hard or objective data (survey/quantitative) over soft anecdotal or subjective data (case studies/qualitative research). Yet policy, the product of much negotiation and conflict, when produced as a text, took on a linguistic coherence not representative of its process of production.

> As the findings of a piece of research become taken for granted, they are finally incorporated into the texts of the discourse without reference to their source . . . achieving facticity obliterates the historical and specific source; the work, the local setting and the authorship of particular texts are forgotten.
>
> (Smith 1990: 66)

The policy text was 'cleansed' of any linguistic terms that could contaminate it politically and ideas were extracted from the context of their production. Thus 'changing masculinity and the boys culture' is written as 'changing cultures as best management practice'. The problem of masculinity went unnamed, thus reconstituting femininity as the issue once again. 'Thus insights of feminist theory which point to hegemonic masculinity are incorporated into official discourses' in palatable ways (Brittan 1989: 184).

By the mid-1990s, three discursive regimes coexisted uncomfortably within the bureaucracy, 'each delivering its own language, imagery, values, relationships and ways of doing things' (Newman 1995: 15). There was the traditional culture, with its mix of administrative and professional discourses, which formally emphasized clear hierarchical role positions and informally pursued patriarchal social relations. There was the competitive culture, which freed up bureaucrats with its market orientation, 'legitimating cowboy styles of operation so that managers can now become "real men", now released from the status of public sector functionaries'. Power now lay 'where the action was and informal hierarchies formed around sexy jobs which are entrepreneurial (e.g. technology). Women can join if they are macho or tough and if they can stand the pace' (Newman 1995: 15). Finally there was the transformational culture, which was value-based. It recognized and valued people and sought to empower staff, emphasizing the soft skills of leadership.

New policies for new times?

These women in the bureaucracy had come to understand policy as process and action, as an open-ended dialogic process that was both contested and changing, always in a state of 'becoming', as they sought to work with often mutually incompatible discourses of 'hard nosed' management and 'women's styles of leadership'.

> Policies are representations which are encoded in complex ways (via struggles, compromises, authoritative public interpretations (and reinterpretations) and decoded in complex ways (via actors' interpretations and meanings in relation to their history, experiences, skills, resources and context).
>
> (Ball 1994: 16)

While keeping particular ideals in mind, the women worked strategically, depending upon the level of commitment and opposition, within specific sites. They realized that gender equity policies were framed in terms of the possible, and not only the desirable, because they had to promote deepseated change through understanding in a context of shifting relationships that were contingent upon a complex interplay of thought and language, process and power (Taylor 1991). Changing discursive practices is difficult, however, and naming the discursive practices of male culture is one important step, a point exemplified in one focus group.

> When all the female staff collectively and publicly agreed that the greatest block for women was the male culture, the male manager was quite shocked. He said: 'Well I will have to do something about that'. And he did, putting it on the executive agenda and establishing a committee of women and male managers who had the responsibility and the power to produce change. We didn't need another group of women without power sitting around agreeing upon what the problem is.
>
> (Evelyn)

Their view of policy also assumed a 'value-critical stance'. Given the different value position emerging with top-down policy frameworks, the success of gender equity policies now rested increasingly, particularly in self-managing schools, with teachers. Teachers therefore also needed to be able (and be prepared) to articulate their own particular value position and interests. In order to contest policy it was necessary to make strategic discursive interventions (Yeatman 1990: 160). Feminist educators learnt to know when to intervene, interrupt or redefine.

> No policy is effective if it is untimely. You have to look at the environment and consider what is going to work now, what conditions you can hook into and the resources you can marshal . . . There has been a tolerance about equity. We are now thinking why didn't it work? Why hasn't the world changed and why aren't women into leadership? We assumed that if you had action plans and targets that women would go right into leadership. So now we have to look at who makes the decisions, and how we lock into them, e.g. performance management contracts. Perhaps we have to get women into power who are closest to being 'normal' according to current male norms and then the next generation produces the radical change. From Karpin, for example, we can argue that it is for everyone's benefit to have more inclusive leadership . . . you would be a better manager if you do so – forget the fairness argument in public but not the long-term principle.
>
> (Evelyn)

There was also the need to build strategic, if not unusual, alliances based on shared and mutually beneficial positions, a 'dialogue across difference' (Burbules and Rice 1992). The women and leadership progam, argued one female bureaucrat,

> would not have gotten off the ground if this male manager had not said 'I want to do that in my region'. He was a most unlikely ally. There are male managers who are recognized as 'genuine feminists'. And then there are the really politically astute ones who see it as the way to go and who can earn some brownie points. Use them as you will.

These are serious strategic issues that gender equity reformers must consider given the principles of market liberalism and devolution that endangers the strategic power of a femocracy. Despite the paternalistic bent of white middle-class male bureaucrats of earlier times, their discourse of public administration privileged service to the public good above sectional interests and they sought to improve the social representativeness and responsiveness of the bureaucracy (Pusey 1991). The ministerialization of policy and shift to a contractual state mediating the market now positions the citizen as an individual client and undermines the representational politics and service orientation of the 1980s (Eisenstein 1996: 203). while not without their own exclusions, women's past citizenship claims were premised upon equal opportunity as a right, to which many groups could, and did, appeal. The new individualizing contractualism of the performative state suggests that a feminist politics for gender equity reform will need to rethink how to work collectively again in a more oppositional manner, but from outside the state. Where will the focus of such strategies be: at the level of the supranational/international, or at the grass-roots level; through formal institutional and legal processes or through the market?

Note

1 Radical conservatism calls upon postmodern discourses about change to protect existing power relations (e.g. market), whereas traditional conservatism opposes change and calls upon old values (family; Giddens 1995).

6　Fixing the feminist gaze on masculinity

Resistance and investment

Feminists, Cynthia Cockburn (1991) suggests, have not engaged sufficiently well with the level of investment most men have in maintaining existing gender relations. Bob Connell (1987) argues that the capacity of hegemonic masculinity to deflect attention away from itself has been a major barrier to effecting change in gender relations. Indeed, 'the most effective opposition to change is one that is kept intangible' (Eveline 1994: 133–4). Amanda Sinclair (1995: 39) refers to how the exclusivity of the Australian executive culture, which inextricably connects masculinity to 'conceptions of executive eligibility, success and performance', is 'undiscussable'. 'The boys' club' was the most familiar, yet intangible, aspect of organizational life to women. Masculinism has been a critical element in obstructing gender equity reform and its ongoing dominance has been achieved in subtle, and not so subtle, ways.

> Organisations chose high profile, cost free measures [with respect to EO] . . . Policies adopted are seldom implemented. Non-compliance is not penalised, nor has co-operation been rewarded . . . There is active resistance by men. They generate *institutional* impediments to stall women's advancement in organisations. At a *cultural* level they foster solidarity between men and sexualise, threaten, marginalise, control and divide women.
>
> (Cockburn 1991: 215)

Joan Eveline (1994: 129–30, 32) argues that feminism has been too preoccupied with documenting, explaining and justifying women's disadvantage, and that it would now be more strategic for feminism to focus upon male advantage:

> The discourse of women's disadvantage reinforces an assumption that processes advantaging men are immutable, indeed normative . . . Men,

for instance, or whites, the highly paid, the abled or those without family responsibilities, are never 'commatised' in a categorical list according to what advantages they have . . . the everyday spectrum of privileges that accrue to men are taken as unremarkable, and instead attention is directed to any instances where the situation seems to be reversed . . . In Australia, the principle of disadvantage becomes a discourse that not only inhibits an articulated reference to advantage, but also obscures the connections between those who are disadvantaged and those who are not. In Australia, in equal opportunity discourses 'disadvantage' is normatively demanded, in fact and in terminology, for claims against inequality.

This discourse of disadvantage translates the lack of advancement of women's leadership into women's need for more 'training' or 'self-esteem'. 'Hence men's position in relation to the male norm is implied but left unproblematised' (Eveline 1994: 134). Gender equity policies have long focused upon changing women to 'cope' with masculinist organisations. The discourse of female disadvantage breaks the 'relational link' to male advantage. Thus the glass ceiling is perceived as a barrier to be penetrated rather than deconstructed in order to seek out what it constitutes, why and how it has been maintained.

Feminism has also produced a subjugated discourse in the powerful field of knowledge of educational administration. As a social movement and set of social practices, feminism has produced counter-hegemonic discourses that have challenged hegemonic masculinities. Kathleen Weiler (1988: 52) views counter-hegemony as the creation of 'a self-conscious analysis' of a situation and the development of collective practices and organization that can oppose the hegemony of the existing order. Resistance, she suggests, is more individualistic, spasmodic, a less organized and politicized response. In this chapter, I consider the cultural resilience and resistance of 'hard core' masculinities that have actively reconstituted themselves by co-opting, incorporating or subverting any counter-hegemonic impulses arising out of feminist political agendas.

The shift from covert to overt male resistance or backlash (the imported American term) arises in the context of a new political conservatism; a media that sees feminism as an issue but conflict within or against feminism as a media event; economic recession, uncertainty and rapid social change; and a radical restructuring of the workplace. Equal opportunity (EO) policies are now under threat as discourses of national crisis, economic rationalism and neoconservative politics privilege efficiency over equity (Blackmore 1997c). Educational restructuring has also provided a strategic opportunity for the mobilization of individual, and sometimes collective, male resistance to gender equity reform. Ellwyn, a Victorian primary principal, referred to this structural backlash as 'the reassertion of old style patriarchy in a new disguise with organizational restructuring and policy shifts, amalgamations, reduced school budgets and new career structures which required reassessment of roles and positions in schools'. More patriarchal forms of leadership have been reasserted as principal power supplants democratic committee systems in schools while industrial agreements that institutionalized gender equity positions and policies disappear (Brannock 1993; Distant 1993). The dismantling of EO policies and units, the withdrawal of government funding from the women's agencies and services, and the supplanting of oppositional feminist voices provide concrete evidence that gender equity is off the agenda. Equity is a luxury in new hard times of national and organizational financial crises; and masculinity, it seems, is also in crisis.

Faced with the seeming failure of gender equity reform policies to alter the gendered division of labour in educational organizations significantly, the attention of gender equity policy and research has shifted away from changing individual women to changing organizational cultures during the 1990s (Cockburn 1991; Baker and Fogarty 1993; Blackmore 1993; Sinclair 1994; Gherardi 1995; Itzin and Newman 1995). Women readily list the exclusionary barriers confronting women seeking leadership: the marginalization of teachers to organizational decisionmaking; the lack of professional development and resources for gender equity reform; the dynamics of selection and promotion panels; the age factor jokingly referred to as 'lies, secrets and half truths'; the lack of female mentors; the triple shift of paid work, home work and community work; narrow community perceptions about women in leadership and so on. Women felt most inhibited in their capacity to act freely and with vigour due to the discursive cultural practices that positioned women as lesser, powerless and undervalued displayed through the symbols, values and patterns of behaviour, the discourse about 'the way we do things around here'; the use of time, resources and energy; the design and organization of work; the architecture and technologies employed; the ceremonies and celebrations, the temporal and spatial structuring of organizational life; the jargon used and dominant ideologies; even the appearance of members (Gherardi 1995: 13). Yet male managers are often puzzled why women do not apply for management jobs or leave soon after reaching the top. They do not understand men's 'paradoxical communication' when they 'simultaneously invite women to become their peers, expressing their distrust of equality, and implicitly threatening those who dare imagine that they may change the rules of the game' (Gherardi 1995: 10).

The boys' club

Organizational cultures are often described as 'how we do things around here' – unproblematically constructing the 'we' as the norm, disregarding its exclusions and biases, and assuming one way of doing things. Discourses of masculinity tap into particular cultures to produce a range of exclusionary practices which 'keep women in their place', either as subordinate to men in power, or as different from men once in leadership. Women in both schools and the bureaucracy were conscious of this positioning:

> I find the male-dominated culture that we live in disempowering. I find the fact that our society's dominated by male values disempowering. I find it distressing that women in order to succeed largely have to accept male values and male culture and have to some extent adopt male behaviour. I find all this disempowering as they are not my values and I have a constant battle in retaining my values.
>
> (Joan)

> I found the culture depowering. I still believe that this organization is run very heavily on male camaraderie and football. It is difficult . . . and you can easily lose energy as you are always required to be assertive and at times one is overwhelmed by it all.
>
> (Belinda)

> This region is one of the worst in the state being particularly closed in terms of masculinity, parochialism and conservatism. At the last principal's conference, the grey suit brigade – The Middleborough mafia – stood out. Their togetherness emanates out of a little nucleus of regular drinking partners. We started a women's principal class network – all five of us.
>
> (Dorothy)

Particular discursive constructions of hegemonic masculinity position women as other and lesser. Such cultures thrive in unlikely environments, but are remarkably resilient over time. Young female staff spoke of how the 'old boys' club' operated in otherwise innovative schools. Progressive educational philosophies did not preclude masculinist behaviours.

> I find it very difficult. The top positions in our school are all held by men. Basically the men make the decisions over the card table – both administration and union. There is a lack of process in decisionmaking which means women are not involved and therefore appear ignorant.
>
> (Anne-Marie)

Many women excluded from the masculinist culture still had close friendships and work relationships with their male colleagues given that institutional alliances, social relationships and activities are premised around particular value systems, shared interests and common tasks. Yet masculinity was the invisible constant. Cynthia, a bureaucrat, commented:

> I perceive a very strong male hegemony, but an interesting one – a group of men, all previously teacher unionists, therefore 'right thinking' in a

sense from my perspective, liberal and progressive, but still men who believe their intellectual (read male) superiority entitles them to set the agenda.

The boys' club was characterized as a range of practices that positioned women as being outsiders – storytelling, male-bonding practices, social rituals, language, talking about football and meeting after work for a drink when many women picked up children. More formally, in meetings, subtle discursive ploys of resistance, outlined by Eleanor Ramsay (1993: 48), came into play to position women as powerless one moment and co-opted the next. A common tactic was 'professional betrayal', when the credit for a woman's work was assumed by a senior male. Another was 'bureaucratic subversion', when formal structures and processes that legitimated the exercise of male power smothered any issue of gender being raised. Anna, a young EO representative on a school administrative committee commented:

> I was the youngest teacher, female, least experienced of two male and two females. It was a facade. I tried to make my opinions heard because in the amalgamation mainly women's positions were lost. It was very clear I had to accept the older men's advice.

> What I find most disempowering is the old time operators who know how to run the system and who just get you on the process. The first time they did it to me I was nearly in tears thinking: 'It's like a big game . . . the way they speak'. I had felt quite effective until that moment. Now I've learned the ropes!
>
> (Debbie)

A different tactic was that of 'masculinist exclusion' where casual and formal conversations were dominated by men's interests and littered with sporting metaphors – being 'caught off side', 'trapped with the ball', 'good catch' and so on – in what Hester Eisenstein (1996) calls the 'football league model of leadership'. A new middle manager, Lyn, recalled:

> I went to a meeting for my first central office meeting. The first half hour was football talk. I didn't know what to do. I was so angry as I was totally ignored. The male with me, with whom I am quite friendly on a one-to-one basis, joined in as was expected. But the topic was initiated by a senior bureaucrat. I considered whether I should interrupt and point out how it was wasting time. Then I decided to sit and watch. But it was insulting.

Of course there was also 'professional containment' when women's professional expertise in, and commitment to, gender equity, was appealed to when asked to add to their workload. Fran, an EO coordinator, realized equity was 'made my thing because I am so good at it'.

But you not only suffer the insults, you are also overloaded with work – the work that was dumped on me as an AST [Advanced Skills Teacher] to do professional development in EO was outrageous.

This effectively removed any responsibility for gender equity from the male principal. For Sarah it meant

any piece of information that arrived on any person's desks which mentioned girls or women was thrust into my hands for me to deal with as EO coordinator, even a suggestion about a beauty contest! I learnt to say 'Well what is your department going to do about it?' Many staff actively developed projects once the responsibility was seen to rest with them.

Other modes of cooption and control included 'conversational colonization', when a woman's ideas were claimed by a man five minutes later. There was also a form of 'social stigmatization' associated with being the token woman who was often simultaneously expected to speak for all women, but still expected to accept that her opinion was self-interested, uninformed, representing particularistic and not universal interests. 'Identity invisibility' was when women were spoken over, treated with condescension or ignored as if not present. Male power was derived from its 'taken for grantedness', as one principal reflected.

I find that while they are not intentionally rude, that men tend to affirm men and never women. I sit and observe at principals' meetings as names are mentioned for jobs. Women are bypassed even where most primary schools principals were women.

(Colleen)

Women in leadership thus felt through these discursive practices the regulatory and disciplining power of particular hegemonic macho masculinities and how they were ignored or relegated to do 'the female things'.

The climate got chillier and rougher higher up. As a new regional assistant manager, Janice, recollects her first meeting in the resources and administration area:

Here I was. One woman among 15 men. The managers themselves were, to a man, 'gentlemen'. They did not put a step out of place. Several offered to assist if I needed anything. They did that individually not collectively as they wouldn't be OK publicly. The male bureaucrats from central office arrived. Everything about their body and verbal language was aggressive and male. They used every four letter word and derogatory phrase you could think of. And I sat there and thought: 'This for my benefit because they actively resent me being here'. Even the handshakes and body language were saying: 'I don't really want to shake your hand but I will'. I remember thinking they were waiting to see my response: use four letter words back; say I am offended and please behave; or will I just shut up and 'suss it out'. I opted for the third strategy and that period passed. Now, apart from the normal individual competitiveness from individuals, I don't feel the bias. Maybe I passed the test or just got used to it.

Moving up through the ranks did not necessarily improve the situation. Resistance just took on more subtle forms. One tactic was to deny access to school and system-wide information gained through involvement in committees and decisionmaking networks. Often issues were caucused and decided upon by key (male) members prior to meetings. It meant that any substantive input by women, already excluded from earlier discussions, was to elicit further information to clarify what was happening, and contest decisions, rather than discuss issues. Thus women were positioned as uninformed, misinformed, troublesome, nonconsensual or just wasting time. These were the forms of 'symbolic violence' frequently used to position women as outsiders (Gherardi 1995).

Even the physical presence of women was threatening to normalizing masculinist cultures that promoted 'masculine' behaviours, technocratic models of management and masculinist images of leadership. Language, symbols, rituals and myths defined insiders and outsiders: position and size of an office; dress; myths about women's incapacity to manage. Kerry was 'tested out' on her arrival as a senior manager in central administration.

There was a competition over this office . . . A guy was meant to move out of the larger office in the row of managers to the smaller office. I knew I had to hold out and be in line with other managers and win an office along this wall. I knew people were watching and that it was symbolically important. And I did it, by speaking to the general manager . . . the boss moved him. A number of people (mostly women) said . . . we're glad you did that because everyone was watching to see if you were going to be strong enough. In their view it was strength, in my view it was bloody ridiculous. After that things were very smooth.

While such competitive behaviour was perceived as strength and showing she 'had balls', other more 'feminine' attributes, such as delegation or consultation, were perceived to be weakness. Women leaders who practised more democratic styles of management were used as examples to perpetuate the myths about women's incapacity to manage. Consultation implied not being able to make the hard decisions. Jenny recalls overhearing senior male bureaucrats commenting about a female executive manager as 'not knowing what is happening, unable to make a decision', quite contrary to many women managers' impressions:

She is a wonderful example of what women are capable of doing. I admire her enormously . . . She knows people by name, she is very warm, has a personal interest in people. Her manner is exemplary. But also very good on communicating outside. She is a very good speaker and thoroughly professional.

(Jenny)

These practices were embedded in organizational structures, processes and cultures. Paul, a senior manager, commented about the tendency for homosocial reproduction in promotion and selection practices:

> There is sort of a private pecking order amongst the boys which says it is your turn next. It is not overt and many men are not conscious of it. But it is a culturally accepted way of working and the norm. It is not aggressively antagonistic towards women getting jobs or against women's rightful place in society and hasn't been for some time. It operates at a subliminal level in the way in which attitudes are formed and certain measures used. For example, the notion of merit. Merit is what I think is good. Well someone else may disagree. And it depends upon the framework in which you measure good. I think something good looks a bit like me.

Discourses about good leadership emphasized bureaucratic rationality, unemotional arguments and hard decisions. Even though few individual men actually fit the images of particular hegemonic masculinities, the discourses of hegemonic masculinity enabled individual men to maintain their advantage.

> There is always an expectation that it is men who go on selection panels . . . and if a woman is assertive or aggressive in interview they say, 'I don't like her much . . . a bit forward with what she said', although the previous male had said exactly the same thing. More so in the country than the city.

(Sandra, principal)

Women learnt different strategies to reposition themselves proactively: initiating interaction, rather than waiting to respond to others' initiatives; balancing out behaviours (being quiet sometimes, outspoken at others); being unpredictable in their predictability; not fitting norms of either wimpish or aggressive femininity; being well-prepared for meetings both in terms of documentation and contacting key actors; taking something new and different to meetings to catch the group off balance; caucusing where possible with other women or men with similar points of view; referring back to their staff when possible to widen debate; refusing to take on more jobs but reminding others of their responsibilities; arguing strongly on small issues, but never compromising on the big issues; and, most of all, by 'staying cool', never getting angry or too passionate. Such moments were tempered, however, by the capacity for men to call upon wider extraorganizational discourses which positioned them as powerful – discourses of efficiency, rationality and increasingly anti-feminist ones.

Discourses of denigration

Masculinist hegemony is fought for, contested and reformulated through a range of discursive practices and discourses of denigration about femininity in general and feminism in particular. While EO provided opportunity structures for many women teachers to gain leadership experience, it was fraught with dangers. Debbie, a teacher of three years' experience commented:

> The older male staff in particular are just gross – they think it's a joke. When I got a Special Responsibilities Payment to do EO . . . they commented: 'You are just a baby in nappies. How can you get a SRP?' It's as much ageism as sexism.

Annette, a teacher of 20 years' experience, saw it as straight out sexism – 'you get it because you are a girl and not because you're young – either way you lose'. There were discourses in some schools that positioned any woman connected to EO (and that meant feminist) as 'butch', 'a ball buster', 'communist leftie' or just 'a bitch'.

> I was Equal Opportunity in a primary school . . . I have been in terribly male-dominated places, taught for a long time and learnt to cope. You get a lot of flack and snide remarks. They try you out, say things like, 'The last EO coordinator was a bitch', make jokes and expect a reaction. While I live equal opportunity, I'm not a leftie (although they call you communist for reading feminist books).
>
> (Vivian)

Discourses of denigration were called into play to 'put down' women who did things well.

> I decided to raise the profile of EO in the school with a professional development day . . . there was a lot of sniggering. Next day on the bulletin board was a nasty comment about some woman going over the top with power. The principal commented at my effort – but not approvingly.
>
> (Joanne)

Then there was the discourse about the humourless feminist who 'can't take a joke'; Liz recalled:

> Older men on staff love to bait me. In a crowded staffroom at lunchtime one deliberately made a joke to get a reaction in front of a range of people. I just ignored him.

Louise remembered how EO was the butt of jokes by the vice principal in the daily bulletin:

> Little puns and jokes about what equal means. How can affirmative action mean equality when its favouring one sex ... things they wouldn't say to your face.

Many EO coordinators felt like moral policewomen. 'You walk into a room', said June, 'and the comment can be heard "Don't say that around her" or "Be careful, here comes June" '.

Changing hegemonic masculinist cultures was seen by many women to be a precondition for women's sense of belonging once in leadership, although many assumed significant cultural change was contingent upon the departure of 'this generation of dead white males' (Louise).

> I still bring it back to the boy's club. There are a lot of them out there. The decisions and the philosophy underlying them indicates that. But there are also SNAGS [sensitive new age guys] out there who relate well to women and who are quite comfortable – ones brought up by their mums to think that women are OK and do not feel threatened. But they are still working their way up. At the minute we have those guys who see men as breadwinners, the big he-man and the one who must get to the top. Too many women in leadership 'unbalances society'. They are afraid of creating weak men or homosexuals or something. We make men feel inferior.
>
> (Maria)

Hegemonic macho-masculinities also disciplined disruptive masculinities (such as homosexuality or SNAGS) through the denigration of them as other or 'too feminine'. Many male teachers carefully disassociated themselves from being seen as SNAGS. Craig, a Victorian primary school principal, saw the term as a derogatory label:

> It makes me feel like a 'poof'. I associate it with gays . . . I think it indicates a weakness, a sense of conforming to how the butch feminists want us to be. A butch feminist wants men to change so that they are weaker – to do anything they want. True feminists want equality. True equality is not where one is better or more powerful than the other.
>
> (quoted in Vanderende 1996: 28)

Craig's was a typical response when male gender identity was under threat. He drew from discourses of macho-masculinity that equated 'wimpish masculinity' to femininity, therefore weak or associated with homosexuality, thus equally suspect in deviating from 'real' masculinity. (Seidler 1994)

> As an ideal the masculine self has left many men with an inherently unstable masculine identity, requiring as it were an ongoing and active

commitment to differentiating oneself from both femininity and homosexuality.

(Douglas 1995: 89)

Reading equality to mean equal treatment, affirmative action was seen to
advantage women. These reactionary discourses, Sue, a principal, argued,
arose because gender equity reform had seriously challenged male dominance and value systems.

EO is treated as a joke, ironically, because it *was* taken seriously and so
has to be seriously resisted. The arguments are that it's discrimination
against the boys and there is not sexism in schools.

Such comments touch on the complex network of the relations of gender
that underpin what many women see as the cultural, institutional, and personal resistances to their advancement into formal leadership. This resistance takes on a variety of forms through the language, practices and social
networks of organizations that have historical, cultural and institutional
power. While the meaning of what constitutes authority, leadership and
masculinity change, it is the ongoing implicit and unquestioned relationship
between particular normative discourses about hard core masculinity from
which women, and some men, are excluded.

At the same time, the emergent global discourses of 'masculinity in crisis'
produce new strategic problems for gender equity. There has always been a
range of discursive practices resisting, transforming, co-opting and subverting deepseated gender reform, largely but not necessarily by men, both at an
individual and institutional level. New hard times have been conducive to its
more overt articulation, however. A senior manager, Paul, commented:

The backlash is a deflection, being visited on 'what about the boys'.
There is a conservative backlash although the cultural imperatives are
now such that it is impossible to come out and do it directly against
women, tell them to go back to the kitchen, although that seems to be
changing.

Deflecting the gaze: masculinity in crisis?

There are an array of discourses about 'masculinity in crisis'. As with
feminist discourses, each has a particular understanding about the nature
of power, the possibilities for change and implications for gender equity
reform policies. There is a much publicized discourse that blames feminism
for the crisis in masculinity, for undermining the social (and gender) order,
for the breakdown of the family, for youth delinquency and crime and even
for even the poor school performance of boys (*The Age*, 7 July 1997: 6). It
taps into both male and female uncertainties about changing gender roles,

into job uncertainties and destabilization of previously secure male career paths, and as promotion opportunities decrease. It appeals to those males who have the greatest investment in maintaining the status quo (Douglas 1995: 188). Its psychological emphasis fails to address the structural and cultural biases that advantage men. This is the reassertion of macho or 'hard' masculinity and a return to 'innate' attributes of natural man premised upon biological essentialism (Kenway 1995). Brannock (1993: 5–7) quotes male principals' responses to feminism in rural NSW schools in the 1990s:

> Mothers have a special place in the home. Militant feminism has decreased femininity in girls and led to crudity and vulgarity in girls.

> The feminist movement is now detrimental to women. Women's strengths lie in their ability to think things through, and to verbalise and not resort to aggression . . . the best situation is when you get both males and females complementing each other. They both have strengths. Women have lost the strength they once had in being the pacifier, being the peaceful one.

> The women's liberation movement is responsible morally for the decline in society. Women are too busy. If they weren't so strung out with career and were home keeping families together there wouldn't be so many street kids and broken families. Women become independent when they have their own money and say: I don't have to put up with this rubbish and leave.

It would appear that: 'An ensnared crisis-ridden manhood is even more dangerous than its "healthy" predecessor' (Brown 1988: 184). Many male teachers referred to how 'political correctness' (another American term imported through the media) silenced opposition and how EO policies led to an overreaction. One vice principal commented:

> People have over-reacted and we are now so guilt ridden that we give women whatever they want . . . if I dare criticise or make comments about how a woman is running a classroom, I'd better run for cover: 'that's a typical sexist remark' or 'you wouldn't do that to your mates.' The reality is I probably would if it was necessary. I'm too scared to say it to women.
>
> (Joe, principal; quoted in Vanderende 1996: 33).

These statements indicate how gender equity policy is subversively rewritten in schools. Male teachers now see themselves as disadvantaged. Restructuring means 'we are now on a level playing field', argued Craig, as merit had replaced seniority for promotion. Such men readily appropriated the individualistic rights orientation of popular EO discourses. The confusion about equality is indicated by Angelo, a senior teacher:

[Women] deserved this help and they got it. But it should have been given out equally. Men could have had the same advantages. There is no Masonic clan or brotherhood who assist each other. Women don't want to be in that role – it is as simple as that. My wife never wanted to be assistant principal. She was quite happy not having any heavy leadership role. Women were happy to help provided their teaching was first. Most women are like that – so what do we do, we give them more responsibilities.

(quoted in Vanderende 1996: 35)

Angelo saw power being bestowed by wrong-headed men upon reluctant women. This discourse of disadvantage was voiced by a district liaison principal (DLP) when commenting on a shadowing program offered only to female principals in a district of 21 principals (19 of whom were male):

There was some uneasiness amongst many male principals about the shadowing program. Many men believed that offering it only to women principals was unfair to men. It's now a level playing field with merit and equity policies replacing seniority.

(Vanderende 1996)

Having lost their advantage, men felt bereft. One extremely vocal male principal in this district opposed women-only programs as unfair to men. He failed to see his appointment as acting DLP, the intermittent career path of his female colleagues due to family responsibilities, or the criteria for principalship prioritizing financial management over human relationship skills, as representing any form of ongoing systemic disadvantage for his female colleagues or advantage to himself. This discourse of male disadvantage attracts the self-interest of males generally. Male teachers now seek access to women-only professional development courses initially established to rectify female disadvantage by providing women with the same opportunities as the informal 'boys' networks' bestowed on men, such as mentorship, succession management, and accessing acting management positions. This discourse became more strident as the stakes got greater.

When we conceive of equality in term of a language of rights we see this fundamentally as an issue of access, and it renders invisible issues about the organisation of institutional power within work. Within this framework, it is relatively easy for men to support the claims of feminism and to think that feminism is concerned about the empowering of women without really challenging the rights of men.

(Seidler 1994: 95)

Brittan (1989: 184) refutes the thesis of a general 'crisis in masculinism' as there is no 'breakdown of heterosexualism and the decline of men's power and authority in the public sphere'. He does admit that the legitimacy of male domination is being questioned increasingly by women and some men, but this has not led to a destabilization of the dominant mode. The challenge of feminist and gay politics is being contained because dominant male hierarchies can tap into a constituency which is unsettled about a range of other factors, re: family and work.

(Brittan 1989: 184)

He sees the viciousness of the attack on gay men and on feminism as indicative of the 'strain on masculinism', as men have 'lost their collective nerve, their self assurance, their sense of certainty. They are uncertain about their potency, their heterosexuality, their status worthiness' (Brittan 1989: 183). Status, in a deprofessionalized and casualized teacher workforce was an issue.

While hegemonic masculinism remains intact, however, it faces numerous 'subcrises which it negotiates, often through incorporating the voices of dissent into its own practices' (Brittan 1989: 188). Not all men are in crisis, and not all men have the same interests. Yet although the economic and political power of men in management is less challenged, they are able to tap into this sense of crisis to reassert their dominance.

Strategic masculinity

The discourse of strategic masculinity is another strand of the discourse of male crisis which derives from the men's movement. It also focuses upon masculinity as problematic, but argues that males have problems in gender formation, albeit different ones. This literature takes issue with the earlier feminist position that 'men-in-general' are responsible for the oppression of women, and sees individual males as the source of the problem, not patriarchy or hegemonic heterosexualism (Brittan 1989). It is a powerful line in that the 'men-in-general' view runs counter to liberal individualism. The problem is class and other forms of inequality but not men. This perspective argues that men are also disempowered by their sex roles, for example they cannot cry in public; that male gender roles are as limiting for men as female gender roles are for women; and that if men do practice 'female styles of leadership' they are not seen to be, as one principal, Harry, said, 'real men'. Men have been socialized to become emotional anorexics. This literature appropriates those feminist accounts of gender relations that de-emphasize gender politics. Its critics suggest that it is not that men lack a relational psychology, but rather that men are selectively relational – consciously and unconsciously. Lyn Segal (1990) comments on the irony that such men have the best of both worlds in that they do a lot of the play work with children (in public) and not 'the grunge' (in private). This strand of thought is ambivalent with regard to feminism, but generally does not advocate making gender relations with women better. There is no analysis of how power/masculinity associations produce different readings for what men and women do that may appear to be the same.

This new discourse of masculinity has produced the image of the sensitive new age guy, or SNAG, who can be publicly sensitive, caring and family-minded without being seen to be 'unmasculine'. In management it produces what Kerfoot and Knights (1993) call 'strategic masculinity'. Thus the SNAG is quite often able, without any redistribution of either institutional power or domestic labour, to colonize and appropriate the better, and usually more public, aspects of childcaring. In this way many men so prepared to change earn 'brownie points' as caring about kids and thus gaining advantage over those males who continue to treat public and private as separate (Kerfoot and Knights 1993: 664). As Andrea, a single mother of three aspiring for leadership, commented:

> A male principal can bring his kids in to work and look good. And some of the women run to help him 'babysit' his own kids! A female principal who did that would be seen to not being able to cope or organize her life. She would no longer be the superwoman everyone thought she was and would be criticized because she had more space to do that than other women teachers because she makes the rules.

The messages of strategic management in which the individual's energies (intellectual, cultural, emotional *and* sexual) are moulded towards the organizational ends by channelling individual careerism towards a corporate vision are conducive to strategic masculinity (Kerfoot and Knights 1993). This mode of masculinity has gained credibility because it is seemingly inclusive of a range of 'feminine' behaviours, yet the asymmetrical power relations based on gender have not altered. Cockburn talks about how women in her study distinguished between the 'cod-piece wearing jocks' of old style masculinities and the 'new men' who, while welcoming of women into work, still position women in a no-win situation. 'These men expect to find women in the public sphere. Nominally at least they welcome women in to this new exciting world because their presence adds sexual spice to the working day' (Cockburn 1991: 156–7). Roper does not see organizations as domesticating men, or men as emotional anorexics. Rather male managers 'deep act' on the behalf of the company as they create and internalize 'corporate feeling rules'. Their passion and emotional investment in management is a form of emotional labour which relies upon 'fierce spirit and bonding' and the reinvention, not disappearance, of passionate 'primitive man' (Roper 1994: 3–4).

Strategic masculinities may work in some institutional contexts and not others, however. In Burridge Secondary College, feminism and EO provided new opportunities for exploiting discourses of strategic masculinity. Trevor, well known for his grass-roots activism in areas of social justice, had been

EO coordinator for four years. He saw 'an EO coordinator as an imple-mentor of policy and evaluator of policy and a real hands on person, a con-tact person for people in difficulty, staff and students'. Being in a 'feminized' gender reform job, Trevor reflected

> sits comfortably, probably more so than a woman in the job. I think people were a little uncomfortable in the first instance about gender equity. Now they say, well he is not really pushing his own barrow! I genuinely believe in the skills of women and the ethos that women approach things differently and often more efficiently. I remind people women have more family responsibilities and leadership – it is a matter of commitment and not time; leadership can be done differently with-out sacrificing family time . . . there is no one 'male way'. Our school workshop on interview techniques changed job descriptions to be more inclusive, changed the language from the assertive 'you will do' to 'work and communicate with others'.

Trevor, as a male, is seen to be neutral and not representing particularist interests (feminism). Yet for Trevor, as for other men now that EO is a paid position in schools, EO was an advantageous career move, gaining him 'brownie points' and thus speeding him up the 'glass escalator' (Williams 1992).

By contrast, in the context of the hard core masculinist cultures of the cen-tral bureaucracy, strategic masculinities were derided as 'wimpish'. A senior male manager, John, felt under considerable pressure

> about the leadership style I am displaying when I talk to my superiors. I am more under pressure to display the normal characteristics of toughness and lack of compassion than I ever have been in my life. I am seen to be a 'wuss' . . . the person who gives in to what principals want. A pushover. Never gets real objectives done, the hard-edged stuff is beyond me. Yet I feel that my outstanding leadership characteristic is to get people to do things, to work for me by being open, to talk to them. Yet when I represent them I am seen as weak by the centre.

Many of the women principals viewed this same manager as being firm but fair, as being able to listen but make the hard decisions, and as being sup-portive without being too directive. He lost his position in the next restruc-turing. Hegemonic 'macho' masculinity in this context saw any debate as opposition, and any ability to work collegially and collectively as weak leadership. Strategic masculinity positioned him as not measuring up against hegemonic discourses connecting hard masculinity to effective leadership. For many men, 'two things are inextricably together – the desire for power and the fear of failure. No other alternative seems to exist' (McLean 1995: 292), but 'while men as a group clearly hold the reins of power, the majority of men experience themselves as powerless' (Segal 1990: 214–5; Connell 1990: 165).

While there are a range of masculinities and femininities at work in schools, the discourses of restructuring and reshaping educational work privilege some masculinities more than others. Alan, a principal, rejected the need for so-called feminine management skills of emotional management, nurturance and communication. He argued it was not unfair that women had to 'put on the leadership suit that we men had designed':

> As long as they don't replace the traditional management styles. In this period of school closures, global budgets, schools need to sell themselves to stay open. We need tough decisions. As a classroom teacher you can afford to nurture, but as a principal you are so busy making financial decisions you don't have time to anymore.
>
> (quoted in Vanderende 1996: 39)

Survival in the market era was not about caring, consultation, collegiality and delegation but about image, performance, and making tough decisions. In its popularization, the discourse of the crisis in masculinity has privileged the 'victim' status of men and marginalized the profeminist literature on masculinity. The latter has focused upon male power and elite privilege in organizational cultures, and therefore provides a more sophisticated way of thinking about how the power relations of gender are changing.

Changing men

The above analysis of masculinist discourses of resistance and denigration supports the view that the operation of power relies upon a multiplicity of resistance points and the capacity to call upon powerful hegemonic discourses to justify gender inequality as 'normal'. It also requires us to think how and why individual women or men change when gender equity reform obviously works against their interests. Gender equity reformers need to better understand the investment individuals have in both changing and resisting change. Many male advocates of EEO came to this position, as 'partners of feminists' and 'fathers of daughters', through the realization of the way discursive practices work to produce gender inequity and discrimination in schools on a daily basis (Sinclair 1994). It was these men's emotional connectedness to those close to them who had experienced overt and covert sexism, structural and cultural discrimination, and often ongoing harassment, which then allowed them to empathize and understand the ways in which women and girls in general were positioned unequally.

Gender reform is also about teachers' investment in their professional and *gendered* work identities. Gender reform challenges teachers' *gendered* subjectivity, threatening long-held institutional and personal practices and beliefs, because it is closely tied up with power relationships at home, school and work. It problematizes what it means to be professional. Whereas curriculum change is acceptable to male teachers on the grounds of 'good teaching prac-tice', changes relating to promotion and allocation of duties or definitions of leadership are difficult because they are testing out everyday gender relations, status, and authority. So while men can clearly describe and elaborate upon the facts of structural discrimination (e.g. the position of women in education) and intellectually engage with the moral discourses about equity for women, they still express feelings of anger and a sense of unfairness because they feel they are losing any advantage in more competitive times. Yet early EO strat-egies naively assumed that once the facts of systemic and indirect inequality were laid bare, that change would follow. Gender reform has been treated as an intellectual activity, failing to recognize the considerable political, emotional and professional investment of many men (and women) in the status quo.

There was also the early tendency for feminism to make all men feel guilty. Profeminist men have internalized the view that they must reject their masculinity, and this has perhaps put many men off going down the path (Seidler 1994).

> Guilt is an emotion with social effects, but . . . they are likely to be dis-empowering rather than positive. A young man (or boy) 'feeling terri-ble about being male' will not easily join with other men in social action, nor can he feel solidarity (except at some symbolic level) with women. Thus guilt implies that men's personalities must change but undermines the social conditions for changing them, an enterprise which requires (as the feminist movement knows) considerable inter-personal support. Nor are there any set of texts to turn to (as again feminism has learnt). In terms of what is widely available, there is little between popular feminism (which accuses men) and mass media (which ridicules feminism).
>
> (Connell 1990: 299)

The 'blame all men' approach has fed an anti-feminist politics and that of the New Right as feminists have been positioned as anti-male. Rather than work from such a negative base of guilt, we need to begin from the position of what men will gain from changing dominant modes of masculinity. We can better promote change in gender relations by working with profeminist men, other marginalized social groups, and those men equally alienated by dominant masculinities, to develop more inclusive discourses about mascu-linity that are open to alternative discourses of leadership.

Part III

RISKY BUSINESS

7   Doing emotional management work: gender, markets and self-managing schools

Seductive discourses

The past decade has been marked by the restructuring of educational work in many western industrialized nation states towards devolved and marketized education systems (Ball 1994; Whitty 1997). Administration, teaching and learning have been expected to change radically in order to meet the demands of postmodern society – a post-Fordist feminized workplace, new information technologies, global markets, changing demographics and the citizenship claims of a more culturally diverse society (Hargreaves 1994). Postmodern educational leadership, the new management literature argues (e.g. Senge 1990; Drucker 1992), requires the capacity to cope with rapid change, insecurity and uncertainty of outcome. Leadership is not about the doing, but also about listening, facilitation and stewardship (Sergiovanni 1992). Leaders do not inform individuals *what* to do, but recognize, support, resource and coordinate others with expertise in the organization to take action at the workface in smaller, more autonomous self-managing units. In learning organizations, personal as well as strategic skills are essential to leadership – the 'people skills' traditionally associated with the 'feminine' aspects: emotional management, nurturance, communication and facilitation (e.g. Senge 1990). Workforce diversity, both group and individual, generates initiative and action, and serves the diverse clientele. Thus conceptually oriented skills (the mental work of planning, analysis, assessing and making decisions) need to be matched by the social capacities to motivate individuals and manage cultural change.

Notions of postmodern leadership, premised upon self-governance and managing diversity, are seductive to feminists. Discourses of self-governance appeal to feminist communitarian ideals and mythologies that the local is necessarily more democratic. Self-governance supplants the notion of the paternalistic state, taps into aspirations for professional autonomy, and promises the space to initiate change locally (Yeatman 1990). Postmodern appeals to consultation and consensus – the features of so-called feminine styles of leadership – affirm women's experiences and perspectives, legitimating them in the public domain. Women would now seem to be positioned favourably in terms of their claims to leadership, but as the following Victorian case study illustrates, postmodern texts of reform, with their promise of greater flexibility, diversity, community and autonomy, can have a downside in that in their implementation of such reforms produces practices that are quite modernist, controlling and conforming and not conducive to women's styles of leadership.

Overworked and under scrutiny: leadership in self-managing schools

Devolution, as outlined by the ensemble of policies associated with the management plan. *Schools of the Future* (SOTF) in Victoria, has produced a distinct shift since 1992 in the governance of public education away from more participatory modes of administrative decentralization within a centralized bureaucratic framework, to a managerialist mode of centralized-decentralization premised upon the principles of market liberalism, deregulation and privatization (Kenway *et al*. 1994; Blackmore *et al*. 1996, Watkins 1996). These reforms effectively appropriated key terms of 1980s reform discourses – participation, community, school reorganization, curriculum and assessment reform and work restructuring – and juxtaposed them beside notions of individual choice, competitive advantage, and deregulation of the economy and of the education labour market in the name of efficiency and effectiveness (see Chapter 2; Caldwell and Spinks 1992; Caldwell 1994).

Schools of the Future (Directorate of School Education 1993) represents a fundamental shift in state/individual/community relations in education. Educational restructuring in Victoria has been characterized, as in other western nation states during the 1980s, by downsizing, devolution, mainstreaming of equity programs, marketization and privatization (Ball 1994; Whitty 1997). The argument made by the conservative Kennett government in 1992 for restructure was that government schools were neither efficient nor effective. Not only did they cost too much, but they did not produce productive, flexible and skilled workers for the global market. Devolution in Victoria after 1992, as elsewhere, was accompanied by the reduction in per capita expenditure of $300 million to government schools to make Victoria the second lowest in per capita funding of education in Australia; the 'voluntary' departure of over 20 per cent of the government teaching labour force; the decimation of the regional support systems in terms of special needs teachers (counselling, integration, disadvantage, health and welfare), curriculum and professional development and EO support. Over 300 schools, largely in the western suburbs and country areas with the greatest cultural diversity and lowest socioeconomic income and where most female principals were located, were closed (Marginson 1994; Blackmore 1996).

Self-management devolved responsibility to principals for staff appraisal (Professional Recognition Program), professional development, administering industrial awards (teacher leave, administrative staff, contract staff); staffing (leave, promotion, appraisal, selection); establishing school priorities through school charters; financial management on a one-line global budget (with an additional equity index); managing new career structures for teachers premised upon performance management appraisal hurdles (Leading Teachers) as well as implementation of centrally determined policy. Bonus payments rewarded high performance. Teachers' work conditions have been undermined with increased class sizes, reduced regional and school support services, increased administrative commitments, increased reporting and recording tasks, less preparation time, as well as new career hierarchies (Bishop and Mulford 1995; Townsend 1996b).

Devolution also required strong feedback systems to the centre. Outcomes-based accountability mechanisms (system-wide and national data collection systems, performance monitoring and standardized testing) have been introduced to make SOTF appear more accountable for public expenditure, and to provide information (in the form of standardized test scores) about individual schools in order to inform parental choice. Such measures have the potential to competitively rank individual students, teachers and schools against each other, but these accountability mechanisms have become more modes of vertical control by the centre than horizontal accountability to the community (Tickell 1994). Parents now sit on school councils as individuals, not as representatives of a constituency of parents as in the past. They are confined to implementing government policy, not informing education policy, as both parent and teacher organizations, as special interest groups rather than stakeholders, are now excluded from policy production at regional and central level. Community has been redefined as the aggregate of individual consumer choices. The public choice theory logic is that individual parents will make rational self-maximizing choices about what constitutes a 'good school' for their child. Such choices, in their aggregation, will construct a market capable of distinguishing effective from ineffective schools (Kenway *et al*. 1993; Marginson 1994; Gewirtz *et al*. 1995; Peters and Marshall 1996).

Effectively, a 'manufactured' crisis of state debt has been 'faxed down the line' (Watkins 1993, 1996). Principals now negotiate within limited school-based global budgets over competing demands for reduced resources – between large class sizes and extracurricular programs (e.g. arts and music); between gifted and disadvantaged student programs; between promoting permanent staff or employing contract teachers. If they miscalculate, the blame rests with them. When schools fail to deliver the services that parents expect (e.g. disability, literacy, gifted or breakfast programs) the school is held responsible for its priorities, and not the government for its failure to resource the school's program or needs adequately. As in self-governing schools in the UK:

> Because devolution appears to be offering self determination and management, thus new freedoms and discretionary power, in reality, because it has occurred in restricted budgets, 'it opens' schools up to blame for the 'failures' of the system, and leaves individual schools with the dilemmas and contradictions inherent in the government policy.
>
> (Bowe and Ball 1992: 72)

The self-managing school, therefore, is the site of many paradoxes for school leaders. Superficially, devolution promises flexibility and responsiveness, but the reality is often control and inflexibility (Bishop and Mulford 1995; Townsend 1996b).

> We have got autonomy but within strict guidelines in curriculum. You are expected to deliver curriculum – Latin, sport and everything is made compulsory – no time to do it. You can be creative, but it is so restricted now it is not creative.
>
> (Ann, principal)

Individual administrators and teachers are confronted with increased parental expectations in an era of economic uncertainty and greater system demands for improved productivity and outcomes at the same time that resources shrink, reducing the discretionary capacities of principals. Principals are expected to implement centrally initiated compulsory programs, prioritize system-wide mandated policy (Learning Assessment Program), while addressing individual student needs through specialist, cost-intensive programs (e.g. music, technology). As one principal commented, 'school leadership has shifted so we are no longer advocates for the kids, but for the department'.

One paradox arising out of self-management is that deregulated quasi-market systems of public education not only tend to exacerbate inequality (as evidence suggests in Victoria, UK and New Zealand) but it also reregulates the daily practices of principals, teachers and students through the accountability mechanisms of school charters, performance management, standardized assessment, centralized data collection systems monitoring outcomes and curriculum frameworks. These technologies facilitate the state's capacity to 'steer and not row' a devolved system (Gordon 1994b; Gewirtz et al. 1995; Blackmore et al. 1996, Wylie 1997). As technologies of self-management, these measures channel individual energies towards system-wide ends as teachers and principals internalize the performativity demands of recording, reporting, appraisal and presentation (Blackmore et al. 1996). Gillian, a rural primary school principal and teacher commented:

The climate and values which are entrenched is that teachers have no control or power over anything except on a day-to-day basis. There is regression to the 1950s here, not progression to the 2000s. The attitude of the system is permeating into treatment of kids; the dominant view is stamp on them before they stamp on you. In the current climate there will be little advancement of EO and social justice. All I can do is control what is happening in my class, and I'm not doing well at this anyway because of increased class sizes and lack of time.

A second paradox is that while the postmodern rhetoric of self-management is about professional autonomy, judgement and expertise, there is a significant shift in power to more executive and less democratic decision-making in schools. SOTF is principal and not teacher-led change, managed change from above rather than managing change from below, signifying more hierarchical and individualized professional relationships (Louis 1994; Ball 1994; Grace 1995). Principals have newfound power over teachers in appraisal schemes, promotion and mobility. They work under different awards with access to bonus pay, but have less time to deal with teaching and learning (Tickell 1994; Blackmore et al. 1996). Ball (1994: 93) refers to a similar reconstruction of the principal's role in self-governing schools in England:

The effective reconstruction of the head's role as budget manager, entrepreneur and promoter of the school, diverts the values, purposes and concerns of the head from matters educational to matters financial and managerial. Thus not only are the priorities of managers and teachers diverging but there is a clear separation emerging between policy concerns, vested in management, and a more limited role of execution, for the teachers.

Many principals saw the increasingly adversarial relationship between principal and teachers as undermining collegiality, encouraging unnecessary conflict between principal and teachers, and producing a competitive environment antithetic to effective change and innovation. Some principals commented on shifting school power cultures with emerging cultures of compliance and competitive individualism discouraging individual teachers from taking risks and encouraging teachers to adopt a siege mentality (Blackmore et al. 1996). Joan, a secondary principal contrasts the work practices of more participative school-based decisionmaking of the 1980s with the 1990s:

It means that the staff reaction is to strike or give in [to policies]. There is little or no scope for the types of creative solutions where you work together and learn ways of talking to each other. We learnt in the old system of participatory school-based democracy in the 1980s where such a dialogue was possible that there were limitations to democratic processes. Because these problems were not resolved it was possible for the new government to highlight them to justify devolution which is non-participatory and managerialist. While we incorrectly assumed that if we got the structures right then everything was OK . . . at least there was some ownership of decisions and collectivity. Now there is neither the dialogue nor the ownership as we are in a moral vacuum as well.

A third paradox is that while the rhetorical emphasis is on quality, the performativity associated with self-management within a quasi-market emphasizes outcomes and image, not process or substance. With the reduction of school budgets, schools are encouraged to be more entrepreneurial and competitive to attract clients and sponsors (Grady *et al.* 1994). The principal's role has become more the business of marketing curriculum and pedagogy, school culture, best practice and leadership in competition with other government and private schools, than practising educational leadership in curriculum (Kenway *et al.* 1993; Gewirtz *et al.* 1995). To achieve the type of curriculum flexibility needed to attract students, principals increasingly hire less experienced (sometimes less qualified) casual teachers on short-term contracts (Blackmore 1997a). As schools increasingly rely upon user pays – parental 'voluntary' contributions and labour – school principals seek business sponsors. All the above shift energy and resources onto image, on criteria for performance pay for principals. As one female campus principal of a multisite suburban secondary college commented:

> It is no longer OK to be just an ordinary school. You have got to physically go to the community and show that you are improving. So you have to have the physical trappings with improvement and not just theory about education. In this competitive climate in an area with lots of private schools, discipline means uniform. If you don't have a uniform you are not disciplined, and therefore not academically successful. And if the uniform is in any way casual you are judged as scruffy – that loses students.

So while the market promises diversity in school provision, the market has normalizing effects, as the dominant image of a good school is of students who are well-dressed, well-behaved and high academic achievers in a pleasant, well-resourced and technologically sophisticated environment. Schools now win or lose students on the basis of their reputation and image. Sponsorships also tend to go to winners not losers, and equity, disadvantage or diversity are not as attractive to sponsors or students as are successful sporting teams. Thus school principals confront significant moral and ethical dilemmas when selling their school to the market (Blackmore 1996).

The market and gender also interact in terms of how women are socially constructed by the market as workers and leaders and represented in the education market (Brah 1994). Jessica, a secondary principal noticed:

> While I think women have got a better chance in a system based on merit, no matter how questionable that can be, than on seniority, it also depends now on a range of other factors. As a member of principal selection panels in the area which has a high number of private schools, I can see a number of government schools who just wouldn't take the risk on a woman as principal because it could lose students. Women are all right as a deputy principal.

Gender does not merely articulate with labour markets, but is a constitutive element of the fabric of labour markets as they have been discursively formed as contingent relations or ideal about how consumers *should* rather than *do* operate (Brah 1994: 151).

The final paradox is that these reforms are represented as being value-neutral and apolitical in the instrumentalist language of the market and management, and yet these market-driven reforms have produced a fundamental value shift in the role of the state vis-à-vis public education. Many women principals felt disillusionment and despair seeing social justice values being supplanted by market values.

> One of the things that really frustrates me is the lack of social justice we have had in the past couple of years. I mean some schools emulate private schools, particularly in this region, where they are all going to be brain surgeons. Our kids aren't, and the days of having the teaching staff and resources to adequately cope are gone. So you look for alternatives. We, for example, have a breakfast program for kids here – many are homeless and it is safer for some to be at school than at home. So teachers spend much of their time doing welfare things before they even teach in order to get the right caring environment.
>
> (Pauline, secondary school principal)

The creation of more competitive relationships between public schools, between students, and between teachers increasingly undermines a collective sense of public education. It also endangers the basis for the types of claims that can be made upon the state with regard to education as a citizenship right. The dominant values of the market-oriented self-managing school premised upon individualism, competitiveness and contractualism also work against gender equity reform values that focus upon integration, care, community, student needs, curriculum and educational issues, disadvantage, inclusion and collegial social relationships.

These contradictory discourses produce a high level of ambiguity and uncertainty and dilemmas for principals in terms of their leadership practice. On the one hand, principals are seen to be increasingly autonomous in financial decisionmaking, expected to be receptive to community and parent involvement in school policymaking; and on the other, as line managers solely responsible to the centre which controls finance and policy through strong feedback accountability measures. Principals are put under considerable pressure to, as one commented, to 'merely do the bidding of the department'. Principals act as a buffer between the centre and the school community of teachers and parents, but also between the centre and the school staff, as they manage the emotions of rapid and radical change – teacher morale, parental anxiety and student alienation. In doing this emotional management work for the system, they unintentionally deflect closer scrutiny away from the centre (Blackmore 1996; Blackmore *et al.* 1996).

While all principals are confronted with the centralizing/decentralizing tensions endemic to self-management in Victoria, it is doubly difficult for women who are being actively encouraged by women and leadership programs to become principals and leading teachers. First, they are overseeing the feminization, casualization and deprofessionalization of teaching (see Chapter 1). Second, with the tendency for women principals to be located in schools with higher levels of student disadvantage and multiculturalism or smaller rural schools, schools most under threat, women principals are more susceptible to being judged as failures according to market norms. Third, many women are appointed principals by local selection committees as change agents and 'caring and sharing' leaders. Yet 'managed change' is about re-engineering along functionalist lines, strong leadership in sense of aggressive entrepreneurship, close coordination and planning, which is about control and hierarchy; and contrived consensus, not collegiality or genuine debate about substantive issues. Many feminist principals expressed concern about the contradictions this raised between their own theory and practice – in being unable to practice their preferred mode of leadership due to the policy imperatives and material conditions of their work. One cannot talk about 'women's ways of leading' therefore, without being aware of the structural constraints and discourses shaped elsewhere that undermine leadership committed to such notions of feminist practice. The following case study elaborates upon the complexities of self-management for one woman principal appointed as a change agent when amalgamating two secondary 'schools of the future'.

Hillcrest Secondary College: a case study of self-management

Judy was selected as a change agent by a local committee to amalgamate a rural secondary school, Hillcrest Secondary College, with the neighbouring Mowray High School. At Hillcrest, leadership was associated with images of hegemonic masculinity due to its long history, previously as a technical school, of male-dominated management. Amalgamation was now necessary for survival as the Schools of the Future program (writing charter, linking programs to global budget etc.) was being implemented. Judy was expected to balance students' needs against teachers' personal and professional needs, as amalgamation could mean up to 25 teachers named 'in excess' of staffing requirements, thus subject to redeployment or redundancy. This sense of personal insecurity was exacerbated by professional and institutional powerlessness in the face of top-down imposed reform, producing localized discourses of despair and discontent, which jostled against extralocal discourses about the crisis of the state and education (that is, teachers) failing to address postindustrial needs (Bishop and Mulford 1995). In response, teachers called upon progressivist professional discourses about child-centred learning, but increasingly tinged with liberal-market notions of individual choice and a stronger client focus. Institutionally specific discourses circulated within each school, positioning Hillcrest as being more caring and collegial, less élitist, more vocational and practical (therefore equitable), and less academic, than Mowray. Mowray staff drew more heavily from feminist and multicultural discourses of the 1980s, and constructed themselves as being more progressive, into quality and gender equity.

Judy came to the school with a history of being a change agent as an acting principal, a facilitator of principal professional development, a master's degree student, an active professional networker, and a self-employed manager in a private business. Her strengths were seen to be her breadth of experience, her consultative style, and her caring approach. When initiating the amalgamation processes, Judy sought to establish structures and processes that facilitated professional collegiality while focusing upon improving pedagogy and creating curriculum possibilities. She would submit a position paper, ask others to do so, and thus promote debate. She spoke often, openly, persuasively and with a clear view about organizational change. Her aim was to encourage staff ownership of change. Change, she argued, was about 'ongoing dialogue between staff working together when possible, to develop policy and translate it into practice'. She juggled between prodding people in particular directions, encouraging self-reflection, and providing time for consultation and review. Teachers needed to know why and how particular innovations would improve the teaching and learning environment. Judy argued:

> You can be a good manager but not necessarily a good leader. In a school you have to be both, because you have the total role. Managers are people who shift bits of paper and do administration and organization and budgets and those sorts of things. Leaders are people who interact with other people, communicate with people, take an interest in people, get people to accept your culture and philosophy and vision and take them on-side. A manager doesn't necessarily have to have those attributes.

She consciously left the 'management' work for home. Her school time was for 'people' work where she was prepared to listen and talk with students, parents and teachers. 'Interruption,' she said, 'is what it is all about'.

Within a few months of her arrival there was a dominant discourse circulating about Judy's outstanding leadership. Staff, teachers and administrative alike, frequently listed her qualities when asked what exemplified good educational leadership. These were being a good listener; being willing to change her mind if convinced otherwise; being prepared to act and make difficult decisions when necessary; being able to follow through when a decision is made; being well-informed about what was going on in the school at all levels, but also willing to delegate as much as possible; being highly knowledgeable, hard working and politically astute; being fair, having a sense of humour and generally pleasant; communicating often; being willing to advise and praise where appropriate; and being supportive to teachers in their personal and professional lives. This converged with Judy's view of good leadership at that time and what she thought she did.

Judy's leadership, however, was framed by the discourse of crisis dominated by restructuring under Schools of the Future policies. Timelines for change were short, with a deluge of new policies changing all aspects of school organization – industrial relations, career paths, principal roles, financial management, school council responsibilities, charters and reviews, performance management, teacher appraisal, professional development, teacher and principal accreditation, curriculum and accountability frameworks and a range of new student-based programs focusing on gifted children, literacy, numeracy and technology. Restructuring was reshaping teachers' personal and professional lives with the invasion of school time into their personal life with meetings, class preparation and correction and professional development no longer undertaken in school time. Alan, the professional development coordinator, reflected on the ambiguities:

> We are having difficulty as the culture at the state level is line management and the culture of this school in the past has been very authoritarian. This has since become more collaborative with the new female principal. It is a very difficult time for collaborative leadership now, given that centrally there are fairly huge expectations being put on leaders within schools not to be collaborative, and in fact to adopt the very line management authoritarian model of leadership and decision-making. But the female principal is seeking to work consultatively and collaboratively, but at the same time trying not to let it all get too bogged down due to system and community pressures.

These contradictions between professional collegiality and line management demands for tough decisions were also played out in the context of community-based discourses associating strong leadership, authority and discipline to particular modes of macho masculinity, which positioned her, as a female, no matter what she did, as not capable of leadership. Her acting vice principal recalled:

> One day an irate father arrived in the front hall of the school. When I said I was the acting vice principal and could I help him, he responded: 'You can't be the vice principal. You're a woman. I want to see the principal'. I replied with pleasure: 'Certainly. I will go and see if I can make an appointment for you with *her* now'!

At the same time, the discourse of crisis that many teachers articulated made them feel disempowered and controlled, and they looked to Judy for support. Top-down reforms were seen to be prioritized as school-based initiatives were measured against efficiency and the capacity to provide quantifiable outcomes rather than substantive solutions to educational problems. Teachers' fears of being 'named in excess'(redundant) interfered with restructuring the curriculum and school organization in terms of what was best for the kids. Teachers saw themselves as readily discardable by the system, with little decisionmaking power, alienated by public discourses blaming teachers, casting them as out of step with current times and resistant to reform. Some called upon the discourses about 'putting the kids first', and withdrew to their classrooms, although classrooms were no longer a safe haven from curriculum and assessment reforms and the market (Coombe *et al.* 1993; Distant 1993). Others tapped into the discourse of performativity, requiring individual teachers to strive to be seen to change, to work harder and longer, to do more outside the classroom so they could be seen to perform, and thus not put themselves at risk. It was 'management by stress', whereby the rapidity and scale of change, together with the intensification of labour, meant people internalized the problems of change, thus quieting resistance and leading to acceptance, if not compliance (Blackmore *et al.* 1996).

While the source of the discourse of crisis was located outside the range of action for schools, principals were held responsible for its obvious effects, for example, the reduced resources of time, money and equipment. Principals, who mediated system level, teacher, parent and student demands, were seen to be complicit in these new disciplinary modes. Judy was fully aware, as she did the emotional management work of counselling and supporting staff, of how the discourse of crisis paralysed individual action. She was acutely aware that she initiated the amalgamation that threatened staff's jobs and so a 'lot of anger is focusing upon me right now'. Her response was to communicate as quickly as possible on critical decisions, to speak about the emotional responses to change – disbelief, anger, then grief. Her way of dealing with the emotional economy of the school was to encourage others to reflect upon how they might change by talking about her own personal responses to change – frustration, anxiety, fear. At the same time, she sought to be positive and productive by providing an innovative proposal about the reorganization of the school curriculum and welfare. She later privately expressed frustration when her radical curriculum plan was rejected in favour of a status quo proposal, but did not take this personally or articulate her frustration publicly.

While Judy was highly regarded for her fairness, there developed significant points of conflict that undermined the developing relationship of trust. In particular, she overruled the Joint Planning Group of the amalgamating schools on introducing single-sex classes in Year 8. Mowray staff, more active in gender equity matters, feared girls would be overwhelmed by the majority of boys and women staff by men in the redistribution of key jobs in the amalgamated college, given the dominance of boys and male staff. Mowray staff advocated girls-only classes at Year 8, a common gender equity strategy in Victoria to redress gender imbalance in school populations (Kenway *et al.* 1997). Judy vetoed the single-sex classes on a permanent basis at any year level on the grounds that it was advertised as a coeducational school and boys-only classes (the consequence of girls-only classes) could disaffect parents. Mowray staff saw girls' needs 'being sacrificed in order to moderate boys' behaviour', a feminist concern given the discourses of male crisis. Judy argued that she could not be seen to disadvantage the *boys* and promised alternatives to address the gender imbalance (such as female teachers as role models in science and maths). She was well aware that in the context of the marketized education system with an expanding Catholic coeducational college nearby that the school's future rested on maintaining enrolments. Single-sex classes for boys were seen to be radical, and indeed could elicit a reaction from the conservative community in the context of media-generated discourse on the underachievement of boys.

While Judy bore the grief and anger of the amalgamation and 'excess' process well, since most staff recognized this was out of her control, the anger that ensued with this decision was palpable. Many staff felt it was a local policy issue they could influence. For Judy, the first female principal, not to act accordingly was distressing. It clouded Mowray's dealings with her for some time, seeing her as being less democratic and consultative than they expected. This dispute was divisive and bitter, and particularly painful for Judy to be seen as acting against girls' interests. She distinguished between being feminist and 'a radical feminist', although all staff saw her as feminist. As many women, Judy chose to disassociate herself with the open use of the word feminist although she was committed to working for women and girls, and showed her commitment in attending and working actively in local EO networks.

This case indicates the dilemmas confronting women in leadership – ethical, professional, political and personal. One was how women dealt with power. While Judy was appointed for her caring and sharing attributes, she also saw herself first and foremost as a leader in highly professional ways (Court 1992; Glazer 1991). Yet she did not feel comfortable with the notion of having power *over* others. Power was a 'male way of doing things', and professionally and ethically questionable. She redefined her power as power through and with others – shared leadership – 'being at the centre of the spokes of a wheel rather than out in front pulling the wagon'. Chase (1995) argues that the tension between culture and experience, between the discourses of professional work and inequality, for example, both limit and empower women in leadership. Cultural practices, for example, tend to deny women speaking about seeking, obtaining and enjoying power. A dominant theme in the interviews with other women in leadership positions was their sense of acting out of a cultural script in which they did not fit or feel comfortable. Valerie Walkerdine talks about 'femininity as performance . . . As girls at school, as women at work, we are used to performing' (1993: 267). Walkerdine's (1993: 267) comment expresses Judy's feelings about power well:

> It is a though the person with her name exists somewhere else, outside her body: this powerful person that she cannot recognise as herself. Instead she feels that she is hopeless, consistently panics about her performance, and appears to have little confidence in herself. She can however, express her views clearly and forcefully . . . It is not the case that here is a simple passive wimp femininity, but a power which is both desired, strived for, yet almost too dangerous to be acknowledged as belonging to the woman herself.

The pleasure gained from being able to influence through power matched by a fear of power was typical of how many women felt about leadership. Power for many women principals had negative connotations, often equated to control, oppression or domination. Likewise, formal authority was seen to impart a status that was not earned. Feeling powerful in themselves was not the issue, although constantly aware of the fleeting nature of power, of feeling powerful one second and powerless the next. Many could be devastated by even a passing comment that positioned them as 'inadequate', and then 'feel strong' and effective the next. A woman 'never knows when a remark based on her gender rather than her work performance is likely to be made' (Sheppard 1992: 151). While being a woman was 'only sometimes', women forgot the centrality of their gender in their lives until such moments when 'maddeningly I am pushed into this female gender' (Riley 1988: 96). Yet they happily used power to produce change, for them power was something 'flexible, mutable, fluid' that had transformative potential (Sawicki 1991: 170). The ongoing dilemma remained, however: to desire or claim power was in itself unwomanly. It was doubly discomforting when both conservative and progressive discourses converged: neither 'feminine' nor 'feminist' women are meant to be powerful. The dilemma for Judy was that despite her preference for community, consensus, collaboration and collegiality, the values driving self-management in SOTF assumed a 'power over' perspective in which the principal is *the* change agent. This positioned teachers as resistant or passive. It also meant women principals were positioned in ways in which they found it difficult to sustain their credibility as good educational leaders or 'good' feminists.

Managing emotions and change management

Another dilemma was how to deal with the emotions of change. Effective change requires not only ownership of change, and professional collegiality but also an environment of emotional stability and attachment to others (Fullan 1993; Hargreaves 1994, 1995, 1996). Emotion is central to understanding why people become teachers and seek educational leadership, because good teaching and leadership is about passionate commitment. Self-managing institutions are particularly 'greedy organizations' – emotionally, physically and intellectually (Cozer 1974). Judy was aware that she had to maintain a constant display of positive energy to keep everything going, despite periods of emotional despair and physical exhaustion.

> After a particularly bad day I just suddenly stopped off on the way home to see *Sleepless in Seattle* and cried through it all. Tuesday was a much better day, because, like the film, it was really nice and things worked happily ever after in the end.

Yet managerialism reduces leadership to technique and not purpose, passion and desire; uncertainty is controlled by the certainty of mission statements; and visionary leadership is more about directives than vision (Louis 1994; Hargreaves 1995). Managerialism argues that a 'strong corporate culture' is the social glue that binds together the messiness of change, but it fails to address the level of emotional investment in bringing about, or resisting, change either at the individual or group level, that is, the emotional economy of organizations (Fineman 1993; Roper 1994). First, it ignores the superficiality of adherence of many workers to strong corporate cultures, driven more by anxiety and fear in uncertain employment times (Flam 1993). Second, any interest in organizational theory about emotions has been largely psychological. It individualizes emotion as stress and ignores the political, ethical and moral dimensions of emotion. Third, it fails to see that the expression of emotion serves a communicative role in developing a sense of community – a tolerance of ambiguity, and greater understanding through empathy – on political, moral or social terms.

The individualizing or denial of emotion is premised upon the gendered divide between emotion and rationality in organizational theory, which has tended to ignore emotions as being irrational and subjective. Once emotions were recognized – in the 1940s' human relations, 1970s' psychotherapeutic management training and 1980s' human resource management movements

– emotion became just another resource to be channelled into organizational ends, that is, the *management* of emotion (Rose 1992). Even social constructivist theories view organizations in 'emotionally anorexic terms of satisfaction and dissatisfaction, alienation or stress, of having preferences, attitudes and interests' (Fineman 1993: 9). Emotion in self-managing schools has become a commodity itself to be exploited through the teamwork that has come to assume mythical status as a technique of maintaining quality, commitment, enthusiasm, stimulating change, and as a change facilitator in highly instrumental ways (Hochschild 1983). What is missing in such 'contrived collegiality' are the value systems and emotional connections that bind groups together (Hargreaves 1994; Sinclair 1995).

Management theory has only addressed the positive emotions – passion, enthusiasm, verve, zest and empathy. Little is said about how 'feeling individuals worry, envy, brood, become bored, play, despair, plot, hate, hurt and so forth', the downside which Judy had to 'manage' to in her schools (Fineman 1993: 10). Indeed, repressing 'negative' emotion – embarrassment, shame and guilt – is a major aspect of organizational control.

> they are emotions which relate to how we think others are seeing us, or how our performances are judged. The discomfort of personal embarrassment can itself ensure that most people do more or less the right (organisational) thing.
>
> (Fineman 1993: 17)

Managing negative emotions is critical to performativity for women leaders, with particular emotional displays (stress, anger, fear, alienation, lack of job satisfaction) seen to be counter-productive. Hargreaves (1995: 12) comments:

> carefully regulated and tempered emotions like warmth, patience, strength, calm, caring, concern, building trust and expressing vulnerability are preferred and privileged over anger, rage, passion and sometimes even love; over emotions which are portrayed as fiercer, more negative, intensive, regressive and unruly in nature.

Thus the very emotions produced by uncertainty and the intensification of work are denied in the colonization of the emotional.

How emotion is viewed and managed is also highly gendered. It is the irrationality of women that is mythologized as they are the 'holders and purveyors of emotions . . . Thus the body politics of women in organisation may be constructed around emotionality and men's around rationality' (Parkin 1993: 170).

> While the myth of rationality was fed by discourses associating masculinity with lack of emotion and asexuality, men continued to dominate the sexual and emotional agenda of organisations through a range of

organisational practices from direct authority through to sexual
harassment, humour and symbolic violence. In the case of the latter . . .
the splitting of power from emotion.

(Parkin 1993: 169)

For women to display negative emotions such as anger, or no emotion is
to be non-feminine and uncaring; to display tears is to indicate wimp femininity, not allowed by strong women leaders, and therefore weakness. Yet
the mythology of masculine rationality is underpinned by a view that

men are too emotional, too much out of control . . . Management men
control the emotional labour of women and less powerful men, who in
turn manage the emotions of others – clients, patients, lay people, members of the public.

(Hearn 1993: 143)

Furthermore, the juxtaposition of masculinist discourses about the
market – the conquest (of new markets) and campaigns (new ideas) – works
against feminized discourses of service that echo to the 'language of care, of
concern for others and relationality' in the learning organization (Gherardi
1995: 11). Indeed, as feminist economists suggest, neoclassical economics
misconstrues what motivates people to act, change or make choices because
it sets up bipolarities between independence and interdependence, rationality and emotionality, self-interest and altruism, which do not reflect the full
range or complexity of human behaviours. Paradoxically, both the rational
self-maximizing individual of the market and the rational decisionmaker of
administration deny emotion. Yet the market relies upon desire, fear, greed
and inequality for its survival, and good leadership relies upon emotional
capacities such as empathy, intuition, trust, passion and care.

Feminist discourses on women in educational administration similarly
emphasize the positive aspects of emotion, thus trapping women into nurturing and nourishing emotions of care, warmth, patience and calm while
doing the emotional maintenance work of 'self-managing systems' (Cozer
1974). Sarah, a leading teacher, commented:

One learns early on not to be emotional or hysterical about things.
Don't show tears. You can get angry but you can't show tears. You have
to have balls – a bit masculine, aggressive and tough.

Women principals are expected to manage their own and others' negative
emotions, often denying their negative emotions of passion and anger for
their own survival, for fear of being seen to be 'weak', non-rational and psychologically inadequate.

The expression of anger has been seen as culturally acceptable for men,
but not for women. Sanctions against women's anger has long been
controlled through denigration and terms such as spitfire, bitch and nag

are applied to women and girls, but not to men and boys. Women's anger is associated here with characteristics of being sharp tongued, cruelly nasty, whiningly unpleasant or persistently annoying, while a woman expressing her anger with tears risks being described as typically emotional or manipulative.

(Court 1993: 151)

So while women principals may be seen to have considerable power, they are both vulnerable and strong (Chase 1995). They are expected to 'manage' productively for the school the unproductive emotions of anger, disillusionment, alienation – those of their teachers, their students (with high levels of unemployment, lack of employment future) and themselves.

Feminist leadership: not just a matter of style

There were a range of strategies that women principals in this research project employed when confronted with political, ethical and moral dilemmas in their work, to counter feelings of increasing anger, frustration and isolation as their early enthusiasm and energy waned. One was to work even harder and longer. Another response was to become highly task-oriented to just get things done (to the extent that they sometimes forgot the big picture). A third tactic was to focus upon procedure and process, but often to neglect the substance of change. Sometimes they distanced themselves from their decisions by stating they had to comply with line management, policy or time/resource constraints. The final option was to exit when the contradictions became too great (Blackmore 1996). Judy commented:

> The last two years have been pretty terrible. Disruptive with a lot of people under stress. Halfway through I felt as though I had hit a brick wall. I suppose it is a matter of working pretty hard and feeling as though I had lost the big picture. Everything was crowding in on me and I was still forced to get down to the nitty gritty daily things that I didn't want to do. I felt as though I was losing direction. Probably too tired and not functioning well and letting little things get to me . . . But it is also about modifying your expectations and being realistic about what you can do. What is important and where your skills are best utilized. Others can focus on specific programs. You can no longer control one area . . . everyone has to share and that is hard. I find it hard keeping on propping people up when one lacks the desire to go on oneself. It has got even more lonely – particularly with the performance pay thing. If you are friendly with anyone, it looks like favouritism.

In moving into leadership, many women have felt they must reject, sublimate or marginalize what bound them to their work as teachers – the interpersonal relationships with other teachers and children. Pat Ford (1995) suggests that a major area of contention for female principals in SOTF was the conflict arising out of balancing accountability to the DSE (Department of School Education) and their local school community and 'how to resolve the conflict of interests in these different groups without losing personal professional integrity' (1995: 28). Feeling compromised about their preference for certain styles of leadership or concern for social justice, some chose to leave rather than move upward, as that was seen to require even more overt commitment to a value system they rejected. These tensions produced moral dilemmas which led to expressions of anger, disillusionment, frustration and despair. Leadership was not just a matter of style to these women, but about valuing certain ways of working and social relationships, it was about promoting inclusive and more equitable educational practices and outcomes. Ann, a principal, commented

> It is difficult to watch the interrelationships within the department itself and the lack of respect they have in the way they deal with people in their own organizations – including principals and senior officers . . . I think this produces a moral dilemma in terms of my own career planning – where I go after being a principal.

Many new female principals were dismayed at the different culture they confronted in the principal class. Eleanor, acting head teacher in a small rural school, recalled how she 'was shocked by the alien culture at a regional Principal's Conference'. Many principals saw themselves as being 'above and beyond teaching', as 'leading from behind the principal's desk'. The individualizing and competitive discourses constituting leadership in self-managing schools exaggerated women's sense of isolation, often making them feel helpless and failures in their own terms.

At the same time, the disciplinary power of self-managing organizations pushed emotions to the limits. As one female primary principal commented when she found she was expected to become an advocate of all government policies, even those to which she was strongly opposed:

> I will follow government policy. I will offer the Learning Assessment Program to give parents a choice. But don't ask me to become an advocate or to try and hoodwink the community that they don't have any rights whether their kids sit the test or not. Some things really shake me. I had to sit back because if I act in anger I will neck myself in public. And I am not on about being a martyr. But there are those types of things we have to think around more. Once they take democracy out of schools, that is the bottom line . . . It is divide and rule.

Not only was her credibility as a principal and professional at stake, but she was being told to change long-held educational and ethical values, and her passion for education. Pauline, principal of a secondary school with over 80 per cent students of non-English speaking backgrounds, amongst them recent refugees, commented:

> I guess the thing at a philosophical or value level that I have found most difficult is lack of acknowledgement by this government that students who have traditionally been seen as disadvantaged (disabled, poor, kids of non-English speaking background, homeless) probably don't deserve anything different. The special needs staffing was slashed away from under us . . . I guess what you do is to try and make the best of what you can. If I had that decision I couldn't have morally made it. But given that it was put upon me, you make the best you can of it . . . I guess it is a coping mechanism, because if you get angry about this you lose your effectiveness, and it is not good to the kids or staff.

In this context, discourses about caring and sharing leadership can act as guilt traps for women principals who seek to maintain their educational as well as management leadership agendas at their personal cost (Hargreaves 1994; S. Acker 1995).

> I find the work emotionally and physically draining. It is because I have to have a presence in the schools with the kids as well. And you don't get that sitting in the office . . . I try to go into classes as often as I can using all sorts of excuses, bits on diaries, so that kids see me . . . Working bees with parents . . . kids see me in jeans and shovelling dirt and a variety of roles. The girls really relate to me well and come and talk often.
>
> (Nancy, secondary college principal)

The never-ending housework of the teacher – as 'mother made conscious' – is now expected of the good principal who mends the social fabric of school communities.

> The image of the teacher (and leader) as nurturer . . . offers service, dedication, patience, and love as the dominant trope for teaching, making teaching women's work, work that needs no financial compensation or reduced loads for the time that is spent . . . The nurturer, then must remain silent and thereby deny the contributions of and reinscribe the invisibility of women's work.
>
> (S. Acker 1995: 40)

Contradictory messages

I have signalled through these stories some of the dimensions of radical change as well as the overt and covert messages in new management discourse about women's special contribution to leadership. The overt message is that women must continue to be feminine, sensitive and caring – otherwise they are not seen to be good leaders (or good women). To be caring and sharing also can set women up for failure, however, for the covert message of the system is of greater efficiencies, strong and hard management, entrepreneurial not educative leadership. Women are now being encouraged to enter middle management (principalship) into SOTF because of the 'special contribution' they can make with regard to their emotional skills to oversee radical change at a time when the profession of teaching is in many ways being dismantled and devalued and the positive aspects the pleasure gained from teaching and leading – care, nurturance – are overshadowed by its negative and painful, aspects: stress, low morale, disillusionment, anxiety, fear and anger. They are expected to deal on a daily basis with the emotional housework of schools centred around the welfare of the school community at times when other community support systems (social welfare, counselling etc.) services have been decimated. While they are expected to be professional, this resort has little comfort. Many women

> fully acknowledge their continuous subjection to gendered and racial inequalities in the profession, and yet they construct individual solutions to collective problems. Through these individual solutions, women seek integration into the professional community so that they can get on with their work . . . however the structural and discursive conditions continue to discourage them from seeking collective solutions to the collective problem of inequality.
>
> (Chase 1995: xi)

The experiences of these women in leadership was that there is no simple dichotomy between professionalism and unionism, or simple equation between decentralization and democracy, or centralization and control. There was a sense that self-management put the burden of guilt on individual women, which had to be countered through more collegial, community-based and collective action as

> the discursive practices, the fine detail through which maleness and femaleness are achieved and sustained, will not change just through minor and exceptional changes in *individual power relations* . . . One woman, who is the exception, is probably . . . someone who has got her gender relations wrong – which of course she has – since the symbolic order which defines how men and women *ought* to be has not changed. Even though that particular woman may find herself more often than previously in a powerful position in relation to others, the struggles she will daily undergo to survive as a 'woman' and as a person with power will mean that one or other of these will continuously be contested as she juggles her contradictory subject positions.
>
> (Leach and Davies 1990: 327)

The self-managing post-Fordist SOTF, as elsewhere in devolved education systems, has been more about 'managed change' rather than 'change management'; about management for efficiency rather than governance for democratic citizenship (Moller 1993; Louis 1994; Whitty 1994; Gewirtz *et al.* 1995; Blackmore *et al.* 1996; Wylie 1997). Many women principals regrouped to work through the market in more collegial and community-oriented ways by developing socially responsible school policies. This meant promoting their schools collectively, not competitively as part of a public system; by sharing school resources and best practice; by using the language of education, not business; and by nurturing collegial support networks. They were still the buffers of a system under stress, however (Blackmore 1996). Women have historically been 'held responsible' for the caring and emotional aspects of education, for the free development of the child, as the moral arbiter of schooling, and now the emotional managers of a quasi-market system. It is a responsibility that brings with it pain and guilt when, due to the material conditions of their work as well as the managerialist and market values driving the system, many women principals are unable to practice feminist educational leadership. Leadership, as an educative and participatory practice, in new hard times is difficult, dangerous and de-valued.

8 Embodied authority: the disciplined but disruptive body of powerful women

Femininity, says Bartky (1990: 65) is an artifice and achievement, 'a mode of enacting and re-enacting received gender norms which surface as so many styles of the flesh'. Women in management mask their gender and sexuality through how they dress, walk and talk in order to minimize their female presence and 'manage the disturbance of difference they represent'. All these strategies are 'continually precarious and leave their credibility and organisational membership in doubt' (Marshall 1996: 6).

> By forcing women with public roles who seek change to personify ideals which do not make sense in everyday life, by divesting them of both passion and angularity, we destroy them . . . The preoccupation with appearance is the clue. It is an indicator of the profound panic around identity, power and desirability.
>
> (Rowbotham 1987: 9)

This chapter explores how women in leadership deal with the masculine embodiment of authority, and how the body itself is a site of resistance as well as domination in gender power relations in educational organizations.

Dressing up

The 'physical sense of maleness and femaleness is central to the cultural interpretations of gender' and 'the social relations of gender are both realised and symbolised in the bodily performances' (Connell 1995: 54). Central to the act of 'performing' leadership is the body. Women leaders made frequent reference to being careful about dress, of dressing for the occasion, of being highly conscious of their bodily appearance, of being different, but not too different. They spoke of the body not as a sociobiological pre-given, or as a 'neutral surface upon which culture works' (Connell 1995: 54), but as a living, breathing and ageing thing. Each performance of leadership is simultaneously symbolic, social, and physical: symbolic in the sense that they are women in male-dominated jobs; social in terms of how they relate to others; and physical in the sense that the very presence of the body of women in authority challenges gender power relations.

Yet organizational life disembodies individuals at one level by privileging the mental over the bodily, and simultaneously embodies them as male and female. Collinson and Collinson (1990) argue that while management did not consciously seek to desexualize organizations, that is the outcome. Rather, they see the overriding organizational theme is that of the domination of men's (hetero)sexuality as a way of reinforcing and sustaining their power through horseplay, the exploitation of sexuality, sexual harassment/discrimination and mutual sexuality. These are the disciplinary modes that discourage women to enter male-dominated workplaces (Collinson and Collinson 1990: 92–3). For women to resist positions them as troublemakers. Compulsory heterosexuality has disciplinary power in that it positions single women in particular as deviant, different and dangerous, either because of their implied lesbianism or sexual availability (Blount 1994; Weiler 1994).

> It is men who use or deploy their sexuality at work far more than women, and yet it is women's workplace identity that is frequently saturated with sexuality . . . the real nub is heterosexuality . . . and within which men establish both their difference from women – as they simultaneously force a male homo sociability – and their power over them.
>
> (Gutek 1990: 63)

It is women's sexuality, not men's, which is constantly made visible because of its potential threat to disciplinary modes of organizational life (Cockburn 1991). Male sexuality and bodies are invisible because their sexuality or use of the body is natural, the norm, but female desire (in particular for power) is 'rabid and dangerous' (Collinson and Collinson 1990: 94).

Gender, sexuality and the body are part of the complex 'technology of control' within organizations, and how women come to be integrated unequally into organizational life. For the minority of women in a predominantly male domain, female sexuality requires more overt control through codes of dress, language and manner because of their visibility (Marshall 1996). So on the one hand it is possible for women to accept that they really are equal to men in terms of capacities in leadership, but then, on the other,

> organise their interactions on the basis of their assigned sex, and all the assumptions that attend that assignment . . . It is not just a cognitive task, but also bodily . . . Each person's body takes on the knowledge of 'maleness' or 'femaleness' through its practices. The most obvious and superficial forms of bodily practices that distinguish male and female are dress and hairstyle.
>
> (Leach and Davies 1990: 319)

In turn, this unstable relation is maintained in the way in which the organization

> reincorporates parts of the person, including sexuality, segmented from each other by organizational definition and redefinition in roles, tasks and job description. Sexuality is constructed as both a separable and a defining characteristic for women differently to men.
>
> (Hearn and Parkin 1992: 153)

Furthermore, the male gaze on the female body is a subtle form of control both within and outside organizations. Sexuality and the body, as social constructs, are sites for control of, and resistance by, the subject. 'Deviant' dress (e.g. women wearing slacks) or language (e.g. swearing) therefore signify organizational opposition.

Acknowledging the body as a site of power makes transparent the connections between masculinity, knowledge and power, thus exacerbating the Enlightenment's 'crisis of reason' and making problematic its 'Cartesian opposition between "the mind and body" in ways which set up "the spirit and rational thought" in opposition to the "emotions, passions, needs"' (McNay 1992: 12). Whereas modernist classical sociology separated body from mind, the primary focus of postmodernist thought is on the commodification of the body possessing both cultural and physical capital. Thus the crisis of masculinity, often portrayed as a crisis of the male body (health), has led to shifts away from the muscular view of men as primary breadwinners. 'The body in consumer culture is a bearer of symbolic value, so there is a tendency for people to place ever more importance on the body as constitutive of the self' (Giddens 1995).

The body enters into the maintenance of social relations of dominance and subordination. When men open doors for women, this is not merely symbolic, but actively constitutes gender inequalities. A man 'steers' a woman (rather like a well trained horse) in a 'light and gentle but firm grip', treating women as faulted actors without the 'normal' capacity for physical exertion (Bartky 1990). Social categories not only define bodies differently, but gendered social practices seek to transform it – change the meaning and nature of people's bodies to conform to images of masculinity and femininity which positions the feminine as the 'weaker sex' physically, which, in turn, is extrapolated to all aspects of social life (e.g. strong leadership). Yet there is often little congruence between the biological aspects of the body and these meanings. Gender difference is constructed based on gender superiority of the male body where such differences are often fantasy in terms of body size and capacity for action. This discrepancy, however, sustains male social power (Connell 1987: 85).

The female body at risk

Foucault (1980b) sees the body as a site both of production and internaliza-
tion of various disciplinary regimes enforced through institutions such as
prisons, clinics and schools. Discourses about the body link powerful knowledges to specific organizational practices. Thus the 'microphysics of power
operates in modern institutional formations through progressively finer
channels, gaining access to individuals, themselves, to their bodies, their ges-
tures and all their daily actions' (Foucault 1980b: 151). In internalizing that
which is feminine, the feminine subject is 'a practiced and subjected body'
(Bartky 1990: 71). Resisting dominant constructions of femininity is to challenge the sense of self as a gendered identity and mastery. To do so is risky.
The body is symbolic of risk which is co-based upon social location and
stratification. Some individuals can take more risks with their bodily appearance than others, for example artists more so than air hostesses. While male
bureaucrats or leaders cannot take risks by not conforming to particular
dress codes, they embody masculinity as the norm. Women, already perceived as a risk, cannot flaunt the norm. Bartky (1990: 67) refers to Iris
Young's depiction of how

> space seems to surround women in imagination which they are hesitant
> to move beyond. This manifests itself both in a reluctance to reach,
> stretch and extend the body to meet resistances of matter in motion –
> as in sport or in the performance of physical tasks – and in a typically
> constructed posture and general style of movement.

Women generally do not sit in meetings with legs splayed widely and hands
clasped behind head, arms openly outstretched to embrace the world.

Women's bodies have been subject to the control of the male gaze, and
this has become institutionalized into a range of repressive practices. The
gendered nuances of how women's bodies have been inscribed as passive,
soft, receptive and submissive are extrapolated into all avenues of social
relationships, whereas men's bodies are preconceived as being active, hard,
initiating and aggressive. Female bureaucrats in particular felt that their
bodily female presence was a primary source of uncertainty and uncomfortableness because it overtly threatened masculinity. Relative to normative masculinity – embodied as white male bureacrats in dark suits, white
shirts and ties – various versions of the 'feminine body' are constructed in
ways that were both different and readily definable. Social practices focus
upon particular norms of 'desirable' femininity. In particular, certain
women who did not fit stereotypic images of the female body were significantly affected by the ways in which they were viewed as bureaucrats – they
were cast as deviant, difficult and certainly not promotable. Judgements
were made on appearances from how women dressed through to their size.
As Bev commented:

This place certainly has all those uncriticized, unconscious discriminatory things which constantly occur. The fact that you don't wear suits, I think, makes you different. A number of us are large. What happens is that people never think about you as doing particular things. And you never come onto their agenda.

Being large, for women, was undesirable. Their sexual undesirability was conflated into their work undesirability, thus undermining their status and authority. Being large, for men, added to their powerful presence as men – being large was an extension of embodied authority or masculinity in general. Thus disciplinary power was not located in particular men or even the institution of the bureaucracy – but it was located in different norms, 'it is everywhere and it is nowhere' (Bartky 1990: 74). It is this absence of formally unidentifiable disciplinarities that disguises the extent to which there are imperatives to be 'masculine' and 'feminine'. To refuse to act out the role is to fear sanction in the withdrawal of male patronage, when and if it is sought. Even then, the disciplinary project of femininity is a set-up in that women inevitably fail to meet the prescribed bodily specifications (Bartky 1990: 72).

The body also brings in emotion. Many women spoke of how what they wore was often an indicator of their emotional state: 'I knew I was feeling low when I went to the wardrobe and took out a red suit'(Angela). We also classify other bodies as our own, and endure the same feelings of embarrassment for others in what we feel embarrassed about ourselves and our bodies. Some of the femocrats felt embarrassed for a female manager who put on too much makeup and wore tight skirted suits and short cropped dyed blond hair, for making a caricature of herself, for not 'dressing down' as a female bureaucrat and by mixing up stereotypic femininity with being a bit too 'butch'. Stigmatized people such as those women who try to pass as normal by 'dressing up' risk having the gap between the image they seek to construct and how they are perceived made transparent.

Dress was also read as a statement. It symbolized conformity or opposition to organizational and often masculinist norms. How one clothed the body meant taking a position in organizational gender politics. All the femocrats and principals in these studies recognized that they dressed for the job of leadership differently from when they were teachers. For some, not fitting a stereotypic female image led to marginalization. One leadership aspirant saw getting promotion relied upon changing her image:

I know I don't dress well. I have never been comfortable with my body – I'm going to take a course to improve my appearance.

Compliance is, according to Connell (1987: 186–8), recognizable in that forms of 'emphasized femininity' accommodate the interests and desires of men – dressing up for them. Emphasized femininity is not hegemonic in the

same sense as dominant hegemonic masculinity which this form of femininity upholds and for which it performs. Those who did not fit this image of
emphasized femininity were cast as oppositional or deviant. Susan, for
example, spoke of how

> you play the game in terms of conforming in ways which are not as
> important. If that means wearing a dress I don't see that it detracts from
> my ability to work for women or asking questions as to why women are
> disadvantaged.

She was therefore amused, but not surprised, on the day she wore tailored
trousers, at the comment by a male colleague: 'So you *are* a feminist!'

Many female bureaucrats spoke of how they dressed to subvert – wearing
strong colours such as red, lipstick and new hairstyles, to symbolize their
power or strength. Dressing against the norm gave them pleasure, but it was
also dangerous, requiring them to carefully balance between fitting 'the
feminine stereotype' without being a 'butch feminist' or being seen to be
'complicit' in reinforcing dominant 'macho and competitive' masculinities
by being too feminine.

> That women dress in 'feminine' suits but with the power shoulders both
> signals desirability and conformity – the colours are neutral and soft,
> but with the touch of femininity – the subtle jewellery, the brooch or
> pin. It also distinguishes women from the ill fitting shirt, cropped hair
> of the 'butch' feminist who dressed in overlarge suits, ties and braces,
> stating that I can both conform and dare not to conform.
>
> (Coward 1985: 35)

Dress was an intense issue for those women who were labelled as 'radical'
and 'feminist'. Many feminists, particularly in male-dominated sites,
actively used the body as a site of uncertainty by dressing up in highly feminine ways to disrupt preconceptions about what it is to be feminist. Feminists now possess a more sophisticated wardrobe and repertoire of skills.

> Many women see the preservation of women's femininity as compatible
> with her struggle for liberation . . . they have rejected the normative
> femininity based upon the notion of 'separate spheres' and the tra-
> ditional sexual division of labour while accepting at the same time con-
> ventional standards of feminine bodily display.
>
> (Bartky 1990: 78)

Yet for women to call attention to the female body, even in jest, was seen
to be disruptive, to break the regulatory codes, because it was not part of the
male discursive positioning of women as objects of desire. It exposed
power/body relations. Thus one femocrat, a strong unionist, was told by her
male superior that her behaviour was inappropriate when she playfully
pinned up a display of shoulder pads, ranked and sorted by size and style,

on the office board above her desk. The offence was not so much that it exposed what women needed to do to 'embody' authority in hierarchical bureaucracies, a joke enjoyed by most women and men working there, but that the white pads provoked other more disturbing images of female sexuality and bodily functions, such as sanitary pads.

Women, both in the bureaucracy and principalship in an era of performativity, were aware that 'impression management' was critical for their credibility in the sense that they could not step over the defined boundaries of their prescribed sexuality. Julie spoke about how particular images of managers meant she had to gain legitimacy first through what she looked like rather than what she said or did.

> When I dressed 'properly', I was more likely to be heard: My long hair had to be up . . . but I didn't wear lipstick. It was helpful that my [female] coworker was older, looked straight and fairly senior . . . Up to that time I had been able to dress and act as the maverick.

As Gherardi (1995: 13) comments: 'cropped hair conveys a sense of excessive masculinisation, whereas overlong hair has a "sexiness" that clashes with the role of woman manager and the authority that conveys'. The female manager's body is carefully scripted against particular ideals. Geraldine, a secondary college principal, spoke about how she was careful to decide what she wore each day given the specific tasks:

> I don't want to look too dressed up for a sports day, but you cannot go in a track suit. I was surprised how the women on the parents' day dressed up, and responded accordingly.

Thus

> In accommodating ourselves to the physical fantasy of women we make ourselves more attractive, and thus find it easier to pass into the established institutional structures, but we also reinforce our own prisons by legitimating the structures of femininity. The repudiation of femininity often associated with professional women replicates the stereotypes of femininity precisely because it is these stereotypes that are being repudiated as the truth of Woman.
>
> (Cornell 1995: 84)

It is the female body that is most visible, particularly when in authority. Students, when asked to characterize leadership in a school with both a female principal and vice principal, referred not only to their work roles but also made frequent reference to the principal's appearance (high heels, suits with shoulder pads and height) and the vice principal's short and slight stature. Whereas women were more often described by appearance, male principals embodied authority. Matthew, a young teacher of three years, was particularly alienated by a male principal who was a very large, physical type person. He got his way by literally brow beating and standing over you – the real bully type . . . But the new female principal is different, she is a negotiator and assessor of people, and in my opinion a far more effective manager.

Being tall was an advantage for women leaders, and was particularly advantageous for women to be physically 'above' many men. It meant, as one female manager argued

I am able to look them in the eye. It is far more difficult for men, individually or collectively, to ignore me when I can insert myself between them when talking in groups and physically, but subtly, demand acknowledgement of my presence. Smaller women are, because of their stature, forced to speak 'up' to men, often using their voices to claim attention in a more overt fashion, and thus appear loud and shrill. As a tall woman it is possible for me to speak softly and be heard.

(Ann)

Being tall, while imparting personal dominance and a commanding presence, was admired in women because it also suggested they were tough. Being tall was not enough, however.

Leadership could also have something to do with the shapes of people. I am a tall person and I impose a bit. But I am also not physically big. I look sort of very, maybe, fragile. But I compensate for that with my drive, my enthusiasm, and what I get done.

(Angela)

The body is a site of regulation. It also indicates the disciplinary power of the managed self as individual's practice self-surveillance. Women's organizational status is often overridden by their sexual and embodied identity because power and authority are embodied in highly masculinist ways, as the following case study shows.

'Bins, bells, bulletins and bad boys': authority and the body

In schools, authority is closely associated with masculinity and student discipline. Indeed, masculinity, as racism, only becomes an issue when associated with student discipline, and then only when connected to overt student violence, not adult male symbolic violence (Mac an Ghaill 1994). This ignores institutionalized power relations and the role particular adult masculinities play in constructing and maintaining masculinist cultures that are conducive to violent behaviours. In this particular secondary school, Chatsworth, there was a dominant discourse that linked macho masculinity to disciplinary authority and school image. It was embodied in a legendary male figure, the former vice principal, Frank, upon whom many of the male staff had modelled themselves. His physical presence alone, I was frequently told by staff and students of both sexes, was able to quell even the most disruptive male students. His authority was clearly associated with the 'masculine' attributes of physicality, rationality, lack of emotion and hardness. A female staff member recalled the power he held on the principal selection panel:

> Well it was the old boys' club, you know. And then we had school council parent representatives who were mums of kids of families that have gone through this school for ages. They idolized the vice principal and just followed him and did whatever he said.

The macho-masculinity/authority association represented by Frank was privileged in conservative community discourses about conventional family life and reinforced through his leadership in male-dominated sporting and community organizations. One less than sympathetic female teacher commented: 'Nobody can step into his shoes – just nobody'. Another recalled: 'He was a very straight person – never showed emotion other than cold anger with kids'. Most staff saw him as overtly strict and physically aggressive with students in public, using implied but often overt physical threats, although privately he displayed other sides. One female teacher recalled, after a difficult staffing decision, being shocked and embarrassed when she found him 'on the verge of tears' in his office. Not all men adhered to his hegemonic masculinity. Jeff commented on the arrival of the female VP:

> In this school there was no doubt amongst the kids that discipline would go out the window and the school would go downhill because a tough person was no longer VP. This was from day one. It was not totally a gender thing. Even as males go, the former VP was more macho than most. Yet behind closed doors he wasn't really like that. He was actually quite caring and quite skilled in dealing with kids. It was just his persona in front of everyone was different. And he was effective because he could play across the range of behaviours . . . so it was a complicated gender politics for the woman who took his place.

The new female vice principal, Helen, had been redeployed from regional office where she had previously acted as a consultant to principals, to work with teachers increasingly cynical about administrators lacking immediate past school experience. Helen also 'took' the job to which many male members of staff aspired. Her appointment intensified the subtle antagonism and mythologies regarding the 'unfairness' to men of equal opportunities policies held by many male teachers, particularly those most attached to the discursive practices of macho masculinity in the school.

On finding no job description, Helen sought to redefine the traditional role of vice principal, traditionally that of 'bins, bells, bulletins and bad boys', to include policy and curriculum matters.

My preferred style was being able to discuss things and to listen to a range of opinions, questions and concerns. I wanted at the beginning of the year to model a more gentle culture, a more caring culture, a more concerned culture within the school, away from the macho heavies.

Staff spoke about how many parents queried within days of her appointment: 'How are you coping since the male VP left? I hear discipline's gone out the window'. Helen recalled some time later parents informing her, 'Oh we were very concerned about standards of discipline deteriorating in the school with a female as vice principal, but it's good to see that it hasn't'. The discourse about the demise of discipline, according to most staff, with the exception of the 'old male guard', was inaccurate. Indeed, many staff indicated that the discipline issues were manufactured by a few threatened male staff. As Harry put it, certain male staff had 'tried the female VP out a bit' by sending up 'difficult boys' to her unnecessarily. This behaviour was, according to a female staff member, 'especially because she is a female and a female known in the community as being prominent, confident and determined to get her own way'. Because 'the links between masculinity and authority have accorded men a measure of cultural capital, building them in others an expectation of their "natural" ability and right to lead organizations', there was an implicit acceptance that to test her out was OK, if not normal (Court 1994: 36).

While many of their male colleagues denigrated in private the behaviour of the male staff in undermining the vice principal's authority as unprofessional, no public criticism was made. Indeed, all men benefit, even if unconsciously, from dominant masculinities. Most male staff were often, if reluctantly, drawn into misogynist jokes about women's lack of effectiveness and harking back to the good old days of a more disciplinary regime. Individual men's 'bad' behaviour is thus supported by the cultural ethos of the school, which naturalizes patriarchy and which 'writes off particular staff on a hard–soft continuum as ineffective, irrational, hysterical and not able' – women, blacks and men who do not conform (Salisbury and Jackson 1996: 20).

The vice principal, shocked at the culture of implicit violence underlying her predecessor's disciplinary approach, developed through a consultative process a new disciplinary policy. This policy sought to redistribute disciplinary responsibilities amongst teachers, coordinators and the vice principal and set up clear procedures, a common approach in schools. This undermined the particularly macho masculinity that was integral to the professional identities, if not authority, of particular male staff. Secondary schools, as active agents in construction of masculinities, make male control (and self-control of the softer emotions) and discipline central.

Boys recognize this power all around them . . . The work of caring and nurturing is inevitably downgraded in such an atmosphere of masculinity power and authority . . . avoiding showing sensitivity and displaying emotions is essential if boys are not to be thought of as weak. Boys recognize the toughening process which is at work as they skilfully avoid the pitfalls of ridicule.

(Salisbury and Jackson 1996: 21)

Mac an Ghaill (1994) refers to schools as masculinizing agencies. Schooling is about the interplay of a 'system of male power and the sense of anxiety around losing that power', an anxiety intensified in a period of radical restructuring (Salisbury and Jackson 1996: 19). This anxiety was manifested in behaviour towards students, but in particular the 'vicious side to fear and anxiety is the male need to exercise power over women' and 'losing face or control means not measuring up to the manly ideal . . . fear drives men to buy into the security provided by strong leadership and patriarchal values' (Salisbury and Jackson 1996: 18–19). Masculinity has to be 'achieved, worked at and accomplished moment by moment in the drive to attain a secure masculine identity and as part of that what it means to be a "real man"' (Kerfoot and Knights 1993: 663).

Within weeks of Helen initiating the new disciplinary procedures based on delegation, an actively subversive institutional discourse of resistance emerged, constructing her as 'weak', and the male level coordinators as 'strong', in propping up her disciplinary authority. As one male teacher wryly observed, this meant the new policy was actually working, not that the vice principal was failing, because level coordinators and teachers were meant to take more responsibility for discipline. Many teachers saw the reliance on the former vice principal's authority, while comfortable for teachers, as an abrogation of professional responsibility. All the female teachers believed Helen's consensual welfare approach converged with their own personal practice. As one female member of staff commented about the authoritarian regime of the former VP:

His was not my sort of discipline. But I suppose Helen is sort of similar to me, as she can't raise her voice and hasn't got this big strong voice to assert her authority. So you do other things. And of course maybe she doesn't want to do it that way, and neither do I. I don't want kids sitting trembling in their shoes. He used to be seen as the head of the school by many parents. He did a lot of the principal's work anyway and so coming in after that image existed was extremely hard.

This subversive discourse positioned the VP in contradictory ways. She was positioned as 'weak' and responsible for 'disciplinary breakdown'. The large number of students who visited her office to 'talk with her' was cited as evidence of her 'being a pushover' and 'soft'. A male year level coordinator, Joe, stated proudly that when he was acting VP 'There were no kids lining up to talk to me!' Gary expressed surprise that the students did not 'take advantage more of the VP's weakness' and that students were 'handling the new mode of operation well'. While this new disciplinary regime under female 'authority' most threatened those male teachers whose proclivity was for the coercive approach to student discipline, it was these same teachers who asserted that the 'strong authoritarian approach' of the previous VP was largely for the benefit of the women teachers who, by implication, had greater disciplinary problems. It was a paternalistic masculinity that

> facilitated a reduction of the tensions surrounding management and individual masculinities by simulating typically patriarchal, family-like relations where power is exercised as a form of 'protection' for the 'good' of the recipient who was unable to protect themselves.
>
> (Kerfoot and Knights 1993: 665)

In this instance both students and female staff were inscribed by this paternalistic discourse as being in need of such protection. As one female teacher commented, however:

> The thing I find hardest is getting the kids' respect and that is perhaps harder having such as strong disciplinarian as the former VP. Ultimately all discipline ended with him and the kids knew it. It undermined one's authority.

The institutionalized discourse of 'macho' masculinity constituted the minds and bodies of individuals as part of a wider network of gendered power relations, however. In particular, this discourse connected the VP's 'weakness' to her physical presence, her femaleness, her smallness in stature, soft voice and quiet, if not sometimes abrasive, manner. The close relationship between the body and authority was clear. It was a discourse that also constructed students as being incapable of accepting new disciplinary modes which were non-authoritarian, thus maintaining a particular version of aggressive, hierarchical authority embodied in the masculinist construction of organizations.

Perversely, Helen was also positioned as unfeminine, aggressive, conflictual and hard when she did call upon her formal authority in informing an increasingly violent teacher that his intimidatory behaviour was unacceptable and she would take action against him if he continued. She felt partially gratified when later her most difficult boys' class told her that 'he doesn't dare do the things he did last year, this year . . . ever since you arrived'. This class, it had been assumed, would

> eat her up and spit her out. Yet she plugged away. I think she has got through to these boys. I saw a change and acceptance of her in their different behaviour.
>
> (Jeff)

So although the discourse associating macho masculinity with disciplinary authority was not drawn upon passively or unselectively by students, as is often assumed, it certainly privileged particular types of masculinities over other masculinities and all femininities in ways which often reinforced like behaviours amongst the boys. Dominant school cultures work through fantasy and desire, as well as fear, and her initiatives put masculinity and authority at risk.

> Our collective imagery, taken from the popular culture of what it is like to be a 'real' man reasserting control, takes over from the inside . . . and gives us the power and security of the 'males on top' identity which was seen to be slipping away.
>
> (Salisbury and Jackson 1996: 19)

While many of the male teachers were not involved actively in subverting Helen's authority, they were, with their silence, complicit in her depiction as unsuccessful. Indeed they could benefit from her demise as the likelihood was that the next VP selected would not be female, and possibly one of them. By not challenging such practices, the naturalness of the association between disciplinary authority and masculinity went unchallenged.

The more masculinity asserts itself, however, the more it calls itself into question. Hegemonic masculinities linking authority to 'hardness' also position many men unfavourably. Matthew, a young male secondary teacher in his 20s who was renowned for his commitment to kids, commented about how he felt guilty at enjoying teaching, but this meant

> The only way I discipline kids is by appealing to them. Once in a while I fantasize total control. Just clap my hands and kids just sit there. The reality is that it is a lot of hard work.

Matthew is putting his masculinity at risk when he states:

> I teach on emotion. I am an emotionally charged person. When I am up, I am really up and life is full and dynamic. I teach through personality – song and dance man, jokes etc . . . I think authority is based on respect . . . the principal needs to be someone who is articulate, has vision, can motivate people through reason, cajoling and encouraging . . . The last two male principals were more gung-ho. Insecure about their decisions, so they had to blast them through and stare anyone down who didn't agree, and that didn't achieve unity. I don't consider myself a typical male anyway. I'm not really a macho sort – I detest the footy club ocker male. They really piss me off.

At the same time the local gendered power relations embedded in the institutional discourse which associated macho masculinity with discipline tapped into extralocal discourses about what constituted good schools – a critical element in the educational market. Teachers, no matter how supportive of

Helen, expressed concern about the effects of her being VP on the school's reputation built around 'good discipline'.

> I thought it was great. I did wonder if it was a bit much too soon. There are a lot of guys on the staff who have been here for many years for whom it will be extremely threatening. They already are highly threatened by the ministry restructuring. But having a female vice principal is closer to home. I think it may be the last straw and they will not be able to handle it.
>
> (Kay, leading teacher)

While Kay, in voicing male fears about radical change, was 'mending the social fabric' of the school by empathizing with a now-redundant mode of macho masculinity, she was acutely aware, as a member of the principal selection committee, of community discourses associating strong leadership with discipline. Attracting and retaining students was now critical to maintain funding in the context of the educational market. Market status is gained by a well-disciplined student population. The market thus privileged particular 'masculinist' images of leadership, and, as in self-governing schools in England and New Zealand, 'culturally produced links between masculinity and authority grounded in skills of numeracy, technical logic and business competitiveness that can be seen to equip men as the people best suited to running schools as business enterprises' (Court 1994: 36; Mac An Ghaill 1994).

Fear of the feminine? masculinity and authority

This case study illustrates how initiatives to develop inclusive leadership practices in schools must deal with the considerable investment most men and some women have in existing gender relations, as well as the gendered association between particular cultural and discursive practices. While recent reforms and the market largely reinforce rather than transform the benchmark male as leader, such images are increasingly difficult to maintain in reality. It also indicates how masculine identity is closely tied up in a network of complex power/authority relationships, and that professional males have been no more progressive in their gender politics than working-class or blue-collar workers (Segal 1990).

There are two sides to this issue. First is the clear manifestation of the fear of the feminine amongst the men whose gendered professional identity was so closely associated with macho masculinity when confronted with women in positions of power and leadership. The 'instability of masculinity', dependent as it is upon the steady confirmation of power from what can prove unstable social institutions and practices, is dependent also upon its hierarchically understood difference from what can prove to be insubordinate 'others'. The dilemma for heterosexual masculinity is both to reject any sense of desire for the feminine or the homosexual while outwardly subordinating both (Segal 1990: 123). Feminist object relation theory explains male fear of effeminacy and their psychology for success in a competitive capitalist world, as a consequence of having to separate from the mother and to reject all that is feminine, as 'not masculine', soft or weak, in order to acquire their masculine autonomous self as aggressive and independent. Gender change will occur, it is argued, when men undertake a more equal role in parenting so that male identity construction does not require rejection of the feminine and fear of intimacy (Chodorow 1978).

Such psychological explanations are inadequate in changing masculinity. Men's absence from childcare is as much due to external (cultural, social and political) than internal (psychological) constraints, because they do not explain the nature, power and privilege bestowed on masculinity through a range of cultural, social and institutional practices. Indeed, they assume that women will continue their conventional maternal functions (Segal 1990: 81). The devaluing of mothering does not explain the symbolic and real power wielded by men. Rather, 'masculinity "becomes an issue" precisely because it is so valued and desirable' (Segal 1990: 82). Nor are men necessarily emotional anorexics requiring the emotional nurturance of women to survive (women as the 'safety valve' for male emotional sublimation); they are just selectively emotive. Men benefit from mothering, but thrive on competitiveness and bonding, highly emotional work in which there is significant ego investment (Bartky 1990).

The other side to this is that 'men and women internalise the notion that a woman with power and authority was anomalous' (Eisenstein 1996: 133–4). Women felt the need to apologize for being in authority. Kathleen Jones argues that feminists have failed to deal with the issue of authority, as distinct from power – treating authority in the public domain as different from that in the private.

> We want authority; we want to explode it; we want those who have not had authority to take it for themselves . . . Yet we insist that we will not practice authority in the same way as the dominant class – those who already have authority – have done; monopolising it and keeping others out.
>
> (Jones 1993: 5)

It is the severance from institutional modes of power (i.e. authority) that is distinctive about women's oppression, and in turn how authority is worked through the body and emotions. Authority is seen to be legitimate power gained through formal position. As with power, however, authority has also been rejected by feminists, many of whom have sought a position of 'safety outside authority' by not seeking it in formal leadership (Jones

1995). A consequence of not dealing with authority as the exercise of legitimate power, because both power and authority are viewed to be repressive and negative, oppressive and masculinist, is the production of a sense of 'victimhood'. One resolution has been to resort to more idealized conceptualizations of power as represented in discourses of maternal power or 'power from within' rather than 'power over' – at the risk of idealizing and sentmentalizing one set of relations, no matter how universal. As I have argued earlier, being caring in itself does not provide an alternative model of political or economic power. The view that one can 'empower' also smacks of paternalism, denying agency (and indeed resistance), which may also mean resistance to 'empowering' feminist discourses.

Carmen Luke (1996) argues that 'feminists face a double bind being in authority and power'. The bind lies with the feminist disavowal of authority as power and desire coupled with feminism's first principle of differences which leads to the 'masquerade of good girl feminism and locates feminist pedagogy [and leadership] on one side of the nurture/authority dichotomy'. After having been powerless for many years, women in powerful positions often act powerless and victimized because they have a lot of trouble with their own authority.

> I think that we never feel in power. I don't know what it means to feel in power. Women and feminists in particular, having tried to theorise it, to think through some different ways of dealing with power and authority, especially power and authority in relation to other women and other feminists – and find it extremely difficult to actually acknowledge that at times they are powerful persons in powerful positions. And for feminists it is doubly troubling as they have a theoretical position to eschew taking the masculinity position of 'power over', the form of hegemonic authoritarianism against which they have rebelled.
>
> (Luke 1996: 285)

Another dimension of this is how power is asserted through the body, the embodiment of authority. To shift this position is to recognize that it is not that women do not enjoy power, but rather that they are more wary about how it is exercised and with what effects, having experienced power as domination, in which physical power is the bottom line. Likewise, they will accept authority, but reject a view of authority that is depicted as disembodied, rational and dispassionate. To shift this position requires dissolving the dichotomy between compassion and authority, contributing to the association of the authoritative with the male voice and which

> normalises authority by opposing it to emotive connectedness or compassion . . . Authority orders existence through rules . . . Compassion cuts across this order universe with feelings that connect us to the

specificity and particularity of actions and actors. Authority distances us from the person. Compassion puts us in a face-to-face encounter with another.

(Jones 1993: 120–1)

It means not positioning women as victims of authority and power, but as exercising power, not domination, and embodying a form of compassionate authority earned through respect, trust and reciprocity in social relationships and not merely formal, symbolic or rational authority associated with particular masculine bodily representations.

9 Dealing with difference

Feminist researchers' understandable desire to emphasize the positive aspects of women's experience in leadership and women's success has often led to the romanticization of women's leadership work and fed populist discourses about women's caring and sharing leadership styles. The focus of research has been on gender equity reform, on exemplary models of leadership and feminist practice, on those seen to be 'good practitioners', 'reformers' and 'change agents', rather than on the women who are cynics, the disinterested or even those resistant to feminism. It has focused upon similarities amongst a relatively homogeneous group of white middle-class women, in part because it is easier to research within the comfort zone of one's own experience of being white, middle-class and academic, and not to step into dangerous areas discussing difference; and in part because this reflects the dominance of such women. I am guilty of all the above research practices.

The populist reading of the feminist discourse of the power of the collective and the sisterhood has also meant any highlighting of difference amongst women, or criticisms of women in leadership, by other women is viewed as disloyal and subversive of the feminist principle of valuing women. As yet, at the institutional and interpersonal level, women lack experience about how to deal with peer relationships when in power and authority, how to negotiate the difficult territory between powerful and less powerful women, and mediate differences based on age, experience, organization power, and political beliefs. For example, a femocrat working in an EO unit in the Victorian bureaucracy was criticized for challenging the feminist collective.

It was because I criticized the totally disabling types of collective practices of many of my feminist colleagues because they never got anything done, because no one would assume responsibility as an individual, and everything had to go through the group. It meant we were viewed as being ineffective, and that was even worse for us in terms of credibility and strategically. They refused to recognize the need for leadership at all, or for some individual to take an issue and run with it in the best way possible. It meant we could not tap into the organizational networks, and were just marginalized.

While a sense of the collective was a source of empowerment, it could become, when not actively reflected upon, a source of control about what could be said and done by 'good' feminists. Similarly, the universalizing tendencies of feminist discourses about leadership provided considerable scope for appropriation by non-feminist women, who benefited from EO policies without any sacrifice for the sisterhood. Even feminist activists, Eva Cox (1996: 13–14) argues, need to recognize the range of ways in which we often sabotage our own efforts:

> By judging ourselves and other women by rules we haven't had a say in making, we act as agents of special control to restrict the activities of women . . . Those who identify with, and or are validated by, the current models act as gatekeepers for them, but, more surprisingly, so do many women who see themselves as change agents. These women often do not see their own complicity in the process of denying other women power.

This chapter focuses on the difficulties of negotiating the discursive terrain of feminist discourses of leadership, about how the conflation of 'being female' to 'being feminist' can produce undesirable effects, and about female complicity in maintaining hegemonic masculinities in leadership. I also argue, in the Australian context, that feminist discourses of leadership continue to ignore how culture, class and race, rather than gender, are foregrounded in the discursive construction of 'self as leader', and in so doing neglect important alternative leadership discourses.

'I'm not a feminist but . . .'

Women in educational leadership exemplify the 'contradictory experiences of achievement and discrimination', although in culturally different ways (Chase 1995: 31; Glazer 1991). While many of the women interviewed in my research projects did not name themselves as feminist, nearly all unproblematically appealed to feminist discourses about women's styles of leadership and the critical mass theory of gender reform (more women in leadership will transform the male culture). Many women rejected being named 'feminist' because it smacked of politics. While the discursive realm of professionalism was taken for granted by many women, the discursive realm of social justice was 'relatively unsettled', 'explicitly ideological' and more 'self-conscious' (Chase 1995: 38). Being professional was about expertise (implying neutrality) and working for social justice (and being feminist) was about overt value commitments that could be labelled as 'ideological', thus undermining women's much sought after public credibility.

Many rejected the term 'feminist' because of its depiction in popular discourses as being 'rabid', 'ball busters', 'man haters' and 'a lesbo', thus equating feminism with abnormality. Being aggressively feminist was also seen not to be strategic, and closed promotion opportunities.

> Bronwyn came out so much a feminist – being a woman and women's rights, the way she dresses – meant that she definitely lost out with the male principal and was discriminated against. She has great skills and abilities but comes on too strong. Whereas the last principal had a personal dislike for her, the new female principal would be too scared to give her power as she would try to take over. Whereas Angela – married, fairly reserved – thinks issues through, speaks quietly and still gets her feminist viewpoint across.
>
> (Jenny)

Even feminist sympathizers were aware of the dangers of 'over the top' feminism. Many believed EO in its early stages had caused significant conflict in schools and often did

> more damage than good. It was affirmative action, thus provided men with a vehicle to argue that women were favoured and had more rights. They felt threatened because it was all supposed to be equal and yet we got more rights. And I think that a number of the perverse bra-burning feminists didn't help the cause and did increase antagonism.
>
> (Terri)

This denial of feminism not only signified ideological differences, but also the uncertainties about gender identity as well as professional risks associated with feminism, particularly in leadership.

While women principals in general adhered to gender equality as desirable, ideological differences emerged when asked to indicate how they worked for equal employment opportunities (EEO) for women teachers. Some sought to promote individual merit (and therefore deserving women) on the assumption that merit was gender-neutral. Others argued that women's differential needs required additional resources and encouragement; and a few sought to actively redefine merit and bend the rules to favour women more. Nancy, principal of a secondary college, while passing on her mentoring skills, did not see herself as a feminist because a feminist would give:

> perhaps less consideration of the male part of the school, be it student or staff, and constantly giving female teachers and female students

priority on all things instead of trying to be fair . . . I seem to conjure up the image of someone a bit more aggressive. I like the idea of being treated as a person without the tagging of gender, as opposed to being called a feminist.

(Nancy, secondary principal)

Yet Nancy also recognized the gender biases and discrimination embedded in school organizations and selection practices, that is, systemic and cultural discrimination.

The process can be fine, but it does not always mean the best person, often a woman, is chosen . . . Committees can say that the process is fine, but people disagree on the relative weighting of criteria informing the process. The basis of judgement was not as objective as should be. The cultural factors are just too much to overcome.

Many women principals' primary criterion of judgement was that of fairness. In seeking to be transparently fair, they were constrained by the fear of being seen to favour women, and thus replicate the patriarchal school leadership in schools of old times when 'only the male staff met in the principal's office on Friday nights after school for a drink and chat' (Dorothy). Looking after one's sisters was deemed to be unprofessional and biased, although EEO policies and practice merely asserted the principle of merit. One rural secondary principal, Glenda, commented:

I think there is probably a suspicion and uncomfortableness with affirmative action here. I am uncomfortable with affirmative action myself probably – more historically than now – it was more aggressive before.

Paradoxically, while the seeming value-neutrality of professional discourses based upon neutral terms of merit could provide a welcome cover for many women in leadership, they were still judged, often quite harshly, not only against the benchmark male leader, but also against criteria of an idealized or simplistic version of 'feminist' leadership that ignored the complexity of leadership in practice for women working in a system not of their own making. The conflation of 'being female' and 'being feminist' leaders further complicated the issue, as those women leaders not seen to be feminist by the sisterhood led to a sense of disappointment, disillusionment and betrayal (Mohanty 1992; Cox 1996). For Sandra, a primary principal,

The things that frustrate me most are women in leadership who, because of their behaviour and lack of what I consider professionalism, put the whole cause of women down, for not doing the job well and not promoting professionalism and the cause of women properly.

For many women, the discourse of managing diversity of the 1990s now being bedded down in official policy, with its gender-neutral language of merit and procedural justice fitted more comfortably.

> I see the merit and equity guidelines as well accepted. I run panels on very formal guidelines. We ask questions specifically to the selection criteria and always brief panels as chairperson on merit and equity. I have trained staff in merit and equity guidelines, so it has checks and monitors. What is not accepted is affirmative action for girls or women – where they are favoured. Our social justice and equity coordinator has a brief to look at what is happening to boys.
>
> (Glenda, secondary principal)

Glenda, as others, by equating 'equal' to the 'same treatment', actively fed media-generated backlash discourses about EEO giving women an advantage and the 'what about the boys' discourse, which runs the line that women are now equal and we no longer need EEO at all. Chase (1995: 183) comments: 'When women talk about their work in gender-neutral ways, it calls upon a gender discourse which conflates masculinity and neutrality'.

By contrast, whereas Glenda felt her credibility as a leader lay with her seeming neutrality, for many principals and teachers, feminism provided a sense of personal empowerment, collective solidarity and a set of principles to guide them in the job of leading. Social justice and professionalism were synonymous to them.

> Feminism has allowed me to make judgements about what I expend my energy on, about keeping my eye on certain things that I value, where I will hold the line at all costs. Without feminism and its focus on social justice principles I would have been lost. Mind you, I don't always achieve what I strive for – but the least I can do is try.
>
> (Sheila, primary principal)

Their feminism also brought with it a sense of guilt about not being able to achieve certain objectives, however, a guilt manifested in the changed context of the self-managing school with its promised autonomy and empowerment. Many felt they were unfairly judged as bad feminists because they were not always collaborative or consultative.

> Most often one's hands are tied as employees of the state. We are bound legally by the specific functions of the principalship which constrain our actions. Some people think we have more power than we do.
>
> (Merilyn, primary principal)

Merilyn spoke of how she had to manipulate the system, which gave no time for consultation with staff, and then inform the staff later about what she had done: 'It is not my way of doing things, and it relies a lot upon their trusting me to do the right thing'.

'Being more boyo than the boys'

The conflation of female leadership into feminist leadership thus ignores political differences amongst women. While some women principals disclaimed feminism, particularly its more extreme forms, others were distinctly anti-feminist (Weiner 1995b). These women – 'social males', 'the queen bees', isolates' – were often described by colleagues as aggressive, dominant, competitive, individualistic and non-supportive, if not antagonistic, to other women. These women often gathered men around them, excluding other women.

> Many of the younger female staff felt they were not listened to by the principal, and she withheld information. She actively undermined those women who were absolute dynamos by not recognizing and valuing what they did, yet propped up an inadequate male teacher. She responded to women's teaching strategies as 'all new fangled stuff. This is the way I've done it and this is the way you'll do it'. There was this jealousy thing about a female senior teacher who had extensive networks and was very knowledgeable as the younger women staff beat a track to her door.
>
> (Jessica)

Being the only female, but also not 'one of the boys', offered such women differential treatment and status that many enjoyed. They took no responsibility to assist, encourage or mentor other women as 'they had made it themselves on their own effort and merit' (Schmuck 1996: 354). They displayed

> an absolute determination not to have anyone challenge them. They actually like being the only woman, not in a sexual way, but the only woman at the centre, of some curiosity, of acclamation as to how wonderful that a woman has got to the top. And they are the ones who are most ruthless in their condemnation of other aspiring women.
>
> (John, manager)

These 'social males' were proof that women leaders were not always caring and sharing. As Paul, a manager, commented,

> You see women criticizing a particular woman manager and think 'Give her a go'. But on the other hand, in some ways, she *is* more boyo than the boys. These women . . . try to be tougher and be more ruthless, less caring and less compassionate in their decisionmaking. To show compassion is a weakness or a feminine trait, therefore they erase it. Even if it's ripping their guts out, they'll hide it. And so you get a coldness, lack of compassion and inflexibility, because any deviation is a weakness.

Many long serving women principals had got into the position with little institutional or personal support in prefeminist eras.

When it was based upon seniority and not merit they believed that they owned the position because they came through the ranks in a totally individualistic system and did not have to compete for it. They didn't have the role models we have, and had only one mode of operation to emulate – the authoritarian.

(Jan)

Whereas many newly appointed female principals of the baby boomer generation had lived through the feminist politics of the 1970s, had fought for equal pay and equal opportunity legislation, and had actively worked as change agents in the 1980s, others had little reason to reflect upon gendered politics once in power. Gender was not part of their sense of individual ability and worth, and indeed to recognize gender would downplay their own success.

Complicity and collusion

The discourse about 'queen bees' was that they had rejected their femininity and internalized masculinist practices, but the discourse of emphasized femininity meant reshaping femininity to bolster up hegemonic masculinities (Cockburn 1991; Connell 1995). Accepting the parameters of male social bonding behaviour (for example, jokes, swearing) was the condition of access for any women principals seeking integration into the boys' network. While humour both sustained and subverted particularly masculinist hegemonic discourses, it more often acted as a means of control used by men against women in the workplace as part of the 'din of domination . . . imposing loud voices, interruptions and put downs' (Harlow *et al.* 1995: 91). Humour 'includes women but marginalises and controls them', because it leads one to be seduced, for fear of not being seen to have a sense of humour, into complicity with the put-down (Cockburn 1991: 153). Jokes reinforced gender-based stereotypes and mythologies: that women gained promotion through their feminine wiles and not merit. Eleanor, a rural primary principal recalls:

At the principal's conference, one of the male presenters made a joke about how women get to the top by sleeping around. This was later reinforced by a joke by the female principal who organized the conference about passing around keys to her room. She told the story about how another female principal suggested: 'In the last resort, to get promoted, put your skirt over your head'.

Connell argues there are a range of discourses of femininity, some complicit in propping up hegemonic masculinities, as above, and others that are cast as oppositional, when women do not play the game by the boys' rules.

Eleanor discussed the instance above with the women principals involved privately, for to challenge them publicly would be to position herself as unprofessional, either a 'rabid feminist' or an anti-feminist, humourless and 'over the top', unable to have 'normal' social interaction, probably resulting in her exclusion from both male and female networks. The professionality (or gender politics) of the women making the jokes was not in question, because it symbolized a gender display of bonhomie and male culture and the rites of passage for some women to get 'into the club'.

While many women principals recognized the exclusionary practices of particular masculinist discourses, others practised what Catherine Marshall (1993) called a 'politics of denial' about their discriminatory experiences. Glenda, the only female principal of rural secondary college in her region, reflected on her feelings about principal conferences. While the male principals always were 'gentlemen' and 'very nice to Glenda', many of them 'took themselves off to tabletop dancing bars in the evening', 'scheduled in half a day of golf', or 'talked a lot about betting and sport'. Glenda commented:

> I do not want to interfere into their friendship and relaxing times – they enjoy talking about the races and betting. I personally oppose gambling. But that is a personal prejudice not to go anywhere supported by gambling. It's a risk to be tagged as 'a wowser'. My interests are tied up with femaleness. My presence will constrict their conversation. So I choose not to travel with them.

Highly discriminatory practices at work conferences were 'normalized' as typical of male friendship. Glenda absolved herself of the responsibility of naming their behaviours as unprofessional by individualizing the issue as her problem, a matter of personal preference, acutely conscious that criticism could lead to ridicule or further exclusion from the network.

> When they forgot to be polite in front of me or jokingly asked what I was doing in the car with another male principal when we came in late . . . the individual who did so would come to me later and say, 'I didn't mean offence'.

She excused these transgressions, allowing individual men not to lose public face, although many were privately in discomfort, thus effectively reinforcing hegemonic macho-masculinities.

> Men do not object to female co-workers out of a misogynist urge. It is not gender per se that is the problem, but rather the cultural traditions surrounding gender. Women have the potential to disrupt patterns of male interaction, possibly without realizing they are doing so. Specifically, men feel constrained in what they may say in front of women: joking and cursing are seen as outside the chivalrous pale.
>
> (Fine 1988: 144)

Outside the gender dynamics of the male group, her one to one interactions with men were not a problem. Silence was the better option for survival.

Wimpish femininity

Then there were the women who do not want to become leaders – the failures of feminism, displaying 'wimpish femininity' (Walkerdine 1993). These are the teachers researchers tend not to talk to as they do not appear to display the passion and overt political commitment to work. They include the 'nine to fourers' who rushed off after school, often depicted in staffroom discussions as women lacking in career ambition and putting their family first. Such discourses ignore the harsh reality of women's life histories – about wanting to have a quality life, about waiting to acquire the necessary experience and skills, about the need to be encouraged to go for leadership. Belinda, a subject and sport coordinator commented.

> Members of my faculty are more experienced than I am and so I am more in a facilitator role. I need to be encouraged. Some of the more senior staff members look down at you and say you are not capable of this. I also think females tend to be socialized into being more reserved and think, 'Someone can do things better than me'. Men do not think that at all. They just apply regardless.

There was also a form of 'gendered ageism' operating which meant that women were either too young and inexperienced to take on leadership or too old and past it (Itzin and Newman 1995).

> There are those who are in their 40s who finally get their kids off their hands and by then it is too late The average age of principals being appointed under local selection is reducing.
>
> (Margaret)

Many women teachers did not seek the principalship because they saw becoming a principal as 'changing your job' and, as Fran commented, 'losing the very thing I love most'.

> It's never been an ambition of mine to become a principal or VP. I became a teacher to teach and that is where I wish to stay. I am doing community education as a sideline out of interest.
>
> (Louise)

Many female teachers saw caring for children as their primary concern and establishing themselves as good teachers first and foremost; leadership seemed too political, about wielding power. Hargreaves (1995: 5) found likewise:

> Those teachers who sometimes seem to care most for their children, whose classroom commitments seem most intense, are precisely those most likely to see educational politics as irrelevant or even counter-productive for their own teaching . . . Politics for such teachers is about careerism, committee work or collective bargaining. Politics is tainted, teaching is pure.

Such teachers tended not to take industrial action, arguing that they put the children first (Acker 1996). The culture of caring for children was seen to be apolitical, as a safe haven for educational practice.

Other teachers sought to disengage from educational politics because of the shift in values with the neoconservative politics of school education. Formal leadership in such a context was seen to demand a negative use of power, not producing the types of change they desired.

> If I looked into the mirror myself and looked at me, I am saying 'my own personal values versus the job'. Do I really want to be a principal? I know I could be, and do a fair whack at it. But I am saying, it's not a power thing for me, it's an empowering thing – empowering oneself to do things I want to do.
>
> (Robin, leading teacher)

Many teachers had, due to the overwhelming changes and the intensification of labour, lost a sense of their capacity to change things – always being cast as reactors to, and not initiators of, change, and thus quietened.

These women, principals and teachers alike, drew upon particular readings of feminist discourses and not others: liberal feminism with its emphasis on individuals and proceduralism, and cultural feminism's advocacy of caring and sharing. The first worked from a premise of gender-neutrality and the latter tended to idealize women as being more nurturing and consensus oriented. Such discourses were more comfortable than radical or socialist feminist discourses which focused upon gender politics, difference and conflictual social relations, promoting an oppositional politics or 'forcible feminism'. Acker (1996) suggests that in particular contexts a 'forcible feminism could be counterproductive' as there is a price to pay if one rebels about sexism. To be cognizant of repressive power (domination) and yet feel powerless can lead to disillusionment and demoralization, discomfort and anger, which in turn leads to political disengagement. Indeed, it was often active political engagement that led many women to decide not to go any further in promotion. Many female assistant class principals and leading teachers were not applying for principal positions because they realized that they were buffered from the difficult moral decisions they would have to confront once they became a principal. Anna, a primary school assistant principal and classroom teacher:

> I am hesitant about taking up a principal class position at the moment because I don't like the way the department's going. If I was a principal

and was told to do something that was not what I thought was best for the school I don't know how I would respond.

This type of 'strategic fatalism' meant adapting to the new material and discursive realities of their lives, modifying their aspirations and commitments, prioritizing their energies, but also alienating them from what they cared about most (Acker 1996: 120). It also fed discourses about women not wanting to be leaders, casting women as the problem and not a range of systemic, cultural and political factors.

The failure to distinguish between the strategic nuances of feminist discourses of leadership leaches out the political nature of leadership and of feminism, reducing leadership to 'just a matter of skills or style' and not values (Weiner 1995b). The implication is that women have a 'natural' propensity towards more democratic, collaborative styles of leadership, nurturance of other women or sense of collectivity. Indeed, there is no one 'feminist' position, but a range of positions within feminism that define gender issues and the strategies for gender reform differently. Yet the system tends to construct it so that 'women in leadership have either got to be superwomen or super bitches' (Paula). Many women considered the women offered up as role models were just too committed, too energetic and too good to be realistic leadership models. Some women's abuse of leadership power was equally dissuading as there was no guarantee of collegiality and support. 'Both images indicated a high level of conflict and ambiguity in the job. And conflict is something women tend to have been socialised out of, whereas men can handle shifting from conflict one moment to mateship the next' (Cox 1996: 150). For those women in leadership who did draw their strength from more politicized notions of what it meant to be a feminist and a leader, but who lacked the power and resources to practice what they valued as desirable forms of leadership, the effect was frustrating. The isolation of the job also alienated them from their initial source of strength from other women which propelled them into leadership. The political impact of the naturalizing (and essentializing) the discourse of female styles of leadership based on the assumption that women are a homogeneous group in which gender is *the* primary social category, is to neglect difference amongst women, whether on the grounds of status, organizational position and politics as well as race, class and ethnicity.

'The stain that will not go away'

Gender is not the determining or overarching factor in all instances and contexts in individual's lives. There are 'multiple factors which conflict and interlink with each other, producing differential effects. An individual's own identification with and investment in different subject positions and power makes it even more difficult to speak of gender as some kind of unifying or bonding experience' (McNay 1992: 65). So while the discourses of women's ways of leading have provided social mobility for an elite of white middle-class women, it has not informed political reality and their relationship to other women (Eisenstein 1996). For Antonia, located as a young working-class teacher of Italian background,

> there is gender *and* class *and* ethnicity. My parents are migrants. But it is not that they brought me up as passive or submissive. As one of two daughters I was able to do what I liked. But basically our perceptions of ourselves as women are not as great leaders due to the culture we came from. My parents came here with five cents in their pockets and nothing in the suitcase. So they had to fight and scrape for everything they got. And when Dad was offered a leadership position in the factory he didn't want it because, first, he thought the Australians would not take a new Australian as boss; and second, he didn't think his English was good enough. I was very shy and we were brought up as good girls who were seen and not heard in the 1950s . . . and this makes us doubly disadvantaged. It haunts us. We were never expected to be leaders, or to beat the boys. And in class I was better than the boys but I had to shut up . . . I never promoted my intelligence in high school because it always got me thumps over the head by other kids – girls and boys. Even smart boys copped it in this school. I can feel all this creep up on me in interviews for promotion now . . . it is ingrained into me, like a stain that will not go away no matter how hard you try to scrub or bleach it out. Women of that time, particularly of migrant parents, have that disadvantage built in.

Antonia's migrant background and 'poorer' English skills, she felt, were additional disadvantages and inhibitors to being a woman as formal qualifications and interviews counted for too much in gaining leadership positions and promotion.

> I don't really see why that is the case. It should be what you have achieved and how others, the principal, have perceived this and not someone who can talk about it only . . . and the thought that I will probably do badly on interview anyway, and that I would be deluding myself that I could get a promotion has meant I have put off working on my c.v.

In Australia, the 1980s politics of multiculturalism tended to view us all as 'equally ethnic', and race was readily incorporated into other forms of difference. As elsewhere, pre-1980, minority women administrators, of whom there are few, were seen to be 'doubly disadvantaged' due to their colour and gender. Multiculturalism was the 1980s' liberal solution to conflict over race and ethnicity (Britzman 1993). By being positive about difference, it assumed that improving the self-concept of individual 'others' would lead to improved performance. Ameliorative multicultural approaches also assumed that all differences work the same, and that racism or sexism could be addressed through the same gender-neutral administrative procedures or concepts such as merit.

Hester Eisenstein (1996: xix) argues that

the overwhelming whiteness of the [Australian] femocrats was one of the unspoken keys to their success. Despite the challenges to patriarchal structures represented by feminist claims, femocrats and women in leadership could be assimilated over time because of their strong cultural links to the men placing them in positions of power.

Linda Tuhiwai-Smith (1993) points out how Maori women treat pakeha (white) feminism with some scepticism, seeing that white women have been complicit beneficiaries of white colonialism in New Zealand (Fleras 1989). There is a significant absence of discourses about leadership amongst indigenous Australians, compared to the USA, England and New Zealand (Walker 1993; Pringle and Timperley 1995). Indeed, the presence of white women in leadership has meant that of indigenous, ethnic and other minority women was seen to be redundant. When black or indigenous women did assume positions of leadership, they have been faced with discourses about their 'failure to represent all Aboriginals', as Aboriginality is treated as a monolithic culture.

Merely 'adding on' oppressions does not provide a full understanding of the qualitative difference of life for a black female principal or teacher. As race gets onto the political agenda in the 1990s in Australia, minority women are being positioned as change agents to work with their communities in particularly difficult contexts. They are expected to bring 'something different' as an outsider inside, because of their commonality with their constituencies. There is a double bind involved with such a positioning for Aboriginal women principals, being symbolic as representing community views but also challenging existing school structures to do so (Court 1992; Ortiz and Ortiz 1994). Minorities are assumed to have the same interests and to behave in particular ways – thus Aboriginal and white women are positioned as working together as women in a mentor relationship. The following case study of such a principal mentor relationship written by its participants indicates the complexity of gender and race relations in the context of a white masculinist administrative culture at a critical moment in Australian history where cultural and national identity is being reshaped by globalization, Aboriginal land right claims and debates about republicanism (Ngurruwutthun and Stewart 1996).

A principal mentor program established in 1988 arose out of dissatisfaction of the local Yolngu Aboriginal community in the Northern Territory with Balanda (white) principals and Balanda school culture in a predominantly Yolngu school community. Yolngu teachers were mentored by Balanda principals working beside them, mediating the complex cultural territory between local Yolngu communities and white male-dominated government education bureaucracies. The conflict in this context was not about gender, but over the competing perspectives of school/community relations between the white Balanda bureaucracies and the Yolngu traditional views of education as symbolized in the authority relations between the white mentor and Yolngu principal, both women. Nalwarri, the Yolngu principal commented:

> One of the difficulties on being a Yolngu principal in a Balanda educational system is the different way we look at being a leader. In Yolngu society, leaders are not placed up above everyone else. They are at the same level as everyone else. Because I am the principal, I have special jobs and responsibilities of the education of djamarrkuli, and to the community. But I still have to listen to the people, the other Yolngu teachers, assistant teachers and other workers in the school. I also listen to the elders, the leaders of our community who give us guidance. I don't think of myself as 'high' – we all listen to each other and support each other. It is important that I am not a bungawa, a boss.
>
> (Ngurruwutthun and Stewart 1996: 13)

In such a society, Ann (the white mentor principal) and Nalwarri explain, a leader is given authority

> by the people and that leader stands with the people, not above them in a hierarchical structure. In fact if leaders start to act in a way which is considered bossy and individualistic, the community will 'pull them down because the authority for the leader to rule comes from the people'.
>
> (Ngurruwutthun and Stewart 1996: 13)

Nalwarri therefore had to work with and across two cultures – not to be too bossy with Yolngu teachers and to be sufficiently assertive for the Balanda teachers, while working collegially with Ann. Ann's role was to advise and consult from the perspective of an experienced principal and feminist educator at a university, as the decoder and communicator of Balanda bureaucracy. She also had to work with the Yolngu community, recognizing Yolngu notions of leadership and the authority of the elders. The perception of the local community and school council, however, was that Ann's constant presence was control by her and not by Nalwarri.

For Nalwarri, the major problem was not her relationship with Ann, but the constraints placed on her capacity to be a Yolngu principal in context of devolution. Educational restructuring in the Northern Territory, as in Victoria, had changed the role of the principal in the previous five years; financial cutbacks, reductions to support staff, increased teacher workload and radical change in curriculum and assessment drew Nalwarri away from what she called the 'real work' of being in the classroom, going out into the community and talking with elders and teachers. Increasingly her own, and other Yolngu principals' work, was focusing upon paperwork. In Nalwarri and Ann's words:

> what became apparent was the fact that despite changes to the rhetoric of government policies which today ostensibly provides 'self management' and 'self determination', the relationships between Yolngu and Balanda established in the early days of colonisation, still contextualise education today and affect the reality of our daily practice.
>
> (Ngurruwutthun and Stewart 1996: 10)

Here the changing role of principal worked actively against what both women were seeking: a recognition of cultural difference and different modes of leadership. While the discourse of self-managing schools positioned Aboriginal principals as being representatives of their race/ethnic communities, they lacked access to system-wide or organisational power, being confined to specific specialist tasks as 'Aboriginal' experts whose expertise was not valued within the bureaucracy. Thus Aboriginal women appointed to principalships because of cultural links to their communities, who actually work *with* their community, challenged the authority structures. Yet they were also readily expendable once the task was achieved or if they did not meet the high expectations laid upon them. Similarly, Ann, as change agent, was appointed as mentor to solve a particular problem in a 'minority' school. She also was an expendable troubleshooter rather than permanent administrator. Her role was to manage the 'problem' of Aboriginality for the system.

This case indicates how the racial politics of organizations worked differently for women of different racial and cultural backgrounds. 'Idealised identities do not lend insight into the mobile and shifting conditions that make identity such a contradictory place to live' (Britzman 1993: 25–6). A number of confusions were at work. First, the focus was upon culture and identity as discrete and fixed categories, rather than on how power and politics work in organizations. By overly politicizing the role, both Ann and Nilwarri were positioned so that the 'potential benefits of diversity and alternative modes of leadership are lost' (Marshall 1994: 167). Second, there is the conflation of being female and black to being feminist and anti-racist, which assumes the experience of being black and female produces a particular feminist sensibility or 'predispose us to a distinctive group consciousness' (Collins 1991: 24–5).

Third, dealing with race and ethnicity means revisiting successful gender equity strategies such as mentoring and role modelling which are so often promoted as a common solution to the 'problem' of the lack of women in administration. Role models are not only forms of 'idealized identity', which push particular normative concepts about gender – assertive but not aggressive, persistent but not loud, caring for others but not angry at injustice – but, in this instance, also about race. Modelling has different repercussions for black women in leadership (Byrne 1989; Britzman 1993). Mirza (1993: 33) argues that research idealizing ideological conceptions such as 'the strong black mother' is readily translated into discourses about 'black superwomen'. This is a discourse that is equally paralysing for women who do not 'fit' the image or highly stressful for those who appear to cope. It also assumes such women have the individual and cultural resources to cope, and thereby portrays their oppression as being a *beneficial* experience in producing 'strong' women. Of course 'aggressive, assertive women are penalised – they are abandoned by their men, end up impoverished, and are stigmatised as unfeminine' (Collins 1991: 75).

Finally, sexual politics also works differently, as sexual harassment facing black women administrators is loaded with racist stereotypes about their 'hypersexuality' and their competence (Al-Khalifa 1989: 91). Jenny Williams (1987) sees race and gender policies still defining women and blacks as the problem. Categorical definitions render gender as a female problem, race a black problem, and sexuality a gay and lesbian problem. It allows white women administrators to identify themselves as women, but not as white women (Adler *et al.* 1993). The white 'race' is, as other groups, seen to be culturally unified with stable or homogeneous entities or 'transcendental essences', but as different not only from more recent arrivals and also indigenous populations (de Lauretis 1990).

Educational policies informed by the reductionist and essentialist tendencies of categorical definitions of difference tend to reduce the issue of gender, racial or cultural inequality to one overriding concern . . . the educatability of minorities and increasing the numbers of minority administrators. Thus administrative texts and policies continue to depict women and minorities as 'special cases' (as if deviant from the norm). Categorical definitions of difference and inequality set up women as competing with racial minority and low income groups, forgetting that many are women. This results in 'buttressing the relatively privileged positions of the white middle- and upper-class women, whilst removing from scrutiny the very privileged position of white professional men' (Sleeter 1993: 221). The upper reaches of employment continue to be markedly populated 'by white men – primarily heterosexual and non-disabled men – a narrow, self-reproducing monoculture' (Cockburn 1991: 172). Different women relate in different ways to this monoculture of the powerful, some more readily incorporated than others due to different personal philosophies and political beliefs, and some ready to 'play the boy's game' with more intensity than others.

There is a need to reconceptualize the notion of how difference can be dealt with in policy and practice beyond the categorical politics of the 1980s by considering how race, class and culture impact on the reception of gender equity policy and strategies, and what that means in terms of producing leadership diversity. Leadership diversity values difference, and all its nuances, without slipping into the regressive discourse about management of diversity which reduces difference to individual preference. Leadership diversity is about leadership *for* and not *of* diversity, negotiating and valuing difference, while remembering that addressing difference amongst women does not mean rejecting the category of 'woman', as women as a 'class' continue to be disadvantaged globally and locally.

Conclusion: a feminist postmasculinist politics of educational leadership

New hard times for feminist work in education?

We are facing new and hard times for feminism in an era of postmodernity. In Australia, as elsewhere, the two decades prior to 1990 were marked by discourses of gender equity reform and social justice (Dudley and Vidovich 1995). It was an era characterized by state welfarism and a sense of collectivism informed by the 'new' social movements such as the women's movement. It was a time when the femocrats and specialist equal opportunities (EO) units worked from within the state for the constituency of women, and of strong state intervention for equity through centralized industrial relations systems and top-down policies combined with grass-roots feminist activism in schools. As a consequence, EO discourses became institutionalized as EO policies and structures became integrated, even if partially, throughout schools and other public sector organizations.

In Australia as elsewhere, however, the anticipated cultural changes are yet to be attained, although there has been significant structural change in school governance in most western nation states. In some instances, the gender gap (both numerical and financial) is increasing with the polarization between manager and worker, a discrepancy only partially explained by downsizing and the structural backlash (Blackmore 1997a). It equally attributable to institutional resilience to change and male resistance to gender equity. Those seeking gender equity for women in schools are now working in a significantly different context. The 1990s has been dominated by discourses of self-management, neoliberal market principles and more conservative social policies. In an era of globalization, social justice discourses premised upon citizenship rights have been replaced by discourses of how diversity can improve national productivity. The state has been reconstituted to mediate 'the market' rather than defend, least of all advocate, the public good, thus undermining public education systems by restructuring them on the basis of abstract principles of market exchange and competition. Equity has been redefined as meeting client (not citizenship) needs within a 'contractualist' or competitive state (Yeatman 1993).

Educational administration has been central to the transformation of educational work in devolved, marketized, contractually-based systems of management. As a field of practice, it has reconstituted itself through disciplinary technologies of surveillance and self-management and discourses of performativity premised around performance management, standardized assessment, policy and curriculum guidelines, and data collection systems. Educational organizations have been downsized and devolved, and, in Australia, responsibility for EO has been mainstreamed down to individual managers and units. Educational leadership discourses has been sidelined by discourses of leadership focusing upon performance, image, efficiency and outcomes within a market or line management framework. What do these shifts mean for feminism as a movement and EO as a discursive practice, and for the capacity of feminist discourses in educational administration to inform educational change?

On the one hand, the discourses of educational change hold many promises for feminism, and indeed for women in leadership, with their appeal to change agentry, student (client?)-focused organizations, professionality, autonomy, flexibility, flatter structures, teamwork and people-centred management. On the other, this study suggests that such claims are not often substantiated when the impact of self-management upon women teachers as a group, or even individual women leaders, in an era of market liberalism and economic rationalism, is foregrounded. That is, the downside of devolution is increased control by the centre through accountability measures, a shift from citizenship to market values predicated upon competitive individualism, and a fundamental change in social relationships and value systems in schools premised around contractualism, together with top-down imposed change in an environment of uncertainty. For many women teachers, educational restructuring has meant less employment security but more flexibility; more opportunities to re-skill coupled with an intensification of labour which invades their personal lives and professional autonomy. For women principals, while it has meant more power over teachers, it has also often meant working within a system that emphasizes managed change from above and not school-based change initiatives; on doing more for less; on promoting an image of a 'productive' school rather than education for active citizenship (including paid work), life-long learning and social justice.

The voices of the women in this research have told us much about leadership, not only about the tensions of being a 'good woman' and being a 'good leader' but also between being a 'good' and 'bad' feminist. It indicated that many, but not all, women leaders sought to create safe havens for their colleagues in quite non-supportive work environments, often at risk to themselves professionally and personally, by acting as a buffer against reforms that many felt were antithetic to good education and social justice. They worked as 'outsiders inside' cultural discourses that were often alienating and antagonistic. They experienced the full range of emotions – guilt, rage, anxiety, pleasure and excitement – arising from leadership in a period of radical change, and most sought to lead with empathy and compassion. They also experienced isolation, with little opportunity for collective reflection or support, always expected to deliver praise and support to others, but rarely to expect any themselves. They learnt to accept that they were simultaneously powerful and powerless in the face of this change. They also came to enjoy power as something that could be used positively to benefit others. They learnt to be opportunistic, to work within the system, while seeking to enact long-term agendas. Importantly, some came to understand the difference between 'spoken and enacted values', hoping that they would be trusted to do the right thing when they were unable to speak in their own voice (Dunlap and Schmuck 1995: 423). All were aware that, as women, they were more open to be judged on a range of different criteria than their male colleagues, often more harshly, by both women and men – either for being too female or not female enough, too feminist or not feminist enough.

Being female was not foremost to women leaders at all times, although all were prompted about their embodied femaleness at unlikely moments to rudely remind them of their difference and/or marginality. For some, the isolates or individualists who detached themselves from issues of equity and privileged the individual over the group, gender was not central to their work identity. Others' professional and work identities, the activists and advocates who worked as openly as possible to change the nature of educational leadership and administration, were infused with a sense of feminism (Dunlap and Schmuck 1995). Many were working on the edge, balancing between being cast out as radicals seeking to change the system, or being socialized into the system's ways of working, 'the way we do things around here'. Indigenous women leaders were not only positioned by dominant masculinist and bureaucratic discourses as the 'other' and therefore a problem, but were also outside the discursive domain of white 'professional' feminism premised around individual merit and academic achievement. For them, the danger lay in the clash of expectations of their communities to maintain the cultural values of practice based upon listening, story telling, reflection and shared decisionmaking while working within mainstream educational bureaucratic cultures predicated upon managerialist values of efficiency, effectiveness, short deadlines and hierarchy and in which they, as individuals, were expendable. Working with and through community was a key element of the 'success', as defined by their colleagues and parents, of many of these principals.

While feminism provides many leading women with principles of practice and a framework for making judgements, and although many non-feminist women articulate the discourse of care, collegiality, commitment, consensus and consultation, there is no essential or intrinsic style of female leadership.

Women's stated preferences for more democratic styles of management and collegiality are discursively produced practices arising from being located in a particular array of communities' (work, home, community) practices and discourses. Education is a community of practice located in a feminized and highly gender-segmented occupation centred around children with institutionally specific professional (and gendered) discourses about what it means to be a teacher, a feminist and a leader. Furthermore, the voices of these women indicate that leadership, as a social practice, is not just an intellectual matter, but also a moral and emotional matter. Good leaders address the moral dimension of change, seek to develop high levels of trust and openness, and display a capacity to make sound ethical judgements, but not from a position of superior moral judgement. Leadership is about trust and passion, changing hearts as well as changing minds, for rationality without compassion is irrational.

Interestingly, these women's voices resonated with the discourses about 'good' educational leadership in provincial secondary and urban working-class multicultural colleges, small rural schools, Aboriginal community schools and within educational bureaucracies, all sites of my research. Teacher discourses, as feminist discourses, also centred around the centrality of interrelationships and community, mutual respect, the utilization of diverse leadership expertise amongst individuals with different power, status and authority; and a sense of inclusivity that recognizes *and* equally values difference. These discourses suggested leadership was about capacity: the capacity of leaders to listen and observe, to use their expertise and overview as a starting point to encourage dialogue between all levels of educational decisionmaking and between stakeholders, to establish processes and transparency in decisionmaking, to articulate their own values and visions clearly but not to impose them and to create conditions conducive to professional autonomy. Good leaders worked from the centre of a network of social relations, exercising power through and with rather than over others. Leadership was about recognizing the difference between domination and power, and the use and abuse of power; about setting and not just reacting to agendas; about problem setting and not just problem solving; about initiating change for substantive improvement for staff and students rather than merely managing change.

Sadly, the more hierarchical structures, competitive practices and economistic discourses framing, but not necessarily determining, leadership in self-managing schools in the 1990s tend not to encourage or facilitate this stance, but indeed undermine many principals' capacity to work in a relationship of trust with each other, students, staff or parents, when the bottom line is always expediency, productivity and cost. What women found was that the communities of practice of the principalship in self-managing schools produced discourses, language and practices that devalued discourses of care, relationality and collegiality. As women, they were simultaneously positioned

as different, but as principals, they were powerful; they confronted the contradictions arising from their desire to be seen as professional and yet work
for social justice, realising how discourses of professionalism often work
against action based on principles of justness.

Centralized-decentralization has therefore produced many leadership
paradoxes. The rhetoric of self-managing schools has focused upon professional autonomy and collegiality, yet produced highly Fordist work practices predicated upon hierarchy, and competitiveness and contrived
collegiality exacerbating distinctions between teaching and administration.
Discourses of good educational leadership stress ambiguity, shared visions,
bottom-up change and creativity; yet self-management has meant top-down,
principal-led and managed change encouraging compliance. The discourse
of managing diversity suggests recognition of a culturally pluralistic society,
yet its implementation focuses upon individualizing difference and denying
systemic inequality. The discourses of self-managing schools promise more
community-oriented local school governance, yet management practice
expects school councils merely to implement government policy. The education market depicts parents as rational self-maximizing individual
choosers, yet relies upon 'irrational' emotions of greed, envy and anxiety.
The leadership literature stresses teaching, learning, and people management in learning organizations, yet self-managing schools prioritize entrepreneurship, financial management, and 'strong', if not authoritarian,
leadership. Leadership in such a fluid, changing and complex context means
being able to address ambiguity and contradiction.

While these paradoxes confront all school principals, they have particularly gendered nuances in that dominant discourses, images and practices of
self-managing schools privilege 'hard masculinity' and 'strong' leadership.
Being 'strong', however, is not how women leaders are seen to be strong:
morally strong, strong on relations, care and collegiality. It was particularly
evident that feminist discourses of community, care and collegiality had
traps for women leaders with the intensification of emotional management
labour in self-managing schools. Acting as an emotional buffer to rapid
change because one cares for colleagues and children had the potential to
encourage teacher dependence on leaders, passivity and compliance rather
than interdependence between autonomous professionals, and often at great
personal cost to women in leadership. The dilemma here for feminism is that
applying the logic of intimate relations to the political life of organizations
is fraught with contradictions (e.g. care and teamwork), as the shared principles of equality, mutuality of respect and consensual decisionmaking in
face-to-face contexts idealized in discourses about women's ways of leading
cannot be so readily replicated in large organizations or systems, but can still
be appropriated by managerialist discourses of consensus, vision and strong
culture (Jones 1995).

Equally important, the continued association of strong leadership with hard masculinity provides no alternative conceptualizations of masculinity for those men who seek leadership, but who, as many women do, reject the values of competitiveness, coercion and control and seek to reconceptualize leadership in more socially just and inclusive ways. The maintenance of connections between macho masculinity and leadership are critical to maintaining gender power relations in schools and bureaucracies. Rarely are the individual behaviours of men and boys connected to wider institutional relations of power. Thus a group of male teachers can happily pay lip service to equal opportunity for girls and then set up the female vice principal by manufacturing discipline problems to 'test her out'.

Women can be equally complicit in perpetuating masculinist discourses. Many women buy into the discourse of EO as being unfair for men or are uncomfortable with the political baggage that goes with EO as it puts their own professional achievements under scrutiny. Many women's sense of identity is closely attached to caring, leading them to downplay their own claims for equality if it jeopardizes caring relations (Weiner 1995b). At the same time, those bureaucrats and principals seen to be feminists were particularly susceptible to the charge of being too pragmatic and 'bad feminists'; of being caught up in the iron law of bureaucracy which assumed that to work with the enemy led ultimately to total co-option. Drucilla Cornell (1995: 83) comments:

> That in constructing 'good' and 'bad' feminisms we indeed reinvent the gender hierarchy. That form of moralising involves the separation, undertaken by feminists themselves, between a 'sensible' feminism committed to a reasonable program of reform, and the 'wild' feminism that seems to leave little of our most basic institutional practices unchallenged ... while feminism sets out to challenge the reigning symbolic order of gender hierarchy, it ironically reinforces it if it succumbs to the fantasy that there are 'good' feminisms and 'bad' feminisms.

To recognize the potential of even the most emancipatory discourses of feminism to also become repressive for women is not to deny the emancipatory capacities of feminist discourses of rights, liberties and justice altogether, but rather to be continuously wary of its truth claims. Pragmatism and idealism are not necessarily mutually exclusive. Cynthia Cockburn (1991) talks about two levels of gender reform. One level is the long-term *strategic* work – that which we desire and aspire for in a more idealistic sense and against which we constantly measure success. The other is the *tactical* work – the ways we work for change to benefit women in situations 'not of our own making'. Feminists have always troubled over the dissonance between what is doable and what is desirable.

Tactical or sensible feminism(s)

Tactical feminism is about working for gender equity on a daily basis in any specific site. Tactical feminism is about understanding and building upon what we have learnt from feminist practices and histories in gender equity reform; about providing sensible alternatives, while also being alert to their dangers. Sensible feminism recognizes that desired social change will not evolve if there is no immanent practical possibility for change – personally, institutionally and politically. It is about working within a range of different sites – personal, organizational and extraorganizational – and understanding their interrelationships, and how discourses articulate across different levels. It is about reading discourses opportunistically, but with a sense of their possible long-term effects. It means considering the disabling and enabling conditions that hinder or facilitate this gender work. It begins by asking what can I do today, how do I best use my time, how can I use gender as an asset? (Dunlap and Schmuck 1995: 432–3).

The ongoing danger for sensible feminism is the understandable tendency to focus upon the doable. It is easier to focus upon changing individual women to better match and meet the needs of such management discourses as managing diversity rather than integrating women's experiences to change management practice, or to challenge the nature, images of leadership or the knowledge base of administration. In focusing upon changing individual women, equal employment opportunity (EEO) tactics have successfully produced many skilled female managers by training them in c.v. writing and interview skills, career counselling, and financial management. Opportunity structures modelled upon male career paths have extended women's experience and organizational learning with mentoring, networking, role modelling, shadowing or acting in leadership positions. Not surprisingly, EEO texts, largely because of their liberal feminist emphasis on the individual and gender-neutral ideas of merit, have been more palatable to men (and many women) in power than those of cultural or socialist feminists who have sought more fundamental cultural or structural change.

Focusing upon acquiring administrative competencies and skill building distracts us from unpacking the cultural biases embedded in organizational structures, processes and cultures, or deconstructing the global management discourses of efficiency and the market shaping leadership practices that marginalize women and promoting particular values that dampen their desire for leadership. Women are being put off leadership, not only because of the unreasonable demands on time and energy, but the contradictions arising out of the ethical and moral dilemmas of formal leadership in a performative state. Emphasizing networking, modelling and shadowing programs, rather than context, tends to mean women work collectively to assist individual women without challenging the dominant discourses of leadership. Likewise, the trend towards teacher and leadership professional development programs based on problemsolving in specific school sites tends to accept the policies unproblematically, prioritize school or system needs, and make professional development the means by which to implement government policies rather than actually meeting the professional needs of individual teachers or developing critically reflective professional discursive practices. In Victoria, Sarah considered

> even the women and leadership programs are telling us how to be principals of Schools of the Future without debating issues of leadership and education rather than infiltrating ideas of feminist leadership into mainstream management.

Locally, feminists need constantly to revisit their conceptualization of leadership, reactivate those EEO networks now being dismantled or reclaim those taken over by men, and create new sites for leadership training work for women during the 1990s, given the demise of the career path provided through institutionalizing EO.

At the extraorganizational level, feminists have learnt to use policy and the state for gender equity. The institutionalization of gender equity in Australia during the 1980s imparted legitimacy, credibility and authority to EO. Equity discourses, even in their appropriation, shifted the frame of thinking and ways of acting. This tactical work was successful due to the combination of strong top-down policies *and* senior management advocacy (both male managers and femocrats) with grass-roots networks and activism; with 'specialist' equity units providing policies, strategies and resources together with strategies mainstreaming equity throughout the organization; with good collegiate networks to spread information and communication, sound personal support systems from colleagues, friends and/or partners and resources dedicated to EO. At the same time, affirmative restructuring, in seeking to develop 'women friendly' workplaces and facilitate women's capacity to juggle the precarious balance of family and work relations, has the potential to make women even more flexible (read casualized), further facilitating the colonization of women's personal time and space by work rather than attacking the unreasonable demands of greedy organizations. Indeed, the intensification of educational work renders teaching, not just leadership, increasingly difficult for many women. What this tells is that EO policies are necessary but not sufficient conditions for change, and they are unpredictable in their effects (Limerick and Lingard 1995). EEO discourses have privileged particularly narrow gender scripts for women in leadership and valued particular tactics (critical mass of women and women's styles of leadership) over others (changing leadership). The danger in performativity-driven quasi-market education systems is that EEO policy will be left at the level of the 'symbolic' rather than 'penetrate into practice'.

In the short term, therefore, we need to exploit the discourses of the market, managerialism and contractualism to work more effectively for feminism. We can demand, as consumers, that equity be built into all levels and aspects of devolved management systems premised upon contractualism: into professional development and performance management contracts of all managers, into school charters, into outsourcing contracts, as well as being one criterion for recruitment, selection, promotion and retrenchment. Resources and reward systems can be attached accordingly for successful gender equity action by individuals, groups and schools. This also requires a high level of transparency about the contractual arrangements and peer review about what constitutes success, however, a transparency not often forthcoming. Similarly, we can argue that school-based policies and practices and principal professional development must address equity, diversity and fairness as these are legal requirements in decentralized employment relations where principals and councils are employers. Discourses linking leadership diversity to productivity can be used to justify policies promoting difference amongst leaders by promoting women and different racial and ethnic groups into leadership, an important point that can be linked to the internationalization of education. Finally we can tap into the 'new' management literature, which sees macho modes of masculinist management as out of date, and which suggests we are moving towards a postmasculinist rather than a postfeminist era (Brown 1988).

At the same time, these discourses shift rapidly with new policy initiatives and as new political ideologies take hold, so we need to be constantly aware of how such shifts may close some possibilities and open others. The 1990s has seen a radical configuration of gender power relations in school systems with the shift of policy production to the ministers and the politicization of educational policy. It now means that femocrats, even those in merit and equity managerial positions, cannot be expected to act openly as advocates for a constituency of women. As for principals, accountability in line management is unilaterally upwards to the minister. There is less space to play. Social justice discourses have little credibility against the resurgence of liberal feminist discourses of individual merit and choice and management discourses predicated on the market, which also provide more space for men to claim 'equal rights' to access women-only programs. While the demise of women-only programs undermines the benefits of women-centred professional development programs – naming gender as an issue, legitimating women's experiences as alternative leadership practices, creating supportive learning environments, networks, and the space to gain courage to speak of imagining being in formal leadership – it also lays open new possibilities to work with men.

> We [women shadowing male principals] are doing more of the teaching than learning as we provide another perspective and new insights as well as demanding a level of self-reflection of male managers' practices, than in other strategies which are premised upon more hierarchical

relationships. Mixed-sex shadowing therefore is one strategy which achieves multiple gains in both informing women aspirants about career possibilities but also changing male management practices.

(Betty)

Similarly, while the critical mass, change agent and female styles of leadership theses central to EEO policies have gained some temporary advantage for femocrats working in alliances with powerful men to develop gender reform policies, it was at the cost of not scrutinizing male advantage too closely because it was 'much easier to sell the policies that will address disadvantage . . . than policies that will take something away' (Sawer quoted in Eveline 1994: 141). Such theses not only made women the problem but also the source of change as women were expected to continue to 'mend the social fabric' of organizations by taking responsibility for gender reform (Kenway *et al.* 1997). Such discourses not only feed into the crisis of masculinity discourses that position men as emotional illiterates, but releases them from any responsibility to change themselves or the social relations of gender. The discourse of crisis in masculinity, however, also provides opportunities for women to work with men from an informed feminist perspective about gender change while continually reminding them that men come from a position of advantage. Christopher McLean (1995: 298) argues that

> While men who baulk that they are in a position of power, I ask them to consider this. While individual men may not possess much power, by the mere fact of their gender, the possibility of power exists . . . A man may be barred from a game by rules about race and class . . . but not on grounds of gender. For women, her gender alone is enough . . . Men therefore are advantaged.

Certain dominant macho masculinities are problematic for many men as well as for many women, and opposition to the values of economic rationalism and managerialism and a passion for education, social justice, antisexism and anti-racism are not the monopoly of feminists. Moreover, such alliances mean that those in subordinate groups can come to appreciate how it is possible for someone who is dominant, in some, but not all respects, to share their interests (Sawicki 1991: 42). Feminists not only need to learn to work with men sympathetic to feminism, but also in power relations with other women. While recognizing political differences amongst women highlights the fragility of feminist discourses about the collective, it leads us to rethink what we mean by feminism, understand the race, class and ethnic as well as generational differences in experiences of feminism, and the difference between being female and feminist. We need to reinvent what we mean by a feminist politics.

Tactically, gender equity reform needs to focus more upon why people change. Change is often cast as an intellectual exercise, reinforcing the emotionality/rationality binary of administrative theory. The presence of women in positions of leadership, while accepted at a rational level by most teachers as not being a problem, was still highly emotional, personally unsettling and threatening to many male and some female teachers and parents. EEO tactics have wavered between rationalist approaches, assuming that people act upon knowledge of inequality, or behaviourist assumptions that imparting guilt would provoke change in powerful men. Raising awareness is the first critical step, and feminists need to counter the perpetual naïveté of 'the advantage of not knowing' about current gender equity research by keeping gender on all professional development agendas in schools (Robertson 1992: 44). We also need to develop 'pedagogies of discomfort', which tap into the emotions of gender change reform, with all its pleasures and fears. We forget about desire and why we want to teach and lead, about the passion invested in teaching and leading, and the sense of achievement, satisfaction and pleasure embedded in social relations premised upon affection and belonging. Reflective practice is not merely a cognitive process of analysis and inquiry, but also about feeling and intuiting (Hargreaves 1995).

Tactical feminism is also about being aware of how oneself is being discursively situated as the object of scrutiny, embodied as female, while keeping an eye open to opportunities as an active subject to rewrite seemingly resistant discourses. Many feminists learnt to exploit the discursive constitution of the female body as 'different' by tapping into the female bodily images' capacity for being subversive as well as conforming, realizing the superficial and performative effect of embodied authority, while holding dear particular sets of feminist principles which become evident in their practice. They learnt to play with management discourses in ways that make it difficult to position them as extremist feminists, being loud and strong when necessary, but often quietly achieving their ends.

To do all this without considering what leadership now means in the context of a self-managing school has little meaning. The change in the principals' work away from the core work of teaching and learning in educational leadership to financial management, image promotion and industrial relations in a hierarchically organized market-oriented school represents not just a shift in emphasis as much as a shift in values (see also Gewirtz *et al.* 1995). In this context, the image of the woman in the principalship for many women teachers is often of someone struggling to deal with the ethical dilemmas arising from the contradictions between their personal commitment to social justice, sense of professionality and policy expectations, as strong (and exceptional) women.

> Despite its high profile about women into leadership, under Schools of the Future, women are more vulnerable now. Those who are determined and strong will be OK, those on the fringes . . . will drop out.
>
> (Barbara)

We have also learnt that EEO reform's reliance upon procedural justice (structures and processes) does not necessarily produce just outcomes. While this strategy was necessary for femocrats to work with men in power, there is no neutral administrative logic to which women can safely appeal. So while one aims for procedural justice, substantive justice requires us to focus upon more equitable outcomes and substantive moral and ethical value positions in a proactive sense. We need to ask: whose 'vision' is followed, whose 'interests' are achieved, who is affected by change and how?

> We are increasingly drawn to the argument that changing education will involve more than improving the credentials and inventiveness of teachers, the climate, or the leadership capacities of the school. And it is perhaps not an 'improvement process' that must be managed, but rather, collective norms and procedures for processing and dealing with ideas that must be addressed.
>
> (Louis 1994: 9)

Strategic or wild feminism(s)

Feminist educational leadership needs to reassert a strong sense of the normative, even though what that may be is hotly contested, at the same time that we need to be open to postmodern possibilities. Education is about values and moral practices. While Foucault feared that the 'laying down of norms inevitably has a normalising effect', many feminists sees normative power as necessary to safeguard against repression (McNay 1992: 8). Gender equity reform studies have indicated how powerful feminism, as a political movement and a social practice, can be in informing and changing discursive practices in schools and systems. There is no shared understanding of what feminism means to women, however, and feminism has displayed its own normative and regulatory tendencies upon which we need to reflect. Iris Marion Young suggests that if we recognize substantive differences (gender, race, class etc), then we also recognize the relativism and situatedness of all discourses about justice. Justice emerges out of contextually and specifically negotiated judgements (Young 1990: 10). The questions framing this process are: why we seek to change, with what intent, whose discourses of justice are we calling upon, and how judgements can be effected most fairly in terms of means and outcomes?

Wild feminism is about debating the ideals of feminism, and developing long-term strategies to work towards them. It is also about scanning for dangers to successful strategies. State feminism as a strategy is, I suggest, in an era of the postwelfare state, now under threat. The strategic dangers of relying upon the protective 'maternalist' state are now obvious as the safety net is being withdrawn and EO infrastructure dismantled. Given the supplanting of the welfare state by the performative/competitive state, feminists may need to employ different strategies, while utilizing prior learning about gender equity reform in order to protect past gains, retain present practices and develop new initiatives. Feminist collective claims upon the state premised upon rights are being increasingly undermined by a neoliberal market orientation and neo-conservative gender politics that reduces all rights to individual choice exercised at the level of the local. Such a view endangers the sociogeographical entity of local community around the neighbourhood school or government education as a public good central to citizenship in a democratic community. Feminists need to reconsider how they will make future claims upon the nation state, previously based on needs, given the reinvention of liberalism's rights-oriented possessive individualism (Fraser 1995).

One challenge for western feminists is how to redefine the individual–state relations in the context of the market in socially responsible ways. Feminist research has begun to unwrap gendered nuances of the education market and economic rationalist ideologies, illustrating how market-liberalism's self-seeking, profit maximizing individual ignores the interdependence between individuals and their need for reciprocity (Kuiper and Sap 1995; Kenway and Epstein 1996; O'Neill 1996). We need to position our claims from a view of individual self-determination that reflects that interdependence and need for community. The second challenge for Australian feminists in a more disparate and diverse feminist 'movement' in post-Mabo times is how to construct an oppositional politics from outside (rather than inside) a conservative state unsympathetic to feminist advocacy for the constituency of women from within the state.[1]

Finally, globalization suggests that there is a need for feminists to work at a range of levels, strategically targeting local, supranational extragovernmental bodies as well as the nation state in women's claims for equity, claims that may be based upon interests, not just rights or need (Yeatman 1992). At the level of the local, one point of active resistance by some women principals against the regressive aspects of school reform was their capacity to mobilize community support against particular policies because of their exemplary leadership. In returning to the local as the site of feminist activity, one needs to be wary that feminists tend to romanticize the local in the same way that they idealize notions of community as bearing a common good that precedes individual interests and that positions individualism and collectivism in antagonism to each other, with the expectation that the individual is sublimated to the collective. In particular Australian feminism developed out of 'a tradition of collective organising on the model of trade unionism or party solidarity', developing a 'strong sense of loyalty to the collectivity' rather than the more 'psychologising' model of American feminism that focused upon individual transformation (Eisenstein 1996: 157). At one level, the discourse of the feminist collective, in which all work and act equally, rejects the notion of leadership as feminist practice. At another, the culture of solidarity is receptive to discourses about women's styles of leadership or ways of organizing that value femaleness, but the collective impulse can also work against any sense of the politics of difference amongst feminists between being female and feminist, or on the basis of race, class or ethnicity.

Feminists need also to be wary of idealized models of feminist organizational practices that are decontextualized. Such exemplary models of feminist communitarian practices are usually local, not responsible for large organizational decisions and goals for their survival, and with a relatively homogeneous membership. Schools are complex organizations, work within large systems and diverse communities, upon which their survival depends, with often contradictory expectations and responsibilities. In many instances the conditions for greater egalitarian participation do not exist – 'small group size, common goals, equal participation, relatively equal knowledge and experience, individual members who are flexible and non-competitive, and a benign organizational environment that supports participatory practices' (J. Acker 1995: 141). Even within small group situations such as committees

> Collective decisionmaking is impossible when there are large differences in knowledge and experiences between participants, accompanied by time pressures for effective action. Excessive focus on internal processes to achieve consensus interferes with action to achieve change in a world that does not wait. Some division of labour and allocation of authority and responsibility is necessary – given the social relations in which we are embedded – to reach organizing goals. But this does not mean that feminist organizers can abandon efforts to keep hierarchy to a minimum and create favourable conditions for democratic participation.
>
> (J. Acker 1995: 141)

Furthermore, the local is not necessarily more democratic. Conservative discourses justifying devolution tapped into communitarian discourses that the local is more equitable, but Australian, UK and New Zealand research indicates that while the structures of devolution and self-management in themselves do not necessarily produce inequality, they tend to do so when driven by the values of market liberalism. Victoria in the 1980s illustrated the capacity for a centralized bureaucracy to deliver, in some way, equity and participation, whereas gender and equity can quickly disappear in self-managing schools (Middleton 1992; Gordon 1994a). Local communities can be highly progressive, but also highly conservative, about gender equality and social justice – they can recognize some forms of difference (race) and neglect others (gender) (Davies 1990).

The ongoing strategic problem for feminism as a political movement is the sameness/difference issue. Feminist claims have wavered between sameness and difference, between the gender-neutral 'I' of universal man and the 'we' of the collectivity of women. Women's claims for access to educational leadership similarly waver between the assertion that women are 'as good as any man' or that women collectively bring something special to leadership that is distinctly feminine and different, the latter position more dominant during the 1990s. Neither position has challenged masculinist hegemony because the public/private, rational/irrational dualisms remain intact. We need to move strategically beyond the claims of sameness and difference as being in antithesis as 'equality is not the elimination of difference, and difference does not preclude equality' (Scott 1990: 138, 146). Neither position provides a viably different alternative for a feminist politics of change because either we become like men or are complementary to men, in both instances leaving the normative male intact. A possible strategy is to challenge liberalism on its own terms and show how 'othered' special groups 'demonstrate the partiality of these institutions and their abrogation of their professed adherence to universalistic standards of right' central to liberalism (Yeatman 1994: ix).

A feminist politics of educational leadership for postmodern times

So what would constitute some guiding principles, given that there is no feminist consensus, for a 'wild' feminist postmasculinist politics of educational leadership in new hard times? A feminist postmasculinist politics of educational leadership would recognize first and foremost the politics of difference; not a difference that dilutes into diversity in the negative, assimilationist sense, but one that values particular first order differences of gender, race, class, ethnicity and sexuality equally. It is the *articulation* (between class, race and gender) that is important, and not the shared common universal experience of womanhood (Butler 1990). Recognizing difference raises issues of voice, representation and privilege in democratic society: 'Who can speak for/as/about whom, who can use the term 'woman' knowingly and authoritatively? It asks whose voice is authoritative, whose voice is not heard, and, more specifically queries the distribution of resources that makes some voices louder than others.

Such a politics demands that 'feminists confront both difference and *privilege*, including the privilege we may unconsciously take on as we pass into established institutional structures and thus seemingly move away from our situation as women' (Cornell 1995: 83). Such a position widens the debate beyond the critical mass theory of women in leadership because it requires women in leadership to address the radically changing materialist conditions regendering educational work that continues to marginalize women as a group, but some more than others.

The political–economic context remains ... and is extraordinarily more fixed and materially more powerful than ever ... systems of law, global economic inequalities, the structured dis-enfranchisement of most women and most men in the world, the influence of the military–industrial complex ... are working to constitute and to fix very specific subjects in very confined and inegalitarian geo-political spaces.

(Jones 1995: 10–11)

It would also focus upon the responsibilities of, and accountability to, women in leadership for other women, but with a keen sense of the complexity of leadership in schools.

Feminists, Amy Allen (1996: 145) argues, 'need a theory of power to do'; they 'need to get to know power better'. This means not seeing power as 'nothing other than the enemy; to recognize power for its potency and not just domination, as exciting and not only dangerous, as productive and not simply repressive' (Brown 1988: 207). The women principals in this research readily exercised the power gained through formal authority as imparting them with the capacity 'to just get things done', yet they remained nervous about the language of power, realizing for a female to be powerful was unfeminine, recognizing that power relations were nearly always one-sided or asymmetrical, and that their power was contingent upon the material and discursive conditions of its practice. Feminism must also be reflexive about its own claims to truth and power, as women cannot automatically claim a higher moral position as marginality does not guarantee critical insight, while never forgetting that men still are institutionally dominant.

A feminist postmasculinist politics of educational leadership would be forever wary of binaries that position 'the feminine private world of nature, particularity, differentiation, inequality, emotion, love and ties of blood as set apart from the public, universal – and masculine – world of convention, civil equality and freedom, reason, consent and contract' (Mouffe 1992: 376), as such dualities produce fixed categories that inhibit change. Thus discourses of rationality (e.g. bureaucratic rationality, economic rationality, the self-maximizing individual rational chooser) undermine equity because rationality artificially excludes compassion and emotion from decisions that impact on equity (Putnam and Mumby 1993: 36). Women in leadership face contradictions between their lived experience as decisionmakers and how they are constructed as compassionate carers. Working in the rationalist culture of organizations, they feel that they too must make decisions on the basis of reason alone. Men, meanwhile, appeal to a particularly abstract mode of rationality that hides their emotional dependency from themselves and 'does not fit the conceptions they have of themselves as independent and self sufficient' (Seidler 1994: 41). 'Men will often talk as if they have taken all the 'rational' considerations into account, so that it is not a matter of dealing with the emotional consequences of the situation' (Seidler 1994: 39). Rationality without compassion in a humane world is irrational, however (Jones 1995).

A feminist postmasculinist politics would 'fix the feminist gaze' on masculinity and the social relations of gender. This requires us, with men, to

> develop a theory of masculinity that makes sense of men's experiences and behaviours, not only to theory makers but to the men themselves, because the crucial task is to get men and boys actively involved in the project of change, in cooperation with, rather than in opposition to, women and other groups that are experiencing the negative effects of dominant, masculine culture. We need a theory of masculinity that speaks to men's experiences of themselves while enabling them to honestly acknowledge their complicity in the collective structures of dominant masculinity and gender injustice. We need a sense that change is possible, and that it is going to be good for us, as men, too.
>
> (McLean 1995: 291)

Such a theory would move away from there being something 'psychologically wrong as individuals or wrong as males' (McLean 1995: 292) but getting men and boys to recognize injustice and the negative experiences of male power, and thus work from the 'inside out' (Sinclair 1995: 41). Institutions promise power, but such promises are illusory for most men. We need to focus less upon rectifying the emotional illiteracy of men, for the male passion for management and power is about emotion, and more on the 'gendered power structures within which emotions are constructed and expressed' (McLean 1995: 297).

A feminist postmasculinist politics would seek to reconstitute professional discourses of care around teaching and leading in which care can be seen as 'labour undertaken out of affection or a sense of responsibility for other people, with no expectation of immediate pecuniary reward', while realizing the dangers of the commodification and reification of care (Folbre 1995). It could begin with a view of caring as neither totally altruistic nor totally self-interested, one that recognizes the value of care as a mutually beneficial engagement that can be learnt through empathy and relationships of trust, without forgetting who benefits and who does not in any caring arrangement (Noddings 1992).

Finally, a feminist postmasculinist politics would substitute the public and democratizing notion of self-governance for the privatizing and controlling notion of self-management. Self-governance recognizes schools as part of a network of social relationships and responsibilities within wider communities. Such schools should encourage tolerance and inclusivity, a respect for difference, egalitarian educational practices and democratic relations. Self-governance links education to citizenship and a sense of the public good in a 'democracy of emotions' where 'individuals who have a good understanding of their own emotional makeup and who are able to communicate effectively with others on a personal basis, are likely to be well prepared for the wider tasks and responsibilities of citizenship' (Giddens 1995: 16). Self-governing schools would therefore work on different principles and judgements of value than self-managing schools.

Conclusion

In this text, I have sought to bring some reflexivity into feminist theory and practice in educational administration by pointing out how feminist discourses about women and leadership have the potential for co-option by, as well as subversion of, hegemonic discourses in educational administration. Feminist discourses also have the proclivity, as any discourse, to produce new regimes of truth that are potentially disempowering as well as empowering for women. I have focused upon what I see to be particular problems for feminism and feminist leaders in the future: the role of the state in delivering gender equity, the entrapments of the culture of care, the paradoxes of self-management, and the inadequacies of theories of educational change.

First, I have argued that feminism needs to theorize more explicitly gender equity reform in the context of the changed education/state relations at the level of policy. I have argued that we need to reconceptualize the state as fluid and re-view the capacity of the postmodern competitive nation state to deliver equity. Second, we need to consider the receptivity of gender reform's gendered subjects in terms of the considerably different investments – emotional, intellectual and political – of men and women in gender reform. Third, we need to problematize the notion of care so that it is less about eternal demand feeding at the maternal breast to one that sees care as an educative process to be learnt and appreciated by both men and women, boys and girls. There is a need to develop institutional understandings about what care, trust and empathy can mean as key elements of tolerant and diverse educational communities that promote notions of difference and active citizenship. Fourth, I have argued for the need to distinguish between 'female' and 'feminist' leadership as a precondition to reconceptualizing a feminist postmasculinist politics of educational leadership, given that 'not any woman will do in leadership' when social justice is a basic tenet of a feminist practice of educational leadership.

Finally, I have argued that despite the foregrounding of difference by poststructuralist feminist epistemologies, postcolonial and black feminisms, which put the category of 'woman' under question, it is both possible and desirable to speak of a normative feminist project, although one that is continuously negotiated and contested. Such a project sees leadership as being an educative practice dealing with substantive educational issues and not just a matter of technique, performance, style, or set of tactics to manage change. This means new alliances and strategies across different genders, races, ethnicities and classes. The point of departure for new alliances I argue, rests with the reconceptualization of the role of education (and leadership) in citizen formation which could be the basis of principles for a feminist postmasculinist politics of educational leadership premised upon revised notions of community, individuality, reciprocity, trust, and inter-dependence. This would promote an empowering view of educational self-governance and active 'subjects' to supplant that of the disempowering notions of self-management and the managed self.

Feminists in educational administration, I suggest, need to focus beyond the issue of women and leadership, to contextualize it and to politicize it by linking leadership more transparently to wider educational debates about social inequality, educational reform and issues of social justice. We also need to theorize gender change better – to consider both its textual nuances and the power of discourse in meaning making, but also to consider more often the material and cultural conditions that produce particular leadership discourses that constrain women. It also means problematizing leadership as a key concept in educational administration and policy – redefining it and even rejecting it – for perhaps the focus upon leadership is itself the biggest barrier to gender equality.

Note

1 In 1992, the High Court of Australia in the Mabo decision made void the notion of Terra Australis Nullius (i.e. the legal position which had been held that Australia was unoccupied at the time of white settlement). The consequent native title legislation and process of reconciliation is now under challenge.

References

Aburdene, P. and Naisebett, J. (1992) *Megatrends for Women: From Liberation to Leadership.* New York: Fawcett Columbine.

Acker, J. (1995) Feminist goals and organizing processes, in M. Ferree and P. Y. Martin (eds), *Feminist Organizations. Harvest of the New Women's Movement.* Philadelphia, PA: Temple University Press.

Acker, S. (1995) 'Carry on caring': the work of women teachers, *British Journal of Sociology of Education.* 16(1): 21–36.

Acker, S. (1996) Gender and teachers' work, in M. Apple (ed.) *Review of Research in Education,* 21. Washington, DC: American Education Research Association.

Adkinson, J. (1981) Women in school administration: a review of the research. *Review of Educational Research,* 5(3): 11–43.

Adler, S., Laney J. and Packer, M. (1993) *Managing Women: Feminism and Power in Educational Management.* Buckingham: Open University Press.

Affirmative Action Agency (1994) *Negotiating Equity, Affirmative Action in Enterprise Bargaining. Monograph.* Canberra: Australian Government Printing Service.

Alcoff, L. and Potter, E. (eds) (1993) *Feminist Epistemologies.* New York: Routledge.

Al-Khalifa, E. (1989) Management by halves: women teachers and school management, in H. De Lyons (ed.) *Women Teachers.* Buckingham: Open University Press.

Allen. A. (1996) Foucault on power: a theory for feminists, in S. Hekman (ed.) *Feminist Interpretations of Michel Foucault.* PA: Pennsylvania University Press.

Anderson, K. and Jack, D. (1991) Learning to listen: interview techniques and analyses, in S. Gluck and D. Patai (eds) *Women's Words. The Feminist Practice of Oral History.* London: Routledge.

Anyon, J. (1994) The retreat of Marxism and socialist feminism: postmodern and poststructuralist theories in education. *Curriculum Inquiry,* 24(2): 114–34.

Arnot, M. (1991) Equality and democracy: a decade of struggle over education. *British Journal of Sociology of Education,* 12(4): 447–65.

Arnot, M. (1993) A crisis in patriarchy? British feminist educational politics and state regulation of gender, in M. Arnot and K. Weiler (eds) *Feminism and Social Justice.* London: Falmer Press.

Arnot, M. and Weiler, K. (eds) (1993) *Feminism and Social Justice. An International Perspective.* London: Falmer Press.

Bacchi, C. (1990) *Same Difference. Feminism and Sexual Difference.* Sydney: Allen and Unwin.

Baker, D. and Fogarty, M. (1993) *A Gendered Culture.* St Albans, Victoria: Victoria University of Technology.

Ball, S. J. (1994) *Education Reform: A Critical and Post-structural Approach.* Buckingham: Open University Press.

Barrett, M. and Phillips, A. (eds) (1992) Introduction, *Destabilising Theory: Contemporary Feminist Debates.* Oxford: Polity Press.

Bartky, S. L. (1990) *Femininity and Domination.* London: Routledge.

Bates, R. (1994) *The Bird That Sets Itself Afire: Thom Greenfield and the Renewal of Educational Administration.* 8th International Intervisitation Program, Ontario Institute of Studies in Education, Toronto.

Beck, L. (1994) *Reclaiming Educational Administration as a Caring Profession.* New York: Teachers College Press.

Beck, L. and Murphy, J. (1994) *Understanding the Principalship: A Metaphorical Analysis.* New York: Teachers College Press.

Belenky, M., Clinchy, B., Goldberger, N. and Tarul, J. (eds) (1986) *Women's Ways of Knowing: The Development of Self, Voice and Mind.* New York: Basic Books.

Bell, C. and Chase, S. (1993) The underrepresentation of women in leadership, in C. Marshall (ed.) *The New Politics of Race and Gender.* London: Falmer Press.

Biddington, J. (1994) 'Something to fall back on: women, work and education in seven Victorian high schools, 1905–45', unpublished PhD thesis. University of Melbourne.

Biklen, S. (1993) Feminism, methodology and the point of view in the study of women who teach, in L. Yates (ed.) *Feminism in Education: Melbourne Studies in Education 1993.* Bundoora: Latrobe University Press.

Bishop, P. and Mulford, B. (1995) Empowerment in four Australian primary schools: they don't really care. *International Journal of Educational Reform,* 5(2): 193–204.

Blackmore, J. (1989) Educational leadership: a feminist critique and reconstruction, in J. Smyth (ed.) *Critical Perspectives on Educational Leadership.* London: Falmer Press.

Blackmore, J. (1991) Corporatism, democracy and teacher unions, in D. Dawkins (ed.) *Politics and Power in Education.* London: Falmer Press.

Blackmore, J. (1993) In the shadow of men: exclusionary theory and discriminatory practice in the historical construction of 'masculinist' administrative cultures, in J. Blackmore and J. Kenway (eds) *Gender Matters in the Theory and Practice of Educational Administration and Policy: A Feminist Introduction.* London: Falmer Press.

Blackmore, J. (1994) Devolution and the new disadvantage, in Deakin Centre for Education and Change. *Schooling: What Future?* Geelong, Deakin University.

Blackmore, J. (1995) Participating parents: a feminist analysis of the relationship between the state, the community and education in Victoria, in B. Limerick and H. Nielsen (eds) *Schools, Community and Participation.* London: Harcourt, Brace and Janovich.

Blackmore, J. (1996) Doing emotional labor in the educational market place: stories from the field of women in management. *Discourse* 17(3): 337–52.

Blackmore, J. (1997a) Level playing field? feminist observations of global/local articulations of the re-structuring and re-gendering of educational work. *International Review of Education: Special Issue, Tradition, Modernity. Postmodernity*, 43 (5–6): 1–23.

Blackmore, J. (1997b) The gendering of skill in twentieth century Australian education, in E. Halsey, H. Lauder, P. Brown and A. S. Wells (eds) *Economy, Culture, Education*. Oxford: Oxford University Press.

Blackmore, J. (1997c) Performativity, self management and self managing schools, working paper. Deakin Centre for Education and Change, Deakin University.

Blackmore, J. (1998) Globalisation, localisation and the midwife state: dilemmas for state feminism. *Journal of Education Policy*, (in press).

Blackmore, J., Bigum, C., Hodgens, J. and Laskey, L. (1996) Managed change and self management in schools of the future. *Leading and Managing*, 2(2): 35–56.

Blount, J. (1994) One postmodernist perspective on educational leadership. Ain't I a leader? in S. Maxcy (ed.) *Postmodern School Leadership: Meeting the Crisis in Educational Administration*. London, Praeger.

Blount, J. (1996) Manly men and womanly women: deviance, gender role polarization, and the shift in women's school employment 1900–66. *Harvard Educational Review*, 66(2), 318–38.

Bologh, R. (1990) *Love or Greatness: Max Weber and Masculine Thinking – A Feminist Enquiry*. London: Unwin Hyman.

Bowe, R. and Ball, S. (1992) *Reforming Education and Changing Schools*. London: Routledge.

Brah, A. (1994) 'Race' and 'culture' in the gendering of labour markets, in H. Afshar and M. Maynard (eds) *The Dynamics of 'Race' and Gender: Some Feminist Interventions*. London: Taylor and Francis.

Brannock. G. (1993) Leading from behind. principal's responses to gender equity. Unpublished paper presented at the Australian Association for Research in Education Conference, Perth, 24–28 November.

Brittan, A. (1989) *Masculinity and Power*. Oxford: Basil Blackwell.

Britzman, D. (1993) Beyond rolling models: gender and multicultural education, in S. Biklen and D. Pollard (eds) *Gender and Education. 92 Yearbook of the NSSE*. Chicago: University of Chicago Press.

Brown, W. (1988) *Manhood and Politics: A Feminist Reading in Political Theory*. Tolowa, NJ: Rowman and Littlefield.

Bryson, M. and de Castells, S. (1993) En/gendering equity: on some paradoxical consequences of institutionalised programs of emancipation. *Educational Theory*, 43(3): 341–55.

Burbules, N. and Rice, M. (1992) Dialogue across differences: continuing the conversation. *Harvard Educational Review*, 61(4): 393–416.

Burton, C. (1991) *The Promise and the Price: Essays on Women and Organisations*. Sydney: Allen and Unwin.

Burton, C. (1993) Equal employment opportunity and corporate planning, in J. Blackmore and J. Kenway (eds) *Gender Matters in the Theory and Practice of Educational Administration and Policy: A Feminist Introduction*. London: Falmer Press.

Butler, J. (1990) *Gender Trouble: Feminism and the Subversion of Identity*. London: Routledge.

Byrne, E. (1989) Role modelling and mentorship as policy mechanisms: the need for new directions, in E. Byrne (ed.) *Women and Science and Technology in Australia, Policy Review Project.* Brisbane: University of Queensland.

Caldwell, B. (1994) Australian perspectives on leadership: the principals' role in the radical decentralisation in Victoria's Schools of the Future. *Australian Educational Researcher*, 21(2): 45–62.

Caldwell, B. and Spinks, J. (1992) *The Self Managing School.* London: Falmer Press.

Cameron, D. (1995) *Verbal Hygiene.* London: Routledge.

Carrigan, T., Connell B. and Lee, J. (1987) The sex role framework and the sociology of masculinity, in G. Weiner and M. Arnot (eds) *Gender under Scrutiny: New Inquiries in Education.* London: Hutchinson.

Casey, C. (1995) *Work, Self and Society. After Industrialism.* London: Routledge.

Chase, S. (1995) *Ambiguous Empowerment: The Work Narratives of Women School Superintendents.* Amherst, MA: Massachusetts University Press.

Chen, M. and Addi, A. (1993) Employment threat, equality of opportunities and educator's response to the rapid feminization of school principalship. Paper presented to American Educational Research Association, Atlanta, April.

Chodorow, N. (1978) *The Reproduction of Mothering: Psychoanalysis and the Sociology of Gender.* Berkeley, CA: University of California.

Cockburn, C. (1989) Equal opportunities: the short and long agenda. *Industrial Relations Journal*, 20(3): 213–25.

Cockburn, C. (1991) *In the Way of Women: Men's Resistance to Sexual Equality in Organisations.* London: Macmillan.

Codd, J. (1992) The knowledge base in educational administration and the restructuring of New Zealand education. Paper presented to American Educational Research Association, San Francisco, April 1992.

Codd, J. and Gordon, L. (1991) School charters: the contractualist state and education policy. *New Zealand Journal of Educational Studies*, 26(1): 34–59.

Collins, P. (1991) *Black Feminist Thought: Knowledge, Consciousness, and the Politics of Empowerment.* New York: Routledge.

Collinson, D. and Collinson. M. (1990) Sexuality in the workplace: the domination of men's sexuality, in J. Hearn, D. Sheppard, P. Tancred-Smith and G. Burrell (eds) *The Sexuality of Organisation.* London: Sage.

Connell, R.W. (1987) *Gender and Power.* Sydney: Allen and Unwin.

Connell, R.W. (1990) Gender, state and politics: theory and appraisal. *Theory and Society,* 19(5): 507–44.

Connell, R.W. (1995) *Masculinities.* Sydney: Allen and Unwin.

Coombe, K., Cocklin, B., Ratallick, J. and Clancy, S. (1993) Women principals in rural contexts. Paper presented to Australian Association for Research in Education, Perth, 22–28 November.

Cornell, D. (1995) What is ethical feminism? in S. Benhabib, J. Butler, S. Cornell and N. Fraser (eds) *Feminist Contentions. A Philosophical Exchange.* London: Routledge.

Cott, N. (1987) *The Grounding of Modern Feminism.* New Haven, CT: Yale University Press.

Coulter, R. (1996) School restructuring Ontario Style: a gendered agenda, in S. Robertson and H. Smaller (eds) *Teacher Activism in the 1990s.* Toronto: Our Schools/Our Selves Education Foundation.

Court, M. (1992) 'Leading from behind': Women in educational administration, in S. Middleton and A. Jones (eds) *Women and Education in Aotearoa 2*. Wellington: Bridget William Books.

Court, M. (1993) 1893–1993: How far have we come in women's employment in education? *New Zealand Annual Review of Education*, 3: 81–126.

Court, M. (1994) Removing macho management: lessons from the field of education. *Gender, Work and Organisation*, 1(1): 33–49.

Court, M. (1995) Good girls and naughty girls. Rewriting the scripts for women's anger, in B. Limerick and B. Lingard (eds) *Gender and Changing Educational Management*. Sydney: Hodder and Stoughton.

Coward, R. (1985) *Female Desire*. London: Paladin Grafton Books.

Cox, E. (1996) *Leading Women: Tactics for Making the Difference*. Sydney: Random House.

Cozer, (1974) *Greedy Institutions: Patterns of Undivided Commitment*. New York: Free Press.

Crawford, J., Kippax, S., Onyx, J., Gault, U. and Benton, P. (1992) *Emotion and Gender: Constructing Meaning from Memory*. London: Sage.

Cuban, L. (1990) A fundamental puzzle of school reform, in A. Lieberman (ed.) *Schools as Collaborative Cultures: Creating the Future Now*. London: Falmer.

Davies, B. (1989) The discursive production of the male/female dualism in school settings. *Oxford Review of Education*, 15(3): 229–41.

Davies, L. (1992) *Equity and Efficiency? School Management in an International Context*. London: Falmer Press.

Deem, R., Brehony, K. and Heath, S. (1995) *Active Citizenship and the Governing of Schools*. Buckingham: Open University Press.

Dehli, K. (1996) Between 'market' and 'state'? Engendering education change in the 1990s. *Discourse*, 17(3): 363–76.

de Lauretis, T. (1987) *Technologies of Gender*. Bloomington, IN: Indiana University Press.

Directorate of School Education, Victoria (1996) Ministerial review of employment equity for women in education. Queensland: Department of Education.

Directorate of School Education, Victoria (1993) *Schools of the Future*. Melbourne: Department of School Education.

Distant, G. (1993) Self managed schooling and the disempowerment of women teachers. Paper presented to Australian Association for Research in Education, Perth, 24–28 November.

Douglas, P. (1995) 'The ugly, the mute and the good': men's responses to feminist reforms, in B. Limerick and B. Lingard (eds) *Gender and Changing Educational Management*. Sydney: Hodder and Stoughton.

Drucker, P. (1992) *Managing the Future*. New York: Dutton.

Dudley, J. and Vidovich, L. (1995) *The Politics of Education*. Camberwell, Victoria: Australian Council for Education Research.

Dunlap, D. and Schmuck, P. (eds) (1995) *Leading Women in Education*. New York: State University of New York Press.

Eisenstein, H. (1996) *Inside Agitators. Australian Femocrats and the State*. St Leonards: Allen and Unwin.

Eveline, J. (1994) The politics of advantage. *Australian Feminist Studies*, 19 (Aut): 129–54.

Ferguson, K. (1984) *The Feminist Case Against Bureaucracy.* Philadelphia, PA: Temple University Press.

Fine, G. (1988) One of the boys: women in male dominated settings, in M. Kimmel (ed.) *Changing Men: New Directions in Research on Men and Masculinity.* Newbury Park, CA: Sage.

Fine, M. (1993) The 'public' in public schools: the social construction/construction of moral communities, in M. Fine (ed.) *Disruptive Voices.* Ann Arbor, MI: University of Michigan Press.

Fineman, S. (1993) Organisations as emotional arenas, in S. Fineman (ed.) *Emotion in Organisations.* London: Sage.

Finn, B. (1991) *Young People's Participation in Post-compulsory Education and Training.* Canberra: Australian Government Printing Service.

Flam, H. (1993) Fear, loyalty and greedy organisations, in S. Fineman (ed.) *Emotion in Organisations.* London: Sage.

Fleras, A. (1989) Inverting the bureaucratic pyramid: reconciling aboriginality and bureaucracy in New Zealand. *Human Organisation,* 48(3): 214–23.

Folbre, N. (1995) Holding hands at midnight: the paradox of caring labour. *Feminist Economics,* 1(1): 73–92.

Ford, P. (1995) Professional development needs of principals of schools of the future: a summary of gender related findings. Paper presented to Ministerial Review of Employment Equity for Women, March 1995.

Foucault, M. (1980a) *Power/Knowledge: Selected Interviews and Other Writings.* Brighton: Harvester Press.

Foucault, M. (1980b) *The History of Sexuality.* New York: Random House.

Foucault, M. (1991) Governmentality, in G. Burchell, C. Gordon and P. Miller (eds) *The Foucault Effect: Studies in Governmentality.* London: Harvester Wheatsheaf.

Franzway, S. (1986) With problems of their own: Australian femocrats and the welfare state, *Australian Feminist Studies,* 3: 45–57.

Franzway, S., Court, D. and Connell, R. (1989) *Staking a Claim: Feminism, Bureaucracy and the State.* Sydney: Allen and Unwin.

Fraser, N. (1995) From redistribution to recognition? The dilemmas of justice in a 'post socialist age'. *New Left Review,* 212 (July/August): 68–93.

Fullan, M.(1993) *Change Forces.* London: Falmer Press.

Gaskell, J. and McLaren, A. (eds) (1991) *Women and Education: A Canadian Perspective.* Calgary: Detselig.

Gewirtz, S., Ball, S. J. and Bowe, R. (1995) *Markets, Choice and Equity in Education.* Buckingham: Open University Press.

Gherardi, S. (1995) *Gender, Symbolism and Organisational Cultures.* London: Sage.

Giddens, A. (1995) *Beyond Left and Right. The Future of Radical Politics.* Cambridge: Polity Press.

Gilligan, C. (1982) *In A Different Voice: Essays on Psychological Theory and Women's Development.* Cambridge, MA: Harvard University Press.

Glazer, J. (1991) Feminism and professionalism in teaching and educational administration. *Educational Administration Quarterly,* 27(3), 321–42.

Gordon, L. (1994a) Whatever happened to the National Policy for Girls and Women in New Zealand? Unpublished paper, University of Canterbury.

Gordon, L. (1994b) Rich and Poor Schools in Aotearoa, *New Zealand Journal of Education,* 29(2): 129–36.

Grace, G. (1995) *School Leadership*. London: Falmer Press.

Grady, N., MacPherson, M., Mulford, W. and Williamson, J. (1994) *Australian School Principals: A Profile*. Glenelg, South Australia: Glenelg Press.

Green, K. (1995) *The Woman of Reason. Feminism, Humanism and Political Thought*. Cambridge: Polity Press.

Greenfield, T. and Ribbins, P. (1993) *Greenfield on Educational Adminstration*. London: Routledge.

Grogan, M. (1996)*Voices of Women Aspiring to the Superintendency*. New York: State University of New York Press.

Gunn, E. (1995) *A Taste of School Leadership: A Feminist Perspective*. Masters of Educational Administration Research Paper, Faculty of Education, Geelong, Deakin University.

Gutek, B.(1990) Sexuality in the workplace, in J. Hearn, D. Sheppard, P. Tancred-Smith and G. Burrell (eds) *The Sexuality of Organisation*. London: Sage.

Hall, V. (1996) *Dancing on the Ceiling. A Study of Women Managers in Education*. London: Paul Chapman.

Hamilton, P. (1990) Inventing self: oral history as autobiography. *Hecate*, 16(1/2): 128–33.

Hannan, T. (1975) Julia Flynn and the inspectorship of Victorian secondary schools 1928–9. *ANZ History of Education Society Journal*, 44(1): 1–19.

Hannaway, J. and Carnoy, M. (1993) *Decentralization and School Improvement: Can We Fulfil the Promise?* San Francisco, CA: Jossey-Bass.

Hansot, E. and Tyack, D. (1983) *Managers of Virtue*. Stanford, CA: Stanford University Press.

Haraway, D. (1988) Situated knowledges: the science question in feminism and the privilege of the partial perspective, *Feminist Studies*, 14: 575–96.

Hargreaves, A. (1994) *Changing Teachers, Changing Times. Teachers' work and culture in postmodern times*. London: Teachers College Press.

Hargreaves, A. (1995) Development and desire, in M. Guskey and M. Huberman (eds) *Professional Development: New Paradigms and Practices*. New York: Teachers College Press.

Hargreaves, A. (1996) Cultures of teaching and educational change, in B. Biddle, T. Good and I. Goodson (eds) *International Handbook of Teachers and Teaching*. Dordrecht, The Netherlands: Kluwer Press.

Harlow, E., Hearn, J. and Parkin, W. (1995) Gendered noise: organisations and the din of domination, in C. Itzin and J. Newman (eds) *Gender, Culture and Organisational Change*. London: Routledge.

Haug, F. (1987) *Female Sexualisation: a Collective Work of Memory*. London: Verso.

Hearn, J. (1993) Emotive subjects. organisational men, organisational masculinities and the (de)construction of 'emotions', in S. Fineman (ed.) *Emotion in Organisations*. London: Sage.

Hearn, J. and Parkin, W. (1992) Women, men, and leadership: a critical review of assumptions, practices and change in industrialized nations, in N. Adler and D. Izraeli (eds)*Women in Management World Wide*. New York: M. Saharpe.

Hearn, J., Sheppard, D., Tancred-Smith, P. and Burrell, G. (eds) (1995) *The Sexuality of Organisation*. London: Sage.

Hekman, S. (1990) *Gender and Knowledge: Elements of a Postmodern Feminism*. Oxford: Polity Press.

Hennessey, R. (1993) *Materialist Feminism and the Politics of Discourse*. London: Routledge.

Hernes, H. N. (1987) *Welfare State and Woman Power*. London: Norwegian University Press/Oxford University Press.

Hill, P. (1993) *A Study of School and Teacher Effectiveness. Results of the First Phase of the Victorian Quality Schools Project*. Melbourne: IARTV Seminar Series paper.

Hochschild, A. (1983) *The Managed Heart: The Commercialization of Human Feeling*. Berkeley, CA: University of California Press.

Hodgkinson, C. (1991) *Educational Leadership: The Moral Art*. New York: State University of New York Press.

Hollway, W. (1984) Fitting work: psychological assessment in organisations, in J. Henriques, W. Hollway, C. Urwin, C. Venn and V. Walkerdine. *Changing the Subject. Psychology, Social Regulation and Subjectivity*. London: Methuen.

Hughey, J. (1989) Equal pay campaign in the Queensland teacher's union, in M. Henry and S. Taylor (eds) *Battlers and Blue Stockings*. Canberra: Australian College of Education.

Hyman, P. (1994) *Women and Economics: A New Zealand Feminist Perspective*. Wellington: Bridget Williams Books.

Itzin, C. and Newman, J. (eds) (1995) *Gender, Culture and Organisational Change*. London: Routledge.

Johnson, L. (1990) Gender issues in education. *Australian Feminist Studies*, 11(Aut): 1–26.

Johnson, L. (1993) *The Modern Girl: Girlhood and Growing Up*. Sydney: Allen and Unwin.

Jones, K. (1993) *Compassionate Authority. Democracy and the Representation of Women*. New York: Routledge.

Karpin Report (1995) *Enterprising Nation. Ministerial Working Party on Management Education*. Canberra: Australian Government Printing Service.

Kelly, U. (1993) *Marketing Place, Cultural Politics, Regionalism and Reading*. Halifax: Fernwood Publishing.

Kenway, J. (1995) Masculinities in schools: under siege, on the defensive and under reconstruction? *Discourse*, 16(1): 59–79.

Kenway, J., Bigum, C. and Fitzclarence, L. (1993) Marketing education in the postmodern age. *Journal of Education Policy*, 8(2): 105–22.

Kenway, J., Willis, S., Blackmore, J. and Rennie, L. (1994) Making hope practical rather than despair convincing: feminist poststructuralism and change. *British Journal of Sociology of Education*, 15(2): 187–210.

Kenway, J., Willis, S. with Blackmore, J. and Rennie, L. (1997) *Answering Back: Girls, Boys and Feminism in Schools*. Sydney: Allen and Unwin.

Kerfoot, D. and Knights, D. (1993) Management, masculinity and manipulation: from paternalism to corporate strategy in financial services in Britain. *Journal of Management Studies*, 30(4): 659–77.

Kuiper, E. and Sap, J. (eds)(1995) *Out of the Margin. Feminist Perspectives on Economics*. London: Routledge.

Lash. S. and Urry, J. (1994) *The Economies of Signs and Space*. Cambridge: Polity Press.

Leach, M and Davies, B. (1990) Crossing boundaries: educational thought and gender equity. *Educational Theory*, 40(3): 321–32.

Limerick, B. (1991) *Career Opportunities for Teachers in the Queensland Department of Education*. Brisbane: Department of Education, Queensland.

Limerick, B. and Lingard, B. (eds) (1995) *Gender and Changing Educational Management*. Sydney: Hodder and Stoughton.

Lingard, B. (1993) Corporate federalism: the merging approach to policymaking for Australian Schools, in B. Lingard, J. Knight and P. Porter (eds) *Schooling Reform in Hard Times*. London: Falmer Press.

Lingard, B. and Douglas, P. (1999) *Men Engaging Feminisms: Profeminism, Backlashes and Schooling*. Buckingham: Open University Press.

Lingard, B. and Porter, P. (eds) (1997) *A National Approach to Schooling in Australia?* Canberra: Australian College of Education.

Louis, K. (1994) Beyond 'managed change': rethinking how schools improve. *School Effectiveness and School Improvement*, 5(1): 2–24.

Luke, C.(1996) Feminist pedagogy theory: reflections on power and authority, *Educational Theory*, 46(3): 283–302.

Lyotard, J.L. (1984) *The Post Modern Condition: A Report on Knowledge*. Manchester: Manchester University Press.

Mac an Ghaill, M. (1994) *The Making of Men*. Buckingham: Open University Press.

Mac an Ghaill, M. (1996) Sociology of education, state schooling and class: beyond critiques of the New Right hegemony. *British Journal of Sociology of Education*, 17(2): 163–76.

McLean, C. (1995) The costs of masculinity: placing men's pain in the context of male power, in *Promoting Gender Equity Conference Proceedings*, Canberra: Department of Employment, Education and Training.

McLeod, J. (1995) Regulating gender: feminist truths and educational reform in Victoria since 1975, Unpublished PhD, Latrobe University.

McNay, L. (1992) *Foucault and Feminism: Power, Gender and the Self*. Cambridge: Polity Press.

Marginson, S. (1994) Emerging patterns of education in Victoria, in Deakin Centre for Education and Change, *Schooling: What Future?* Geelong: Deakin University.

Marshall, C. (1994) The politics of denial: gender and race issues in administration, in C. Marshall (ed.) *The New Politics of Race and Gender*. London: Falmer Press.

Marshall, C. and Anderson, G. (1995) Rethinking the public and private spheres: feminist and cultural studies perspectives on the politics of education, in J. Scribner and D. Layton (eds) *The Study of Educational Politics*. London: Falmer Press.

Marshall, C., Patterson. J., Rogers, D. and Steele, J. (1996) Caring as career: an alternative perspective for educational administration. *Educational Administration Quarterly*, 32(2): 271–94.

Marshall, J. (1996) *Women Managers Moving On: Exploring Career and Life Choices*. London: Routledge.

Martin, J. (1994) Methodological essentialism: false difference and other dangerous traps. *Signs*, 19(3): 630–57.

Mayer, E. (1992) *Employment Related to Key Competencies*. Melbourne: Mayer Committee.

Middleton, S. (1992) Equity, equality and biculturalism in the restructuring of New Zealand schools: a life history approach. *Harvard Educational Review*, 62(3): 310–22.

Miller, P. (1986) *Long Division, State Schooling in South Australian Society*. Netley, South Australia: Wakefield Press.

Milligan, S., Ashenden, D. and Quin, R. (1994) *Women in the Teaching Profession*, Commissioned report 32. National Board of Employment, Education and Training, Canberra: Commonwealth Government Printing Service.

Mills, A. and Tancred, P. (eds) (1992) *Gendering Organizational Analysis*. New York: Sage.

Minichiello, V., Aroni, R., Timewell, E. and Alexander, L. (1995) *In-depth Interviewing: Principles, Techniques and Analysis*. London: Longman.

Minister, K. (1991) A feminist frame for the oral history interview, in S. Gluck and D. Patai (eds) *Women's Words: The Feminist Practice of Oral History*. New York: Routledge.

Mirza, H. (1993) The social construction of black womanhood in British educational research: towards a new understanding, in M. Arnot and K. Weiler (eds) *Feminism and Social Justice*. London: Falmer Press.

Mohanty, C. (1992) Feminist encounters: locating the politics of experience, in M. Barrett and A. Phillips (eds) *Destabilising theory: contemporary feminist debates*. Cambridge: Polity Press.

Moller, J. (1993) Restructuring in the Norwegian context: a combination of efforts towards decentralization and centralization. Paper presented to Ontario Institute of Studies in Education, Toronto, April 1993.

Morrison, A. (1992) *The New Leaders: Guidelines on Leadership Diversity in America*. San Francisco, CA: Jossey-Bass.

Mouffe, C. (1992) Feminism, citizenship and radical democratic politics, in J. Butler and J. Scott (eds) *Feminists Theorize the Political*. Cambridge: Polity Press.

Newman, J. (1995) Gender and cultural change, in Itzin, C. and Newman, J. (eds) *Gender, Culture and Organisational Change*. London: Routledge.

Ngurruwutthun N. and Stewart, M. P. A. (1996) 'Learning to walk behind; learning to walk in front': a case study of the mentor program at Yirrkala Community Education Centre. *Unicorn*, 22(4): 3–23.

Noddings, N. (1992) *The Challenge to Care in Schools: An Alternative Approach to Education*. New York: Teachers College Press.

O'Neill, A. (1996) Privatising public policy: privileging market man and individualising equality through choice within education in Aotearoa/New Zealand. *Discourse*, 17(3): 403–16.

Office of the Public Service Commissioner, Victoria (1994) *Merit Equity and Managing Diversity Guidelines*. Melbourne: Victorian Government Printers.

Ortiz, F. and Ortiz, D. (1994) Politicising executive action: the case of Hispanic female superintendents, in C. Marshall (ed.) *The New Politics of Race and Gender*. London: Falmer Press.

Ozga, J. (1993a) Teacher de-professionalisation: hard lessons from England. Paper presented to the Australian Association for Research in Education, Perth, 24–28 November.

Ozga, J. and Walker, (1995) Women in educational management. theory and practice, in B. Limerick and B. Lingard (eds) *Gender and Changing Educational Management*. Sydney: Hodder Headline.

Parkin, W. (1993) The public and the private: gender, sexuality and emotion, in S. Fineman (ed.) *Emotions in Organisations*. London: Sage.

Pateman, C. (1988) *The Sexual Contract*. Cambridge: Polity Press.

Patrick, J. (1994) America 2000/Goals 2000: moving the nation educationally to 'a new world order'. Citizens for Academic Excellence.

Peters, M. and Marshall, J. (1996) *Individualism and Community. Education and Social Policy in the Postmodern Condition.* London: Falmer Press.

Picot, B. *et al.* (1988) *Administering for Excellence: Effective Administration in Education (Picot Report).* Wellington: Government Printer.

Piercy, M. (1980) *The Moon is Always Female.* New York: Alfred Knopf.

Pillinger, J. (1993) *Feminising the Market.* Basingstoke: Macmillan.

Poiner, G. and Wills, S. (1990) *The Gifthorse.* Sydney: Allen and Unwin.

Poynton, C. (1993) Naming women's workplace skills: linguistics and power, in B. Probert and B. Wilson (eds) *Pink Collar Blues: Work, Gender and Technology.* Melbourne: Melbourne University Press.

Pringle, J. and Timperley, H. (1995) Gender and educational management in New Zealand: co-option, subversion or withdrawal? in B. Limerick and B. Lingard (eds) *Gender and Changing Educational Management.* Sydney: Hodder and Stoughton.

Pusey, M. (1991) *Economic Rationalists in Canberra.* Cambridge: Cambridge University Press.

Putnam, L. and Mumby, D. (1993) Organisations, emotion and the myth of rationality, in S. Fineman (ed.) *Emotion in Organisations.* London: Sage.

Ramsey, E. (1993) Linguistic omissions marginalising women managers, in D. Baker and M. Fogarty (eds) *A Gendered Culture. Educational Management in the 1990s.* St Albans: Victoria University of Technology.

Reiger, K. (1985) *The Disenchantment of the Home: Modernising the Australian Family 1880–1940.* Melbourne: Oxford University Press.

Riley, D. (1988) *Am I that Name? Feminism and the Category of 'Women' in History.* Minneapolis, MN: University of Minnesota.

Robertson, H.J. (1992) Teacher development and gender equity, in M. Fullan and A. Hargreaves (eds) *Understanding Teacher Development and Gender Equity. Professional Development.* London: Cassell.

Roper, M. (1994) *Masculinity and the British Organisation Man since 1945.* London: Oxford University Press.

Rose, N. (1992) *The Governing of the Soul.* Newbury Park, CA: Sage.

Rowbotham, S. (1987) Feminism under stress. *New Society,* 20 March: 8–9.

Sadker, M. and Sadker, M. (1988) *Equity and Excellence in Educational Reform: An Unfinished Agenda.* Washington DC: American University.

Salisbury, J. and Jackson, D. (1996) *Challenging Macho Values: Practical Ways of Working with Adolescent Boys.* London: Falmer Press.

Sampson, S. (1986) Equal opportunity, alone, is not enough or why there are more male principals in schools these days. *Australian Journal of Education,* 31(1): 27–42.

Sampson, S. (1987) But women don't apply: a discussion of teacher promotion in Australia. *Unicorn,* 13(3): 139–43.

Sawer, M. (1991) Why has the women's movement had more influence on government in Australia than elsewhere? in F. Castles (ed.) *Australia Compared. People. Policies and Politics.* Sydney: Allen and Unwin.

Sawer, M. (1994) Feminism and the state: theory and practice in Australia and Canada. *Australian–Canadian Studies,* 12(1): 49–68.

Sawicki, J. (1991) *Disciplining Foucault: Feminism, Power and the Body.* New York: Routledge.

Schmuck, P. (1996) Women's place in educational administration: past, present and future, in K. Leithwood *et al.* (eds) *International Handbook of Educational*

Leadership and Administration. Dordrecht, Netherlands: Kluwer Academic Press.

Scott, J. (1986) Gender: a useful category of historical analysis. *American Historical Review*, 91(5): 1053–75.

Scott, J. (1990) Deconstructing equality-versus-difference: on the use of post-structuralist theory, in M. Hirsch and E. F. Keller (eds) *Conflicts in Feminism.* New York: Routledge.

Scott, J. (1992) Experience, in J. Butler and J. Scott (eds) *Feminists Theorize the Political.* New York: Routledge.

Segal, L. (1990) *Slow Motion: Changing Masculinities, Changing Men.* London: Virago Press.

Seidler, V. (1994) *Unreasonable Men.* London: Routledge.

Senge, P. (1990) *The Fifth Discipline: The Art and Practice of the Learning Organization.* New York: Doubleday.

Sergiovanni, T. (1992) *Moral Leadership: Getting to the Heart of School Improvement.* San Francisco, CA: Jossey Bass.

Shakeshaft, C. (1987) *Women in Educational Administration.* Newbury Park, CA: Sage.

Sheppard, D. (1992) Women managers' perceptions of gender and organizational life, in A. Mills and P. Tancred (eds) *Gendering Organizational Analysis.* Newbury Park, CA: Sage.

Simpson, R. and Simpson, I. (1969) Women and bureaucracy in the semi-professions, in A. Etzioni (ed.) *The Semi-Professions and Their Organization.* New York: The Free Press.

Sinclair, A. (1995) The seduction of the self-managed team and the reinvention of the team-as-group. *Leading and Managing*, 1(1): 44–62.

Sinclair, A. (1994) *Trials at the Top: Chief Executives Talk about Men, Women, and the Australian Executive Culture.* Melbourne University: Melbourne Business School.

Sleeter, C. (1993) Introduction, in C. Capper (ed.) *Educational Administraton in a Pluralistic Society.* New York: State University of New York Press.

Smith, D. (1990) *The Conceptual Practices of Power.* Boston, MA: Northeastern University Press.

Smyth, J. (ed.) (1993) *A Socially Critical View of the Self Managing School.* London: Falmer Press.

Spivak, G. (1993) *Outside in the Teaching Machine.* Routledge: London.

Stanley, L. (1993) On Auto/biography in sociology, *Sociology*, February: 41–52.

State Board of Education, Victoria (1986) *Equal Employment Opportunity for Women in Schools.* Melbourne: State Board of Education.

Steedman, C. (1985) 'Mothers made conscious': the historical development of a primary school pedagogy. *History Workshop Journal*, 20: 135–49.

Still, L. (1995) Women in management. Glass ceilings or slippery poles? in B. Limerick and B. Lingard (eds) *Gender and Changing Educational Management.* Sydney: Hodder and Stoughton.

Strachan, J. (1993) Including the personal and the professional: researching women in educational leadership. *Gender and Education*, 5(1): 48–71.

Stromquist, N. (1992) Sex equity legislation in education: the state as the promoter of women's rights. *Review of Educational Research*, 63(4): 379–408.

Taylor, S., Henry, M., Lingard, B. and Rizvi, F. (1997) *Policy and the Politics of Education.* Sydney: Allen and Unwin.

Taylor, S. (1991) Equity and the politics of change: education policy making in context Perth. Paper presented to the London Institute of Education, London, June 1991.

Theobald, M. (1987) Humanities, science and the female mind: an historical perspective. *Unicorn,* 13(3), 162–5.

Theobald, M. (1996) *Knowing Women.* Melbourne: Cambridge University Press.

Tickell, G. (1994) Principal as line manager or educational leader? in Deakin Centre for Education and Change *Schooling: What Future?* Geelong: Deakin University.

Tong, R. (1989) *Feminist Thought: A Comprehensive Introduction.* Boulder, CO: Westview.

Townsend, T. (1994) The self managing school: miracle or myth? *Leading and Managing,* 2(3): 171–94.

Townsend, T. (1996a) *Restructuring and Quality: Issues for Tomorrow's Schools.* London: Routledge.

Townsend, T. (1996b) The self managing school: miracle or myth? *Leading and Managing* 2(3): 1–34.

Townsend, T. (1997) Schools of the future: a case study in systemic educational development and afterward, in T. Townsend (ed.) *Restructuring and Quality. Issues for Tomorrow's Schools.* London: Routledge.

Tuhiwai-Smith, L. (1993) Getting out from under: Maori women, education and the struggles of Mana Wahine, in M. Arnot and K. Weiler (eds) *Feminism and Social Justice in Education. International Perspectives.* London: Falmer Press.

Vanderende, J. (1996) Masculinity and Men's Reactions to Equal Opportunity Policies in Victorian Education System. Masters in Educational Administration research paper. Geelong: Deakin University.

Venn, C. (1984) The subject of psychology, in J. Henriques, W. Hollway, C. Urwin, C. Venn and V. Walkerdine (eds) *Changing the Subject. Psychology, Social Regulation and Subjectivity.* London: Methuen.

Victorian Department of Education (1996) *Ministerial Review of Employment Equity for Women Teachers.* Melbourne: Victorian Government Printing Service.

Walker. C. (1993) Black women in educational management, in J. Ozga (ed.) *Women in Educational Management.* Buckingham: Open University Press.

Walkerdine, V. (1986) Post structuralist theory and everyday social practices: the family and the school, in S. Wilkinson (ed.) *Feminist Social Psychology: Developing Theory and Practice.* Buckingham: Open University Press.

Walkerdine, V. (1993) Femininity as performance *Oxford Review of Education,* 15(3): 267–79

Waring, S. (1990) *Taylorism Transformed: Scientific Management Theory since 1945.* Chapel Hill, NC: University of North Carolina Press.

Watkins, P. (1993) Passing the crisis down the line, in Smyth, J. (ed.) *A Socially Critical View of the Self-Managing School.* London: Falmer Press.

Watkins, P. (1996) Decentralising education to the point of production: Sloanism, the market and Schools of the Future. *Discourse,* 17(1): 85–99.

Watson, H. (1988) The impact of the second wave of the women's movement on policies and practices in schools, in S. Middleton (ed.) *Women and Education in Aotearoa.* Wellington: Allen and Unwin.

Watson, S. (ed.) (1990) *Playing the State: Australian Feminist Interventions*. Sydney: Allen and Unwin.

Weiler, K. (1988) *Women Teaching for Change. Gender, Class and Power*. South Hadley, MA: Bergin and Garvey.

Weiler, K. (1994) Compulsory heterosexuality and the married teachers bar. Paper presented to Australian Educational Research Association, New Orleans, LA, April.

Weiner, G. (1995a) *Feminisms in Education*. Buckingham: Open University Press.

Weiner, G. (1995b) A question of style or value? in B. Limerick and B. Lingard (eds) *Gender and Changing Educational Management*. Sydney: Hodder and Stoughton.

Wernersson, I. (1989) Gender equality – ideology and reality, in S. Ball and S. Larsson (eds) *The Struggle for Democratic Education*. London: Falmer Press.

Whitty, G. (1994) Devolution in education systems: implications for teacher professional development and pupil performance. Paper presented 'Decentralisation and Teachers'. Melbourne: National Industry Education Foundation, March.

Whitty, G. (1997) Creating quasi-markets in education: a review of recent research on parental choice and school autonomy in three countries. *Review of Research in Education*, 22: 3–48.

Williams, C. (1992) The glass escalator: hidden advantages for men in the 'female' professions. *Social Problems*, 39(3): 253–65.

Williams, J. (1987) The construction of women and black students as educational problems, in M. Arnot and G. Weiner (eds) *Gender and the Politics of Schooling*. London: Hutchinson.

Wylie, C. (1995) Contrary currents: the application of public sector reform framework in education. *New Zealand Journal of Educational Studies*, 30(2): 149–64.

Wylie, C. (1997) *Self Managing Schools Seven Years On: What Have We Learnt?* Wellington: New Zealand Council of Educational Research.

Yates, L. (1993) Feminism and Australian state policy. some questions for the 1990s, in M. Arnot, and K. Weiler (eds) *Feminism and Social Justice*. London: Falmer Press.

Yeakey, C., Johnston, G. and Adkinson, J. (1986) In pursuit of equity: a review of research on minorities and women in educational administration. *Educational Administration Quarterly*, 22(3): 110–49.

Yeatman, A. (1990) *Bureaucrats, Technocrats and Femocrats*. Sydney: Allen and Unwin.

Yeatman, A. (1992) Women's citizenship claims, labour market policy and globalisation, *Australian Journal of Political Science*, 27: 449–61.

Yeatman, A (1993) Corporate management and the shift from the welfare to the competition state. *Discourse*, 13(2): 3–9.

Yeatman, A. (1994) *Postmodern Revisionings of the Political*. New York: Routledge.

Young, B. (1992) On careers: themes from the lives of four western Canadian women educators. *Canadian Journal of Education*, 17(2): 148–61.

Young, B. (1993) *Not 'There' Yet: Another Perspective on Canadian Educational Administration*. Edmonton: University of Alberta.

Young, I. (1990) The ideal of community and the politics of difference, in L. Nicholson (ed.) *Feminism/Postmodernism*. London: Polity Press.

Zetlin, D. and Whitehouse, G. (1996) Citizenship and industrial regulation: a –feminist perspective. Paper presented to the 'Culture and Citizenship Conference', Griffith University, 30 September–2 October.

Index